Studies in the Patriarchal Narratives

Studies in the Patriarchal Narratives

WILLIAM McKANE

Professor of Hebrew and Oriental Languages
St. Mary's College, University of St. Andrews

1979

The Handsel Press

Published by
The Handsel Press Ltd.
33 Montgomery Street, Edinburgh

ISBN 0 905312 03 1

Printed and bound in Great Britain by
W. M. Bett Ltd., Tillicoultry

Contents

Preface

The publication of this book has been made possible through the generous financial support of the British Academy, the Carnegie Trust for the Universities of Scotland, and the University of St. Andrews. I am grateful to Mr David Dorward who has been closely involved in the negotiations associated with publication. I am indebted to the Principal of the University of St. Andrews, Dr J. Steven Watson, for the interest which he has shown in the book and the encouragement which he has given to me. I am indebted in a special way to the Principal of St. Mary's College, Professor Matthew Black, for his energetic efforts to have the book published. Its appearance owes more to him than to any other person, and I cannot adequately express my thanks to him for his concern, persistence and expertise which have brought the book to the point of publication.

Professor Rendtorff's book, *Das Überlieferungsgeschichtliche Problem des Pentateuch* (*BZAW* 147, 1977) appeared after this book had been completed, but the view expressed in it, that Promise is an aspect of a theological *Bearbeitung* of the patriarchal narratives, is similar to opinions which I have discussed. A long review of Rendtorff's book, written by me, will appear in a forthcoming issue of *Vetus Testamentum*.

My colleague, Mr Peter W. Coxon, has generously given up time to help me with the proof-reading of this book, and I am most grateful to him.

Abbreviations

AASOR	Annual of the American Schools of Oriental Research
ANET	Ancient Near Eastern Texts relating to The Old Testament
ARW	Archiv für Religionswissenschaft
ASTI	Annual of the Swedish Theological Institute
BA	The Biblical Archaeologist
BASOR	Bulletin of the American Schools of Oriental Research
BJRL	Bulletin of the John Rylands Library
BWANT	Beiträge zur Wissenschaft von Alten und Neuen Testament
BZAW	Beihefte zur Zeitschrift für die Alttestamentliche Wissenschaft
DLZ	Deutsche Literaturzeitung
ET	The Expository Times
FRLANT	Forschungen zur Religion und Literatur des Alten und Neuen Testament
HKAT	Handkommentar zum Alten Testament
HTR	Harvard Theological Review
IEJ	Israel Exploration Journal
JBL	Journal of Biblical Literature
JBR	Journal of Bible and Religion
JNES	Journal of Near Eastern Studies
JSS	Journal of Semitic Studies
KS	Kleine Schriften
OLZ	Orientalistische Literaturzeitung
Pr.M	Protestantische Monatshefte
RA	Revue d'Assyriologie et d'Archéologie Orientale
RB	Revue Biblique
SBT	Studies in Biblical Theology
SThU	Schweizerische Theologische Umschau
StTh	Studia Theologica
TGUOS	Transactions of Glasgow University Oriental Society
ThLZ	Theologische Literaturzeitung

Th.R	Theologische Rundschau
VT	Vetus Testamentum
VTS	Supplements to Vetus Testamentum
WO	Die Welt des Orients
ZAW	Zeitschrift für die Alttestamentliche Wissenschaft
ZDMG	Zeitschrift der Deutschen Morgenländischen Gesellschaft

Introduction

The purpose of this book is to deal with aspects of the study of the patriarchal narratives which have fallen somewhat into the background at a time when interest has been focused on historiographical questions, and, particularly, on attempts to use archaeological evidence in order to give positive answers to these questions. The ground has been well covered and the methods employed have been subjected to searching criticism. Thompson[1] has argued that archaeological and other external evidence cannot demonstrate the historicity of the patriarchal narratives in a second millennium B.C. setting, nor effect the recovery of the historical patriarchs. He has maintained that the Execration Texts do not give proof of a migration westwards into Palestine of groups with the same type of personal names as the patriarchs, and has urged that this type of name is not so particular as to point to a well-defined historical period. His attitude to the Nuzi evidence is very reserved and recalls in some respects the final view of de Vaux in his *Histoire*.[2] A point which Thompson makes, namely, that we should not set out with the assumption that the patriarchal narratives are a kind of historiography which await confirmation by external testimony, is the one with which this book is largely occupied.

Van Seters[3] also holds that the social and legal usages reflected in the patriarchal narratives cannot be effectively correlated with a second millennium B.C. background. He discounts the arguments for an early second millennium setting based on the names of the patriarchs and dissolves the connexion which has been established between *Ḥapiru* and Hebrews. He supposes that the Abraham traditions are to be located in the neo-Babylonian period and finds an historical allusion to Nabonidus in the tradition of a migration from Ur to Harran. He posits five stages in the literary

[1] T. L. Thompson, *The Historicity of the Patriarchal Narratives* (*BZAW* 133, 1974).   [2] See below, p. 8, n. 2.
[3] J. van Seters, *Abraham in History and Tradition* (1975).

I

transmission of the Abraham traditions, the earliest of which is to be dated in the late pre-exilic period and the latest of which is post-exilic.

It is not my intention to deal in a detailed manner with archaeological matters, but in order to justify and explain my approach to the patriarchal narratives I propose to say something about them in this introduction. The premise which is contradicted by this book is that the application of external, archaeological evidence to the patriarchal narratives has a special objective status; that the operation can be carried out and the results ascertained, while a judgement about the genre of the narratives, which depends on an internal criticism, is held in suspense. On the contrary, the interpretation of the archaeological evidence and the manner of its application depends on the particular view of the nature of the genre held by those who are employing that evidence. When the patriarchal narratives are described as 'epics',[1] a judgement is being made about their genre, namely, that they are a kind of literature in which historical reminiscences are preserved, and the significance which is attached to the external, archaeological evidence is coloured by this judgement.

It has been said that Noth refused to make use of archaeological data,[2] but what ought to have been said was that Noth's understanding of the genre of the patriarchal narratives is such that archaeological evidence does not have for him the significance which it has for those who assume that the narratives are a kind of historiography. The conclusions which are drawn from archaeological evidence depend on the sum of the considerations which enter into the critical decision, and there is an interaction of internal critical techniques and what is adjudged to be external evidence.[3] For example, Gressmann's position was that the patriarchal narratives were essentially imaginative literature, but that they were sources for cultural history in so far as they reflected the pre-sedentary culture of stock-rearing semi-nomads on the fringes

---

[1] G. E. Wright, *Biblical Archaeology* (2) (1962), p. 40; J. Bright, *A History of Israel* (1959), pp. 66, 68 (Unchanged in *A History of Israel* (2) (1972), pp. 73, 75); R. E. Clements, *Abraham and David: Genesis xv and its Meaning for Israelite Tradition. SBT*, second series, 5 (1967), pp. 57 f.

[2] G. E. Wright, 'Archaeology and Old Testament Studies', *JBL* lxxvii (1958), p. 48.

[3] Cf. J. Soggin, *BA* xxiii (1960), pp. 95-100; M. Greenberg, *The Bible in Modern Scholarship*, edit. J. P. Hyatt (1965), pp. 37-43; M. Weippert, *The*

of the settled lands of Syria-Palestine.¹ On this view the archaeological attestation could achieve no more than a clearer and more complete picture of the historical and cultural conditions of the second millennium B.C. out of which the stories come. Thus the assertion that determination of genre does not settle questions of historicity (Wright,² Bright,³ de Vaux⁴) is hardly right. If the patriarchal narratives are derived from *Märchen*, as Gunkel and Gressmann supposed,⁵ this would be a demonstration that they represent a kind of literature without an historical kernel. The 'balance of probability' of which Bright⁶ speaks in relation to the witness of archaeology comes down on the side of the historicity of the patriarchal narratives only if there is a prior assumption that the narratives are in some sense a historiographical genre. If the patriarchs are characters of imaginative literature, they cannot be changed into historical individuals by any amount of archaeological evidence. Nor if they are founders of cults, as supposed by Alt and Noth,⁷ can they be the subjects of a biographical treatment which draws on archaeology to reconstruct the Mesopotamian origins of the historical patriarchs. The meaning of the phrase 'balance of probability' is conditioned by the view which is taken of the genre of the patriarchal narratives, and it is not a magic formula for severing the critical connexions between determination of genre and historicity.

A position somewhat similar to that of Bright is found in de Vaux who says of the patriarchal narratives: 'The nature of the events which they report and the character of the men they show in action do not permit the hope of ever finding in extra-biblical sources mention of these events or of these men'⁸ (similarly

---

Settlement of the Israelite Tribes in Palestine (*SBT* second series, 21), 1971, p. 136, '*There must always be literary, formal and traditio-historical criticism*'.

¹ See below, pp. 44 ff.

² G. E. Wright, *JBL* lxxvii (1958), p. 47; *ET* lxxi (1959/60), p. 292.

³ J. Bright, *Early Israel in Recent History Writing: a Study in Method*, *SBT* 19 (1956), p. 82.

⁴ R. de Vaux, 'Les Patriarches Hébreux Et Les Découvertes Modernes', *RB* liii (1946), p. 327 (cf., however, the detailed and judicious discussion in *Histoire Ancienne D'Israël: Des Origines A L'Installation En Canaan* (1971), pp. 157-253).

⁵ See below, pp. 44 ff.

⁶ *Early Israel*, pp. 88 f.; cf. J. Soggin, *BA* xxiii (1960), p. 99.

⁷ See below, pp. 111 ff.

⁸ 'Method in the Study of Early Hebrew History', *The Bible and Modern Scholarship*, p. 28; cf. *RB* lxxii (1965), p. 27; *Histoire Ancienne*, p. 247.

4 STUDIES IN THE PATRIARCHAL NARRATIVES

Bright[1]). In view of this admission of the privacy of the narratives, de Vaux's balance of internal criticism and external testimony cannot be achieved on the terms which he lays down. If no decision can be made about the genre of the patriarchal narratives by processes of internal criticism – and this is de Vaux's contention – the impact of external testimony by itself cannot produce a general probability that they are a kind of historiography. It is not the weight of external evidence which justifies the quest after the historical patriarchs on which de Vaux embarks. This is clear from his own statement that we are not to expect archaeological attestation which will directly confirm the existence of the historical patriarchs. His detailed reconstruction rests on the persuasion that the stories themselves are full of reliable historical reminiscences. It is clear that de Vaux is not simply concerned to relate the patriarchal narratives to a background of political and cultural history in the second millennium B.C. He does not merely say that the society out of which the stories come is proto-Aramaean, since this would leave the question open whether the literature is historiographical or of some other kind, and whether those who feature in it are historical persons or creatures of literary invention. Because de Vaux is persuaded that the narratives are historiographical, he concludes that the patriarchs are historical individuals belonging to an ethnic group which can be called proto-Aramaean.[2]

Noth's view is that archaeological evidence has provided a framework of political and cultural history in the second millennium B.C. within which the Israelite patriarchs are to be located, but he does not conclude that the patriarchal narratives are an historiographical genre.[3] In the light of his decision that the narratives are cultic

[1] *A History of Israel*, p. 67 (unchanged in *A History of Israel* (2), p. 74: 'We know nothing of the lives of Abraham, Isaac and Jacob save what the Bible tells us, the details of which lie beyond the control of archaeological data.'

[2] De Vaux's view is that both Amorites and Aramaeans derive from a reservoir of peoples in the Syrian desert. These nomadic tribes exerted a continuous pressure on the area of the sown throughout the second millennium B.C., but were unable to penetrate it except in periods when it was not effectively policed by a strong power. The Amorite invasion followed in the wake of the fall of the empire of Ur about 2000 B.C., and the Aramaean invasion was made possible by the disintegration of the Egyptian and Hittite empires around 1200 B.C. The term 'proto-Aramaean' has the advantage of displaying the racial continuity which exists between the Amorites of the patriarchal period and the Aramaeans of the eleventh and tenth centuries B.C. (*Histoire Ancienne*, 185-189, 199 f., 244-253).

[3] 'Der Beitrag der Archäologie zur Geschichte Israels', *VTS* vii (1959), pp. 264 ff.

history no more can be said about the patriarchs as historical individuals than that they were founders of semi-nomadic cults similar
in type. The patriarchal narratives themselves are concerned with
post-settlement Israel, and the historical and cultural circumstances reflected in them belong to that age.[1] It is only incidentally
in respect of personal names[2] or legal usages[3] that they furnish
evidence of their connexion with the more general, second millennium setting out of which Israel originated. Hence Noth questions
the propriety of references to the 'patriarchal age' and is impressed
by the privacy of the patriarchal narratives and the difficulty of
penetrating them by means of external attestation.

The difficulty of the concept of a 'patriarchal age' in relation to
the biblical representation of a family history spanning three generations is illustrated by the diversity of definitions of this age which
are offered. These range from 2100/2000 B.C.[4] to the fourteenth
century B.C.[5] If the 'patriarchal age' is fixed by a chronological
approximation with Mari (c. 1800 B.C.), it cannot also be dated in
the fifteenth century B.C. (Nuzi). Here Bright is vulnerable to
Noth's criticisms: if the Execration Texts and the Mari material
bear directly on the age of the historical patriarchs, the Nuzi texts
do not (so de Vaux[6]). Since Bright dates the 'patriarchal age' between the twentieth and the seventeenth or sixteenth centuries
B.C., he ought not to cite Nuzi material as evidence of the Mesopotamian origins of the patriarchs. If they originated at Harran at
the beginning of the second millennium B.C.[7] and were part of an
Aramaean migration to Palestine, and if the lower limit of the
'patriarchal age' is the sixteenth century B.C., no direct historical

---

[1] See below, pp. 113 ff.
[2] 'Der Beitrag der Archäologie zur Geschichte Israels', pp. 269 f.; 'Mari und
Israel: eine Personnennamen Studie', *Beiträge zur historischen Theologie* 16
(1953), pp. 127-152; 'Thebes', *Archaeology and Old Testament Study*, edit. D.
Winton Thomas (1967), pp. 21-33; cf. H. B. Huffmann, *Amorite Personal Names
in the Mari Texts: a Structural and Lexical Study* (1965).
[3] 'Der Beitrag der Archäologie zur Geschichte Israels', p. 270.
[4] N. Glueck, 'The Sixth Season of Archeological Exploration in the Negeb',
BASOR 149 (1958), p. 10; 'The Seventh Season of Archaeological Exploration
in the Negeb', *BASOR* 152 (1958), pp. 18-38.
[5] C. H. Gordon, 'Abraham and the Merchants of Ura', *JNES* xvii (1958),
pp. 28-31; 'Hebrew Origins in the Light of Recent Discovery', *Biblical and
Other Studies*, edit. A. Altmann (1963), pp. 13 f.; 'Abraham and Ur', *Hebrew and
Semitic Studies*, presented to G. R. Driver (1963), pp. 77, 84.
[6] *RB* lxxii (1965), pp. 25 f.
[7] J. Bright, *A History of Israel*, p. 78 (*A History of Israel* (2), pp. 85 f.).

relations between the patriarchs and the fifteenth century Nuzi texts can be supposed.[1]

Noth is impressed by the difficulty of dating a 'patriarchal age' by the use of external attestation and also by the difficulty of illumining the details of the patriarchal narratives by setting them in a framework of political and cultural history in the second millennium B.C. In this connexion he emphasizes the privacy of the narratives and the indispensability of internal criticism: 'Whoever will discourse on the patriarchs must begin from the Old Testament tradition and cannot evade the literary and traditio-historical problems which are given with the tradition. Only when he attends to the internal criteria can he expect effective help from extra-biblical testimony.'[2]

A different direction to the quest after the historical patriarchs is given by those scholars who not only interpret the patriarchal narratives and the patriarchs within a second millennium framework of political and cultural history supplied by archaeology, but who also correct the impression of the patriarchs which is gathered from the book of Genesis in order to accommodate them to the postulated second millennium framework. Thus Gordon[3] does not so much confirm the historical accuracy of the patriarchal narratives by an appeal to pieces of archaeological evidence as reconstruct them in order to make them fit the historical and cultural setting which he has devised for them. He has little regard for the internal testimony of the narratives and appears clearly as a corrector of them rather than as one who uses archaeology in order to elucidate their extant form. The patriarchs are not semi-nomadic stock-breeders, but merchants from the Hittite realm operating with the permission of the Hittite king, and using their flocks and herds as a kind of currency in addition to silver and gold, in which Abraham is said to have been rich (Gen. 13.2; 24.35). Nor are their pursuits peaceable, as a reading of the patriarchal narratives would lead us, for the most part, to suppose, for they are aristocrats with their own militias who fight battles with kings and rulers.

The claim that archaeology has brought a new objectivity to the study of the patriarchal narratives dissolves before such an ap-

---

[1] *ibid.*, pp. 78-82. There is additional material but no significant change of position in *A History of Israel* (*2*), pp. 85-91.

[2] 'Der Beitrag der Archäologie zur Geschichte Israels', pp. 270 f.

[3] See above, p. 5, n. 5.

proach. The variety of conclusions reached by those who have set out to rediscover the historical patriarchs is at least as bewildering as the consequences of internal criticism of the narratives. In Gordon's case everything is staked on the Amarna Age being the 'patriarchal age', but there are those employing the archaeological approach who are equally adamant that everything must be staked on the first two or three centuries of the second millennium B.C.[1] Speiser[2] seeks to correct the patriarchal narratives and to relieve them of distortions by providing the archaeological framework necessary for their interpretation. In connexion with the wife-sister representation of Gen. 12, 20 and 26 he argues that there are elements of misunderstanding and distortion in the extant stories, and he recovers what he believes to have been the original form of the stories by virtually rewriting them: 'Both Abraham and Isaac were married to women who enjoyed a privileged status by the standards of their own society. It was a kind of distinction which may well have been deemed worthy of special mention in the presence of royal hosts, since it raised the standing of the visitors. Status has always been an important consideration in international relations as far back as official records can take us. But popular lore has seldom been internationally orientated.'[3] The wife-sister theme has been preserved in a botched way because of the biblical concern with the purity of the race, the same concern as finds expression in biblical genealogies. But then a virtue is made out of the straitened understanding and lack of perceptiveness of the biblical writer: 'The manifest fact that the author no longer knew the explanation, yet set down the details – details which prove to be reflections of a forgotten civilization – can mean but one thing: his aim was not to

---

[1] Albright also supposes that Abraham was a merchant, but locates him at the beginning of the second millennium B.C. He led caravans of donkeys which the texts of that period (2000-1800 B.C.) often mention, and operated along a route from Ur to Harran, to Damascus, Palestine and Egypt. Abraham was a great merchant in the cities with which he was connected (Shechem, Bethel, Hebron, Gerar) and *'abrām hā'ibrī* (Gen. 14.13) is a designation of his profession: *ḫapiru* means 'dusty man' – Abraham, as a donkey caravaneer journeys through the dust of the desert (W. F. Albright, 'Abraham the Hebrew', *BASOR* 163 (1961), pp. 36-54). Saggs also like Albright contests Gordon's identification of Ur with Ura (H. W. F. Saggs, 'Ur of the Chaldees', *Iraq* xxii (1960), pp. 200-209).

[2] A. E. Speiser, 'The Biblical Idea of History in the Common Near Eastern Setting', *IEJ* (1957), pp. 201-216; 'The Wife-Sister Motif in the Patriarchal Narratives', *Biblical and Other Studies*, edit. A. Altmann (1963), pp. 15-28.

[3] 'The Wife-Sister Motif', p. 28.

question or to reason why, but only to record faithfully what tradition had handed down to him. His task was to retell not to originate. He might lavish his genius on the form but not on the substance.'[1] This is an extraordinary argument. Stories which (*ex hypothesi*) are distorted versions of their originals are historically valuable because they are faithfully transmitted. Their author was only dimly aware of the significance of the material which he was handling, but he preserved this ill-understood substance and exercised his skill and creativity on the 'form'. Against this it must be affirmed that the extant patriarchal narratives have an aesthetic and artistic *raison d'être* and that they are not to be explained as botched historiography with the element of literary creativeness confined to the 'form'.[2]

Speiser's remarks in another place are not altogether reconcilable with the position just described. He now stresses rather the correctness of the historical reminiscences in the patriarchal narratives, although they are not 'conventional historiography': 'The author retells events in his own inimitable way: he does not invent them. What is thus committed to writing is tradition in the reverent care of a literary genius. Where that tradition can be independently checked, it proves to be authentic.'[3] The tendency to use the word 'tradition' in the sense of 'reliable historical reminiscence'[4] is another aspect of the concentration on historiographical questions in the study of the patriarchal narratives. This evaluative use of

---

[1] 'The Biblical Idea of History', p. 214.

[2] Cf. R. de Vaux, *RB* lxxii, pp. 22 ff.; *Histoire Ancienne D'Israël*, pp. 234 f. De Vaux also has the idea that the patriarchal narratives are botched historiography. He says that when the story of Rachel's theft of Laban's gods was fixed in writing, the legal significance of the idols had been forgotten and that the extant narrative (Gen. 31.19 ff.) has a burlesque aspect. He supposes that the accounts in Gen. 12, 20 and 26 may have been botched: 'It is possible that the primitive sense of these episodes would have been different, and that Abraham and Isaac would have wanted to boast before their royal hosts about the honourable rank held by their wives' (*RB* lxxii, pp. 22 f.). De Vaux's attitude to alleged Nuzi parallels to the patriarchal narratives is more negative in his *Histoire* than it was in his earlier work. He now says that the resemblance between the Nuzi ban on expelling the offspring of a slave girl and the Hagar/Ishmael story is superficial (p. 234). He rejects the wife-sister legal arrangement as an interpretative key for Gen. 12, 20 and 26 (pp. 234 f.), and he dismisses the suggestion that there are traces of *errebu* marriage in Gen. 24 and 27. He discounts the hypothesis that Jacob was Laban's adopted son whose legal status was disturbed by the subsequent birth of a natural son. He minimizes the connexion between Gen. 15.1-3 and Nuzi contracts of adoption (pp. 235-237).

[3] 'The Biblical Idea of History', p. 210.

[4] So John Bright, *Early Israel*, p. 55.

'tradition' is distinct from its historiographically neutral sense in 'history of tradition', and the neutral as well as the evaluative sense is to be found in Clements.[1] That a traditio-historical method may yield negative rather than positive conclusions in relation to the historicity of the patriarchal narratives is illustrated by Clements' observation that the genealogical scheme Abraham-Isaac-Jacob is secondary and unhistorical,[2] and that the association of Abraham with Shechem, Bethel and Beersheba is secondary.[3] Thus a study of the history of the tradition of the patriarchal narratives can be undertaken on the assumption that the genre is a non-historiographical one, and this is the character of Noth's history of tradition of these narratives.

I return to a final example of the rewriting of the patriarchal narratives in the light of a construction placed on historical and cultural conditions of life in the second millennium B.C. Yeivin[4] urges that the patriarchs were not merchants (against Albright and Gordon) but 'haulage contractors' and that the migration from Ur is to be explained by the circumstance that the demand for caravans of asses to transport merchandise was declining in that place.[5] In Harran the Terahites came into conflict with other groups which had a vested interest in hiring donkeys, and it was this situation which led to the further migration of the 'Abrahamites', while the 'Nahorites' remained in Harran.[6] The reason why the patriarchs are represented in the book of Genesis as stock-breeders and not caravaneers is that the business of hiring donkeys had declined and they had been forced to seek another means of livelihood. The split between the 'Abrahamites' and the 'Lotites' is perhaps to be connected with this change of occupation. 'The high roads of international commerce were becoming more and more hazardous, and international trade, at least, being reduced to a mere trickle. Consequently economic stress had to be shifted more and more to stock-breeding.'[7] But the 'Nahorites' had made the same shift of occupation and consequently needed more *Lebens-*

---

[1] *Abraham and David*, pp. 30, 31 f., where the sense is evaluative.
[2] *ibid.*, pp. 30 f.
[3] *ibid.*, p. 56.
[4] S. Yeivin, 'The Age of the Patriarchs', *Revista degli Studi Orientali* xxxviii (1963), pp. 276-302.
[5] *ibid.*, pp. 279, 285.
[6] *ibid.*, p. 285.
[7] *ibid.*, p. 292.

raum. The squeeze exerted on them by expanding Hurrian kingdoms in northern Mesopotamia forced them into the steppe border
lands beyond the Euphrates, and the deterioration of the relationship between Laban and Jacob is 'probably to be attributed to the
consequent curtailment of the areas available to these pastoral
clans. With Jacob's return to Canaan the rift is complete, with a
definite demarcation of the zones in which Abrahamites and
Nahorites respectively shall move in the future.'[1]

When the patriarchal narratives are 'corrected' as they are by
Gordon, Albright, Speiser and Yeivin, and the patriarchs and
'patriarchal age' are described in accordance with an interpretation
of external evidence bearing on historical, social and economic
conditions in the second millennium B.C., the narratives themselves, in their particularity, are no longer being taken seriously.
The method does not inspire confidence, and it has not produced
uniform results, but even if it were argued that this is the way to
arrive at the truth about the patriarchs and the 'patriarchal age',
it cannot be said to constitute a study of the patriarchal narratives
in the form in which we have them in the book of Genesis. My
interest, however, is not to win an easy victory by opposing
excesses or aberrations, but to bring the discussion back to the
central contention that a well-balanced criticism of the patriarchal
narratives cannot be achieved unless adequate consideration is
given to the question of their genre. The significance attached to
external, archaeological evidence cannot be freed from a dependence on an assumption about the kind of literature to which it is
being applied. Even those who, like Gordon, Albright, Speiser and
Yeivin, deal in a somewhat free fashion with the extant patriarchal
narratives, nevertheless make an assumption that they are a kind
of historiography and that their value consists in the corrected
historiography which can be gathered from them with the help of
external evidence.

The consequences which flow from a neglect of a proper consideration of the genre of the patriarchal narratives are to be seen
even where there is no marked enthusiasm for archaeology, or, at
any rate, no exaggerated expectations of what external evidence
will yield, and this can be shown with reference to the work of
Rowley.[2] While Rowley assumes that the patriarchal narratives

[1] *ibid.*, pp. 293 f.
[2] H. H. Rowley, 'Recent Discovery and the Patriarchal Age', *BJRL* 32
(1949/50), pp. 44-79.

are historiography and that the patriarchs are historical individuals, he appeals to internal biblical evidence rather than to external, archaeological evidence, and his position is different from those who argue that the latter is the decisive factor in the historical evaluation of the narratives. Although Rowley holds that the patriarchal narratives fit into the historical and cultural framework of the second millennium B.C., and employs archaeology and other extra-biblical sources in order to elucidate the world of the patriarchs and the part which they played in it, he observes that it is 'a gross exaggeration to say that there is any external proof of this'. He continues: 'Our sole evidence for the existence of Abraham or for his residence in Ur is to be found in the Bible.'[1] In the same note he remarks, 'I see no reason to doubt the Biblical statement that Abraham once lived in Ur', and this is an indication that the possibility of the patriarchal narratives being a non-historiographical genre is one which he does not begin to entertain. The narratives are rudimentary history, whatever imaginative accretions they may have gathered, and the scholar's task is to employ archaeology and other external evidence in order to illumine the patriarchs' world and their role in it.[2]

If considerations of genre were to lead one to the conclusion that the patriarchal narratives are not historiographical in any sense and that the patriarchs are not historical individuals, Rowley's premise would be denied and his massive undertaking in *From Joseph to Joshua* would lose its point. Even if such a negative position is not assumed, Rowley's lack of method in relation to the genre of the patriarchal narratives is a disconcerting aspect of his work. It is most clearly seen in relation to Jacob and his 'sons', where a tribal-historical interpretation of the 'sons' of Jacob is combined with the belief that the 'sons' of Jacob were historical individuals. Thus: 'In the Biblical account the Shechem incident (xxxiv) is placed before the descent into Egypt. We find in that age two separate groups, one in the neighbourhood of Hebron and one at Shechem, but in touch with one another. Joseph is sent by his father from Hebron to his brethren in the Shechem area, and since Hebron lay in the area of Judah's activity, this would be consistent with the view that Judah, Simeon and Levi advanced

[1] *ibid.*, p. 45, n. 1.
[2] H. H. Rowley, *From Joseph to Joshua: Biblical Traditions in the Light of Archaeology*. The Schweich Lectures of the British Academy for 1948 (1950), pp. 26, 77, n. 2, 114 f., 116 ff.

together from the south, while Simeon and Levi pressed further north. It would accord with conditions of the Amarna Age, when there was Ḥabiru activity south of Jerusalem and also in the Shechem area.[1]

Jacob and Joseph are apparently historical individuals, father and son, and the other 'sons' of Jacob are described as 'brethren' of Joseph, and so are also presumably envisaged as historical individuals who are sons of Jacob in a plain sense and who have become leaders of tribes. That this is how Rowley understands the matter is clear from the following: 'In the Biblical tradition of that age, while Simeon and Levi have bands of followers and are able to attack towns, Joseph appears as a single individual. There is therefore no tribe of Joseph at this stage. Neither is there any tribe of Benjamin. For at an even later stage in the story Benjamin is represented as still a boy at home, who is not with his brothers.'[2] Rowley uses the scheme of Jacob and his 'sons' as a case of tribal history represented by family history, that is, the 'sons' are Israelite tribes. At the same time he treats Jacob as an historical individual and he envisages a situation where, as it were, some of the sons of Jacob have left home and have become leaders of tribes and personifications of tribes, while Joseph and Benjamin are still at home and merely have the status of individuals. Joseph eventually becomes the leader of a tribe and its personification and so does Benjamin. Rowley represents a father and his family of sons who all in the course of time become leaders of tribes, so that their names become the names of tribes. Joseph's career in Egypt is described in detail and the narrative is said to have substantial historical value.[3] The birth of Manasseh and Ephraim in Egypt is understood literally, and is, so to speak, how Joseph makes a beginning in the acquisition of a tribe.

Tribal history and the history of individuals cannot be credibly combined in this way. Since we know that the 'sons' of Jacob were Israelite tribes, we should certainly conclude that the scheme of Jacob and his 'sons' is a device for dealing with the history of tribal groups and that the 'sons' of Jacob are tribes and nothing but tribes. This applies also to Joseph, although there is here the

---

[1] *ibid.*, p. 115.
[2] *ibid.*, p. 115; cf. pp. 120 f., 141.
[3] *ibid.*, pp. 116 ff.

special problem of relating the tribal Joseph to the Joseph story and especially to the Egyptian Joseph.[1]

This book reflects a conviction about the need for an interest in the history of the criticism of the patriarchal narratives. The description of biblical criticism as a 'science' is not entirely unjustified, but in so far as it conjures up the view that prevailing fashions are normative science which has relegated to obsolescence all previous essays in criticism the nomenclature is misleading. It is in the nature of science that textbooks go quickly out of date and have an interest for those who are historians of science rather than for scientists. Biblical criticism, on the other hand, requires that we should always have a sense of the cumulative gains of criticism – an awareness that other men have laboured and we have entered into their labours.

I have reacted against an excessive concentration on new 'evidence' and too much conjuring with the word 'research' in the recent study of the patriarchal narratives. It is right that scholars should be exercised with new evidence, but there has been a miscalculation of its effects on the study of the patriarchal narratives. There is the view that it revolutionizes their study and that earlier critics have no more to teach us. There is always a narrowness and a certain obsessive character about any modern fashion of scholarship which has to be corrected. Undue concentration on one line of approach constitutes an impoverishment of the study of the patriarchal narratives and we need a vision of a many-sided and ample subject to which there are different avenues of approach and which like a precious stone has many points of brilliance.

In particular, an aspect of imbalance which I have sought to correct is the too great concentration on the question of the degree of historicity which is to be attributed to the patriarchal narratives. I have acknowledged that this is an important matter and that it has a bearing on the theology of the narratives which may be thought crucial, but justice cannot be done to the patriarchal narratives as literature, if the approach is too much dominated by this concern. When we have asked in what sense if any these stories are historical sources, we have hardly entered the province of literary appreciation. The patriarchal narratives also demand aesthetic analysis and the voice of Gunkel should still be heard.

It is necessary to guard against the narrow use of the term

[1] See below, pp. 72 ff., 87 ff., 101 ff., 146 ff.

'literary criticism' which is customary in biblical studies. Literary criticism is equated with source criticism and documentary hypotheses, but this is only a small part of the meaning of the term in wider fields of literature. Gunkel is a literary critic in the restricted sense in so far as his understanding of the patriarchal narratives takes off from a particular version of the documentary hypothesis. A more distinctive methodological orientation is his concern to establish the *Gattung* of the narratives, since this has a decisive effect on his interpretation, and his change of mind between the first and third editions of *Genesis* is to be correlated with it. Over and above the areas which are subject to such methodological influence there is in Gunkel a type of literary criticism which approximates to the wider non-biblical use of that term and which addresses itself to the merit of the stories as literature.

It was this which led him to speak of them as 'poetry', to savour their fragrance and to enter into a minute description of their mechanics and how they secured their effects. He was treading on dangerous ground, for Old Testament critical scholarship, with its respect for solidity and for philological competence, has not made many concessions to the soul of a poet, and it is understandable that Gunkel was thought by some to be 'an aesthete and an impressionist'. It may be that this anxiety was not entirely misplaced, that there was something of the romantic fallacy in Gunkel's approach, and that a man who had taken up the torch of Herder needed to be watched. We may say if we like that this was an idiosyncratic approach and that it did not deserve to acquire a representative significance. Or we may think of it more highly, as I venture to do, and say that it bears the marks of genius and is studded with brilliance.

An interesting fact which emerges from the study of the patriarchal stories as tribal history is that a method of interpretation can survive and be vigorously and ably represented long after it has ceased to be a fashion of scholarship and when it no longer enjoys general support and approval. Steuernagel's book published in 1901 may be regarded as the high-water mark of this type of interpretation, and in Gunkel's first edition of *Genesis* (1901) it is a kind of vestigial relic which accords ill with his principal contention that the patriarchal narratives are developed from stories about gods. In Gunkel's subsequent editions of *Genesis* the tribal-historical element of interpretation almost disappears, and it is explicitly rejected by Noth as incompatible with his view that the kernel of the patriarchal narratives is cultic history. It appears to most scholars now that it has only a narrow sphere of relevance to the patriarchal narratives, but it is prominent in Eissfeldt and is important in connexion with a consideration of the 'sons' of Jacob who were Israelite tribes.

The work of Alt and Noth enabled me to illustrate that archaeological evidence is susceptible of different interpretations and that there is an indissoluble reciprocity between the view which is taken of the archaeological evidence and the genre to which the narratives are allocated. It seemed to me a serious enterprise to examine in detail Noth's treatment of the patriarchal narratives and to show how his complicated argument is related to a nuclear concept that the genre is cultic history. If at the beginning of the history of the tradition of the narratives a post-amphictyonic situation is reflected, the ongoing cultic history to be inferred from these narratives and the subsequent processes of literary elaboration must *a fortiori* be located in the post-settlement period. The key which Noth uses to unlock the significance of the stories does not allow them to be historical traditions in a plain sense. They can tell us nothing about the lives of the patriarchs or the historical circumstances of Israelite tribes prior to the settlement in Canaan. The most that can be said about the patriarchs themselves on the basis of the kernel of cultic history is that they were founders of a particular type of semi-nomadic cult. Such historical connexions as the stories possess are not communicated directly and have to be inferred. By this process they can, to some extent, be correlated with the post-settlement, historical circumstances of the Israelite tribes in Canaan.

Any discussion of the religion of the patriarchs is also controlled by the view which is taken of the genre of the patriarchal narratives. If these are 'historical traditions' or 'epics' which record the movements of Abraham, the father of Israel, from Mesopotamia to Canaan, and the subsequent movements of the patriarchs in and around Canaan, it is possible on this basis to enquire about the religion of the patriarchs: to ask whether they brought El religion with them to Canaan or appropriated it there; to discuss how they combined a family or clan religion with the religion of El. If, however, the patriarchal narratives are thought to be cultic history, the patriarchs are founders of cults who never set foot in Canaan, although their descendants, who had adhered to these cults, did settle there. If this is the state of affairs, the only information which we can pick up from the patriarchal stories is the nature of the relationships between 'god of the fathers' cults and Yahwism, or 'god of the fathers' cults and the cult of El, or the cult of Yahweh and the cult of El. In brief, we can recover cultic history from the patriarchal narratives, but not *Religionsgeschichte* – that is, not the religion of Abraham, Isaac and Jacob. We cannot speak directly about the religion of historical individuals, if the genre is cultic history. Another possibility opens up if the narratives are defined as *Märchen*. Given that the stories are literature of this type, there can be no question of historical patriarchs, but it can be argued (as Gressmann and the later Gunkel do) that the stories reflect a semi-nomadic culture on the fringes of Canaan, that the cult of El was located in this cultural context, and that it was brought into Canaan by the Israelites when they moved in to the settled land.

In the final chapter the problem of the theology of the patriarchal narratives is raised and the background to this enquiry is the entire, foregoing complex of critical considerations. That the question about the degree of historicity attaching to the patriarchal narratives has some theological importance should be acknowledged, but there is room for disagreement about how central and crucial a matter this is. The establishing of the historicity of the patriarchal narratives does not by itself confer abiding, theological significance on them. For this we need more than assurances that Abraham, Isaac and Jacob are historical individulas of deep antiquity. On the other hand, it is not a matter of indifference to those who are exercised with the theology of the narratives whether or not there is such an historical infra-structure. Without it there is perhaps a docetic taint, or the danger that the theology which has been erected is poised over a great void. It is more satisfactory to relate a theological structure to men who shared our experiences of life and death than to men who are no more substantial than characters in stories. But we should not carry this argument so far as to urge that the only significant theology of the patriarchal narratives to be achieved must rest on the premise that they are a kind of historiography.

CHAPTER I

The History of the Genre

I

In his first edition of *Genesis* published in 1901 Gunkel[1] is more reticent than some of his predecessors in relating the patriarchal narratives to astral-mythology and in asserting that the patriarchs and their wives were originally deities. He is, however, as Weidmann's book[2] shows, influenced by their approach to the stories. Gunkel's account of the history of the genre, which traces the patriarchal narratives to an origin in myth, is indebted to Meyer[3] and Luther,[4] and the thought that the patriarchs are Canaanite figures, on which Gunkel insists in *Genesis* (*1*), is found in Baentsch.[5] Moreover, while he avoids the astral-mythological speculations of Winckler[6] and does not make the error of supposing that these are consistent with the assertion that the patriarchs were historical individuals, Winckler's insight that the date of a document does not necessarily supply the date of the smaller units which constitute it is one which was subsequently to prove fruitful in Gunkel's work.[7]

According to *Genesis* (*1*) the origins of the patriarchal narratives are, for the most part, non-Israelite:

A portion of these legends, perhaps very many, did not originate in Israel, but were carried into Israel from foreign countries.[8]

[1] Hermann Gunkel, *Genesis* (*HKAT*, herausgegeben von W. Nowack, 1901), hereafter *Genesis* (*1*).

[2] H. Weidmann, *Die Patriarchen und ihre Religion im Licht der Forschung seit Julius Wellhausen* (*FRLANT* 94, 1968).

[3] E. Meyer, *Die Israeliten und ihre Nachbarstämme*, 1906.

[4] B. Luther, 'Die israelitischen Stämme', *ZAW* 21 (1901), pp. 1-76; 'Die Persönlichkeit des Jahwisten' in E. Meyer, *op. cit.*, pp. 105-173.

[5] B. Baentsch, *Altorientalischer und israelitischer Monotheismus* (1906), p. 54.

[6] H. Winckler, *Die babylonische Geisteskultur in ihrer Beziehungen zur Kulturentwicklung der Menschheit, Wissenschaft und Bildung* 15 (1907); cf. W. Klatt, *Hermann Gunkel: Zu seiner Theologie der Religionsgeschichte und zur Entstehung der formgeschichtlichen Methode* (*FRLANT* 100, 1969), p. 135, n. 36.

[7] For an ampler discussion and for fuller bibliographical information see Weidmann, *op. cit.*, pp. 69-94.

[8] H. Gunkel (translated by W. H. Carruth), *The Legends of Genesis* (1901), p. 88. This is a translation of the Introduction to *Genesis* (*1*). It has been reissued as a Schocken paperback (1964, 1966).

Now if we recall that Israel lived upon a soil enriched by the civilization of thousands of years, that it lived by no means in a state of isolation but was surrounded on all sides by races of superior culture, and if we consider further the international trade and intercourse of the early ages, which went from Babylonia to Egypt and from Arabia to the Mediterranean by way of Palestine, we are warranted in assuming that the position of Israel among the nations will be reflected in its legends as well as in its language, which must literally be full of borrowed words.[1]

The patriarchal narratives are sagas[2] and, as such, are an international genre whose themes and characters are disseminated throughout the Ancient Near East and beyond it.

Hence we have to reckon with stories which have a universal character, which are not originally or essentially Israelite and which were first appropriated by Israel in Canaan. The patriarchal narratives are Canaanite forms of an international culture and nothing distinctively Israelite is expressed in their action and characterization.

The legends of worship in Genesis we may assume with the greatest certainty to have originated in the places which they treat. The same may be said of other legends which ascribe names to definite places. Accordingly it is probable that most of the legends of the patriarchs were known before Israel came into Canaan.[3]

The legends of the beginnings are in the main Babylonian, the legends of the Patriarchs are essentially Canaanitish and after these come the specifically Israelitish traditions. This picture corresponds to the history of the development of civilization; in Canaan the civilization grows up on a foundation essentially Babylonian and after this comes the Israelitish national life.[4]

The earliest expressions of Israelite national consciousness are found in a different genre, namely, the heroic tales collected in the book of Judges, whose warlike character contrasts with the pacific temper of the patriarchal stories, and which emerge about 1200 B.C. when the formation of the patriarchal narratives was complete.[5] The horizons of these heroic tales are narrower, and their cultural milieu more restricted than that of the patriarchal narratives. They reflect the early stirrings of a national awareness in a community precariously lodged in Canaan, still unassured of consolidation and progress towards nationhood and culture. The transition from

---

[1] *ibid.*, p. 89.
[2] Carruth translates *Sagen* by 'legends'; cf. Albright's introduction to the 1966 reprinting, p. xi.
[3] *ibid.*, pp. 91 f.   [4] *ibid.*, p. 93.   [5] *ibid.*, pp. 24, 92, 137.

one genre to another is an illustration of the correlation between Israelite literary history and the total history of the community.

Consistent with this view that the patriarchal stories are a far-travelled genre, which Israel first appropriated in the cultural context of Canaan, is Gunkel's flirtation in *Genesis* (*I*) with the theory that saga is ultimately to be derived from myth. He observes that Sarah and Milkah are the names of goddesses of Harran with which the biblical figures Sarah and Milcah may have been connected. He correlates Laban and *lebānā* 'moon' and says,

The fact that Laban is represented as being a shepherd would correspond to his character as a moon god: for the moon god may be represented as the shepherd of the clouds.[1]

He continues,

In ancient as well as in modern times the attempt has repeatedly been made to explain the figures of Abraham, Isaac and Jacob as originally gods. There is no denying that this conjecture is very plausible. The whole species of the legend (saga) – though not indeed every individual legend – originated in the myth; at least many legends are derived from myths.[2]

Among the extant patriarchal narratives not many pieces

can be interpreted with reasonable certainty as remnants of mythical narratives,[3]

but Gunkel reproduces Winckler's theory that Abraham's three hundred and eighteen servants (Gen. 14.14) may be elucidated as a lunar myth – the moon is visible for three hundred and eighteen days of the year.[4]

Jacob's wrestling with God suggests that this Jacob was really a Titan, and consequently we can scarcely avoid seeing here a faded-out myth.[5]

There is evidence here that Gunkel is still under the influence of the astral-mythological theories of Winckler and others and is still attracted by the hypothesis that the patriarchs were originally deities who have been demoted to human stature. The position in *Genesis* (*I*) is that he recognizes the need for caution. The hypothesis is unproven but he hopes that one day it may be more fully substantiated.

But before we are warranted in declaring with regard to a figure in Genesis that it bears the imprint of an earlier god we must demand not merely that certain elements of a story *permit* a mythical interpretation but that whole legends shall possess striking resemblances to known

[1] *ibid.*, p. 119. [2] *ibid.*, p. 119. [3] *ibid.*, p. 120.
[4] *Genesis* (*I*), p. 259. [5] *Legends*, p. 120.

myths, or that they can be interpreted as myths in perfectly clear and unquestioned fashion. Such a demonstration as this has not been given by investigators hitherto. Let us hope that those who attempt it in the future may be more successful.[1]

Hence Gunkel finally adopts an agnostic position:

Accordingly we are unable to say what the figures of Abraham, Isaac and Jacob, which chiefly interest us, may have signified originally. But this is by no means strange. These matters are simply too primitive for us.[2]

So far the genre represented by the patriarchal narratives has been described by Gunkel as an aspect of international culture and as possessing a high antiquity. The aetiological contribution to the definition of the genre is in accord with these indications. The patriarchal narratives supply answers to questions which are evidence of intellectual or even scientific curiosity. Thus the ethnological stories are 'the first rudiments of a philosophy of history',[3] the etymologies are the 'beginning of a science of language',[4] the cultic stories 'the beginning of a history of religion'[5] and the geological legends pre-scientific answers to scientific questions.[6] In every case the answer is given by telling a story and the fundamental implication of an aetiological interpretation of these narratives is that they are not what they seem to be. They appear to be historical, because the question, whatever its nature, is always answered by telling a story, but they have no value as historiography, because the primary phenomenon to which the question refers is non-historical. The intellectual curiosity which the story seeks to satisfy is, for the most part, non-historical. I say 'for the most part', because there are 'ethnographic' narratives which Gunkel describes as historical[7] and 'ethnological' narratives[8] whose content is fictional but which address themselves to historical matters. Gunkel remarks,

Such ethnological legends, which tell a fictitious story in order to explain tribal relations, are of course very difficult to distinguish from historical legends which contain the remnant of a tradition of some actual event. Very commonly ethnological and ethnographic features are combined in the same legend: the relations underlying the story are historical, but the way in which they are explained is poetic.[9]

Gunkel knows that the patriarchal narratives are not poetry in a strict sense,[10] but he has special reasons for maintaining that they

---

[1] *ibid.*, pp. 120 f.   [2] *ibid.*, p. 122.   [3] *ibid.*, p. 27.
[4] *ibid.*, p. 27.   [5] *ibid.*, p. 34.   [6] *ibid.*, p. 34.
[7] *ibid.*, p. 24.   [8] *ibid.*, pp. 25 f.   [9] *ibid.*, p. 26.
[10] *ibid.*, pp. 37 f.

are poetry rather than prose, saga rather than historiography. In connexion with his understanding of aetiology his intention is to indicate the sway of poetry over ratiocination at this stage of man's intellectual and cultural history. Ancient man has forms of intellectual curiosity but he is not a scientific animal. His creativity, his instincts for elucidation, are imaginative rather than scientific, and the vehicle of release for questions of any kind which nag at him is poetry rather than science. Science is present in the form of some of the questions, but the frame of mentality out of which a scientific method could come does not yet exist. The answer of the aetiological tale comes from the childhood of the world.

The answer which the child gives itself and with which it is for the time satisfied is perhaps very childish and hence incorrect, and yet, if it is a bright child, the answer is interesting and touching even for the grown man. In the same way a primitive people asks similar questions and answers them as best it can. The questions are usually the same that we ourselves are asking and trying to answer in our scientific researches. Hence what we find in these legends are the beginnings of human science, only humble beginnings, of course, and yet venerable to us because they are beginnings, and at the same time peculiarly attractive and touching, for in these answers ancient Israel has uttered its most intimate feelings, clothing them in the bright garb of poetry.[1]

It is because of the 'poetic' nature of the answer which is given that Gunkel can say that the stories are aetiologies and yet are not expressly or prosaically didactic.

As has been shown above many of the legends are intended to answer definite questions. That is, these legends are not the thoughtless play of the imagination acting without other purpose than the search for the beautiful, but they have a specific purpose, a point which is to instruct. Accordingly if these narratives are to attain their object they must make this point very clear. They do this in a decided way, so decidedly that even we late-born moderns can see the point clearly and can infer from it the question answered. The sympathetic reader who has followed the unhappy Hagar on her way through the desert will find no word in the whole story more touching than the one which puts an end to all her distress. God hears. But this word contains at the same time the point aimed at, for on this the narrator wished to build the interpretation of the name Ishmael.[2]

Again:

The art of the story-tellers consists in avoiding every suspicion of deliberate purpose at the same time as they give prominence to their point. With marvellous elegance, with fascinating grace, they manage to reach

[1] *ibid.*, p. 25.   [2] *ibid.*, pp. 74 f.

the goal which they have set. They tell a little story so charmingly and with such fidelity to nature that we listen to them all unsuspecting: and all at once, before we expect it, they are at their goal.[1]

Since the answer is supplied in 'poetry', that is, by a form of story-telling which commands interest and awakens wonder because of its own intrinsic aesthetic merits, one is made to forget that there is an intention to teach and is, as it were, instructed by stealth.[2]

Some examples may now be given of Gunkel's different categories of aetiological stories and then enough will have been said about aetiology so far as *Genesis* (*1*) is concerned.

Ethnological and Ethnographic Stories.[3] The story of the escape of Lot from the doomed town of Sodom explains why his descendants, the Moabites, live in the east Jordanian hill country (Gen. 19). The notice that Reuben had sexual intercourse with Bilhah, his father's concubine, is intended to explain why the tribe Reuben lost its original primacy (Gen. 35.22). The story of the treaty between Jacob and Laban explains why the border between Israel and the Aramaeans is at Gilead (Gen. 31.51-54). Gunkel's distinction between 'historical' and 'ethnographic' is illustrated by his evaluation of the treaty of Beersheba[4] (Gen. 26.23-33; 21.22-34): the account of why Beersheba belongs to the Israelites and not to the people of Gerar is historical reminiscence rather than inventive aetiology.[5] The distinction between 'ethnographic' and 'ethnological' is nicely made with reference to the Ishmael story (Gen. 16; 21) which is ethnographical in so far as it accurately describes the nomadic character of Ishmaelite life and is a valid piece of cultural history, and is ethnological in so far as the story of Hagar's flight is fiction.

Etymological Stories[6]. Jacob receives his name because at birth he held his brother by the heel (Gen. 25.26). Beersheba ('the well of seven') is so-called because Abraham there gave Abimelech seven lambs (Gen. 21.28 ff.), or, according to another aetiology, it means 'the well of oath' because Abraham and Abimelech made a covenant there (Gen. 21.31 f.). Isaac got his name from the circumstance

[1] *ibid.*, p. 76.
[2] Cf. *Genesis* (*3*), p. xlix.
[3] *Legends*, pp. 24-27.
[4] *ibid.*, p. 24.
[5] *ibid.*, p. 35.
[6] *ibid.*, pp. 27-30.

that his mother laughed in derision when his birth was foretold to her (Gen. 18.12 ff.). Gunkel observes that the point of a story is never merely etymological – etymology is always a subordinate aetiology or, at any rate, it is not the sole aetiological element.[1]

Cultic Stories.[2] Stories which associate the patriarchs with Canaanite sanctuaries represent that they are the founders of these sanctuaries or, at least, are intended to legitimate these holy places as centres of Yahwistic worship. More specialized cultic aetiologies are the story of the intended sacrifice of Isaac, which explains why the sacrifice of a lamb has been substituted for human sacrifice at Jeruel (Gen. 22), and the story of Jacob at Penuel. The latter explains the origin of a limping dance which was a feature of the cult there and also a dietary peculiarity of the Israelites (Gen. 32.23-33). Lahai Roi is a sanctuary of the tribe of Ishmael, because Hagar was comforted there by a deity (Gen. 16; 21).

Geological Stories.[3] The barrenness of the area around the Dead Sea is explained by the story of the destruction of Sodom and Gomorrah (Gen. 19). Why is the territory around Zoar an exception to the general desolation of the area? Because Yahweh spared it as a refuge for Lot (Gen. 19.17-22). A peculiar rock formation ('a pillar of salt') is explained by the story of Lot's wife (Gen. 19.26).

Mixed Stories. On the Hagar story Gunkel says:

The flight of Hagar is to be called ethnographic, because it depicts the life of Ishmael; ethnologic, because it undertakes to explain these conditions; in one feature it is allied to ceremonial (i.e., cultic) legends, its explanation of the sacredness of Lacha-Roi; furthermore it has etymological elements in its explanation of the names Lacha-Roi and Ishmael.[4]

On Beersheba he says:

The legends of Beersheba (xxi 22 ff.; xxvi) contain remnants of history, telling of a tribal treaty established there, and at the same time certain religious features, as the explanation of the sanctity of the place, and finally some etymological elements.[5]

On Penuel:

The legend of Penuel explains the sanctity of the place, the ceremony of limping and the names Penuel and Israel.[6]

[1] *ibid.*, p. 35.
[2] *ibid.*, pp. 30-34.
[3] *ibid.*, p. 34.
[4] *ibid.*, pp. 34 f.
[5] *ibid.*, p. 35.
[6] *ibid.*, p. 35.

II

Gunkel's criticism of the patriarchal narratives is much influenced by his conviction that they are essentially short stories throughout which a single mood (*Stimmung*) prevails. His concern is to discover the constitution and range of their aesthetic unity, and he decides that this is to be found not in larger entities which are the result of a combination of individual stories but in the individual stories themselves. The short story is constitutive of the genre and each one is a perfectly formed little gem. The short story is the *Gattung* and the art of criticism consists in identifying these original aesthetic units, each of which has its own beauty and completeness, and of describing minutely wherein consists its excellence and dramatic effectiveness.[1] It is not too difficult to disentangle the individual story from the massive literary context in which it now exists, for each story has a clear beginning and an easily recognizable conclusion.[2] This is an aspect of Gunkel's criticism which is stable and more or less unaffected by the changes in his position between the publication of *Genesis* (*1*) in 1901 and *Genesis* (*3*) in 1910. The reason for the stability of these views is their purely aesthetic character and their consequent relative isolation from his shifting opinions about the origins of the patriarchal stories and the extent of their aetiological function.

Gunkel is offering here a detailed analysis of what he alluded to in his discussion of aetiology,[3] when he noted the artistic or poetic quality of the story which supplied an answer to the question asked. Now the aetiological aspect disappears from the discussion and it is the beauty of the story itself, irrespective of its aetiological function, to which criticism is entirely devoted. But the success of such criticism depends on the capacity of the interpreter to enter the antique world of these stories. They belong to the childhood of the world and one must journey into antiquity and become a little child in order to understand them. The modernizing critic whose concern is to demonstrate the contemporaneousness of the stories will misunderstand them and do violence to them. Their beauty can be rediscovered and appreciated only in the world in which they were told and heard.[4] In a letter to his publisher, dated the 16th March, 1897, Gunkel says:

Dillman despite his great merit, particularly in relation to Genesis, is no

---

[1] *ibid.*, pp. 42 f.
[2] *Genesis* (*3*), p. xxxii.
[3] Above pp. 20-23.
[4] *Genesis* (*3*), p. xii.

more than a dessicated scholar by whom the beauty and naïve childlikeness of the old stories have not been properly understood, while Delitzsch everywhere substitutes modern, harsh tones for the simple unpretentious colours.[1]

Paradoxically Gunkel combined his insistence that the stories must not be modernized, but must be recovered and displayed in the depth of their antiquity, with the conviction that this exercise would be a contribution to the effective communication of these stories to his contemporaries. In a letter to his publisher, dated the 3rd of June, 1910, relating to a 'popular' work on Genesis which was projected, he says:

Our lay people are aesthetically conditioned to an outstanding degree. They are thankful when aesthetic enjoyment is given to them. . . . Who among our laymen takes Genesis into his hands in order to enjoy it? There is no layman to-day who is capable of such immediate enjoyment. Rather it must first be communicated to the layman in what respects Genesis has its own beauty. . . . The way to the content for him is through delight in the aesthetic form. The procedure of the literary-critical method is quite different. . . . My special art is to uncover and portray the aesthetic.[2]

That Gunkel is a critic in search of beauty may be gathered from an essay dating from 1904:

Since the great Herder communicated the grandeur of the Old Testament to the world with a tongue of flame there has never been a complete lack of those who have testified to the beauty of that creation.[3]

Form and content of a work of art do not fall apart as Dear Mr. Philistine supposes; they have the closest relation to one another, for the right form is the necessary expression of the content.[4]

On this Klatt remarks:

By aesthetic consideration Gunkel means nothing less than the appraisal of a work of literature by analysis of its form and content, so as to elucidate in what way this work calls forth the impression of the Beautiful.[5]

How complex a person Gunkel is appears from the circumstance that, despite his praise of beauty and his search after it, there is a religious earnestness in him which will not be quenched and which, in the last analysis, regards the aesthetic as no more than

[1] Cited by W. Klatt, *op. cit.*, p. 117.
[2] Cited by W. Klatt, *op. cit.*, p. 118.
[3] 'Ziele und Methoden der Erklärung des Alten Testamentes', *Zeitschrift für praktische Theologie* xxvi (1904), pp. 521-540; *Reden und Aufsätze* (1913), p. 22.
[4] *ibid.*, p. 23.
[5] *op. cit.*, p. 120, n. 19.

a means to a higher end. This is indicated already when he says of the laymen about whom he has been speaking,

The way to the content for him is through delight in the aesthetic form.[1]

Or again:

For the artistic beauty of the Old Testament is for us only a flower which we find on our way. We should not be such barbarians as to pass by such charming beauty without recognizing it. But we must go on to the end of the road, for we are not aesthetes but theologians.[2]

Nevertheless, he sets his face against the indiscriminate use of the stories as paradigms of piety or quarries for dogmatic theologians. Everything is not to be overlaid with gold, else the antique colour will be lost. A sympathetic appreciation of the old stories is at the same time a willingness to see them as they are and not as piety would like them to be. That which is of little value or even scandalous is to be acknowledged with candour.[3]

Klatt[4] observes that the aesthetic obtuseness and insensitivity of Old Testament scholars in relation to the patriarchal narratives awakened a certain hostility in Gunkel. An artist or a child could appreciate the ancient stories, but a scholar hardly at all. On Gen. 38 he says, 'How difficult it is for theological exegetes to understand an ancient story!'[5] On Gen. 25 he remarks that exegetes who speak here of 'spiritual treasures' betray their total lack of a sense of humour.[6] On the other hand, a letter found in Gressmann's desk informs us that Gressmann, Gunkel and Meyer had been branded by the adherents of Wellhausen as 'aesthetes and impressionists'[7]. There is an inconsistency in Gunkel's work at this point of which Klatt[8] is aware and whose implications will be explored more fully in another chapter.[9] In brief, the difficulty is that although Gunkel inveighs against the pietists and dogmatic theologians, he is, nevertheless, in the last resort, brought into contradiction by his own form of religious earnestness and missionary zeal. This is so despite his insistence that he is a scientific exegete whose theology is a contribution to knowledge and is not merely an

[1] Above, p. 25.
[2] 'Ziele und Methoden der Erklärung des Alten Testamentes', p. 24.
[3] *ibid.*, p. 16.
[4] *op. cit.*, p. 128, n. 14.
[5] *Genesis (1)*, p. 378.
[6] *ibid.*, p. 272.
[7] W. Klatt, *op. cit.*, pp. 73 f.
[8] *ibid.*, p. 121.
[9] Below, pp. 225 ff.

aid to edification and dogma.[1] His account of how the stories acquire religious seriousness and ethical refinement is inconsistent with the indissolubility of form and content in a work of art which is a cardinal part of his analysis of beauty.

Ignoring for the moment the weakness of this dichotomy of aesthetic and theological in Gunkel's criticism of the patriarchal stories, let us enquire further into his aesthetic observations on the genre. This part of his enterprise is in Klatt's view 'perhaps the most brilliant chapter of his Introduction'[2] (i.e., the introduction to *Genesis (3)*).

Popular legends (Gunkel says), in their very nature exist in the form of individual legends; not until later do compilers put several such legends together or poets construct of them greater and artistic compositions. Thus it is also with the Hebrew popular legends.[3]

As examples of such short stories which 'extend over scarcely more than ten verses' Gunkel[4] cites Abraham's journey to Egypt (Gen. 12.10-20), the trial of Abraham (Gen. 22), Hagar's flight or the exile of Ishmael (Gen. 16; 21.9-21), Jacob at Bethel (Gen. 28.10-22) and at Penuel (Gen. 32.23-33).

The first step of criticism is the identification of these small units, and, in order to show what makes them an aesthetic success, criticism must then go beyond generalizations and make a minute inspection of each short story. It is this nice scrutiny which will disclose the literary quality of these stories, and will enable us to describe accurately the simple but delicate machinery which makes them work so faultlessly and which secures their aesthetic effects. The self-contained character of each short story is indicated by the unity of mood or sentiment which characterizes it.

Thus in the story of the sacrifice of Isaac emotion is predominant; in that of Jacob's deception of Isaac humour; in the story of Sodom moral earnestness.[5]

The effect of a story would be spoiled if it were followed immediately by another with a different and discordant mood.

Many stories are entirely spoiled by following them up immediately with new ones which drive the reader suddenly from one mood to another. Every skilful story-teller, on the contrary, makes a pause after telling one such story, giving the imagination time to recover, allowing the hearer

---

[1] 'The goal of scientific exegesis is not edification but knowledge' ('Ziele und Methoden der Erklärung des Alten Testamentes', p. 25).
[2] *op. cit.*, p. 138.   [3] *Legends*, p. 43.   [4] *ibid.*, p. 46.   [5] *Legends*, p. 44.

to reflect in quiet on what he has heard, while the chords which have been struck are permitted to die away.[1]

From this point of view the combination of stories would appear always to be a misguided enterprise – a botching of a smaller perfection in an attempt to create a larger literary unity.

The more independent a story is the more sure we may be that it is preserved in its original form. And the connexion between individual stories is of later origin in many cases, if it is not simply an hallucination of the exegete.[2]

Another consideration which influences Gunkel's thinking is his understanding of the context or setting in which the stories are told and heard. They have a 'folk' or 'popular' setting and are so integrated with this context that they are the cultural property of the group. Presumably they owe their origin to the creativity of individuals, but they win acceptance only in so far as they have been accorded the recognition of the community and have established a sociological place for themselves.

Moreover, for the very reason that the legend is the product of the whole people, it is the expression of the people's mind. And this is a point of the greatest importance for our interpretation of the legends of Genesis. We are warranted in regarding the judgements and sentiments presented in Genesis as the common possession of large numbers of people.[3]

Klatt[4] notices that the expression *Sitz im Volksleben* appears for the first time in 1906.[5]

In *Genesis* (*3*) (1910) Gunkel again asks the question: What is the fundamental unit which we should seek out and enjoy? He replies that the main object of investigation should be the individual story, because this is the form of the narrative which existed in oral tradition. The story is folk art and as such it expresses not only the thoughts and feelings of those who composed it, but also those of the whole circle in which it originated and was narrated. The normative literary unit is determined by the aesthetic form and the sociological place of the patriarchal narratives, which are a communal cultural product whose brevity corresponds with the capacity of the story-teller and the power of receptivity in those who listen.[6] All of this is gathered up in the *résumé* of the properties of the genre which appears in 1925.[7] The patriarchal narrative is

[1] *ibid.*, p. 44; cf. *Genesis* (*3*), pp. xxxii f.   [2] *Legends*, p. 45.
[3] *Legends*, p. 40.   [4] *op. cit.*, p. 127, n. 6.
[5] H. Gunkel, *Die israelitische Literatur* (*1*), p. 55.
[6] *Genesis* (*3*), pp. xxxi-xxxiv.   [7] *Die israelitische Literatur* (*2*), p. 57.

an ensemble of thoughts within a single mood, which has been given an appropriate form and which operates in a sociological context (*Sitz im Leben*), where form and content are sociologically effective. For a full understanding of the functioning of the genre extra-literary factors demand special consideration. The stories belong to an area of public performance rather than of private reading. The ancient story-teller is like the actor in a theatre whose art consists in finely modulated variations of voice and tone, in gestures and in subtle movements of the face and aspect. All of these belong to the total pattern of communication in a living social situation where there is a strange bond between the teller and listener and an intuitive response to audience stimulus.

Between narrator and hearer there is a bond other than the word. There is the tone of the voice, the look on the face or the movement of the hand. Joy and sorrow, love, anger, jealousy, hate, compassion, and all the other moods of his hero which the narrator feels within himself, he communicates to his hearers without saying a word.[1]

The short, independent, story, we may say, is like an individual picture. Pictures are not enjoyed in the mass; every individual picture has to be savoured and analysed as a complete entity. Here concreteness is sovereign – and so it is with each story. This is the first and fundamental stage in the critical appreciation of the genre and is indispensable to any more comprehensive, synthetic account of its literary history. Once the excellence of the primary artistic entities has been appreciated it will be possible to attempt a broader treatment of the history of the genre. This is a method which, according to Gunkel, is valid for Old Testament literature as a whole, where progress in describing its history is always conditional on a prior and correct delineation of *Gattungen*.

The researches which, in the first place, were directed to the consideration of a particular, extant work of art lead the researcher, for his own part, to gather together his observations and to compound them into a history of literature, that is, the aesthetic consideration leads to a literary-critical one.[2]

It will be seen that Gunkel's *Gattungsgeschichte* is allied to a particular view of the sociological setting of the patriarchal narratives – a *Sitz im Volksleben*. He envisages this *Sitz* both in connexion with the theory of *Genesis* (*1*) that the narratives are derived from myths, and with the view in *Genesis* (*3*) that they are a devel-

---

[1] *Genesis* (*3*), p. xlii.
[2] 'Ziele und Methoden der Erklärung des Alten Testamentes', p. 23.

opment from *Märchen*.[1] His change of mind relative to the history of genre does not affect his understanding of the social context in which the narratives are operative. In all this his concept of the professional story-teller, who is an artist and who gives a performance which plucks at the heart-strings of his audience, plays an important part. It is in this kind of setting – an audience gathered to listen to a public performance – that the stories have their life and are appropriated as expressive of a 'popular' culture. Nor is Gunkel's insistence that the artistic unit in this kind of literature is the short story entirely separable from this view of *Volksleben*. The story which does not last too long, which is highly dramatic in its conception and moves swiftly towards its climax, impatient of adornment or complication, is felt to be appropriate to the oral performance which is postulated and to the limited grasp of the assembled audience. Hence, where there is evidence in the patriarchal narratives of lengthier composition or of a greater concentration on sentiment or characterization, which no longer seems to fit this *Sitz im Volksleben*, Gunkel is inclined to say that something of the glory of the stories has departed.[2] At any rate it will be obvious that if one starts off with a different definition of genre and description of *Sitz*, this will have a profound influence on the interpretation of the stories. Thus Noth[3] begins with the assumption that the narratives are cultic history and that they have a credal kernel, and this clearly involves a different sociological setting from that envisaged by Gunkel. One has now to think in connection with the West Jordan Jacob stories of an audience in a cultic setting rather than at an artistic performance and of stories which set forth credal claims and record cultic history.[4]

What then are the aesthetic properties of these stories and how do they achieve their dramatic effects? Their brevity, which is an indication of limited creative powers, nevertheless contributes to a tightness of construction and an economy of detail which allow the main stages in the unfolding of the story to appear with perfect clarity in a series of scenes. On the tightness of construction Gunkel says:

The primitive man demanded from his story-teller first of all action; he demands that something will happen in the story to please his eye. But

[1] See below, pp. 43 ff.
[2] See below, pp. 35 ff.
[3] See below, pp. 59 ff.
[4] See below, pp. 112 ff.

the first essential of such a story is to him its inner unity; the narrator
must furnish him a connected series of events each necessarily dependent
on the preceding.[1]

Again:

> The narrators have no fondness for digressions or episodes in which
> narratives and epics of more highly developed literatures are so rich, but
> they strive with all power and assurance towards their climax.[2]

With regard to economy of circumstantial detail, Gunkel notes
that this is the rule wherever detail is not essential to the further-
ance of the action. In the story of the sacrifice of Isaac (Gen. 22) the
three days' journey is covered at a bound, while the short passage to the
place of sacrifice is described in all detail. . . . Similarly the experiences
of Abraham's servant on the day when he sued for the hand of Rebeccah
are reported very minutely, while all the days consumed in the journey
to the city of Nahor are disposed of in a breath.[3]

This is not to say, however, that there are no degrees of complication, since apart from these there would be no story. Interest
must be excited and uncertainty awakened in those who hear about
the train of events which has been set in motion.

> Thus all the stories are more or less exciting. The child-like listener holds
> his breath and rejoices when the hero finally escapes all the threatening
> dangers.[4]

In the interests of concentration and comprehension the number
of characters is kept to a minimum. Sometimes there are only two
and when there are more only a few are developed as differentiated
characters. Even in the artistically elaborate Joseph story the only
characters which are fully drawn, apart from the leading character
Joseph, are those of Benjamin and Reuben (Judah).

> But this is the extent of the narrator's power to characterize; the remain-
> ing nine all lack individuality; they are simply the brothers.[5]

Very early in these stories it is obvious who the leading characters
are and attention is concentrated on them, while the subordinate
characters receive no more than they deserve and do not distract
attention from the main actors.

> In attempting to discover the method by which the characters are depicted
> we are first struck by the brevity with which the subordinate personages
> are treated. Modern literary creations have accustomed us to expect that
> every personage introduced be characterized if possible with at least a

---

[1] *Legends*, p. 69.   [2] *Genesis* (*3*), p. xlvi.   [3] *Legends*, pp. 68 f.
[4] *ibid.*, p. 73; *Genesis* (*3*), p. xlviii.   [5] *Legends*, p. 50.

few touches as an independent individual. The method of the primitive saga-man is entirely different. The personages whom he considers altogether or temporarily subordinate receive little or no characterization. . . . The narrators did not even consider it necessary to mention the sin of the two chamberlains of Pharaoh (xl 1) or the feelings of Dinah (xxxiv) or those of Sarah on the journey to Egypt (xii 10 ff.).[1]

Even the leading characters are not drawn in detail. There is no exploration of the many-sidedness of the individual or of the inner and irreconcilable tensions which contribute to the mystery and complexity of individuality. Nor is there any dynamic aspect to the portrayal – to portray development in the characters of the personages is not part of the artistic purpose.[2] This would presuppose an emphasis on characterization and a degree of priority accorded to it which could not be reconciled with the artistic aims of these stories. They are not so interested in the interior details, that is, in psychological convolutions, and they do not become too involved in the recesses of sentiment and motivation.

We are struck by this paucity in these legends, since we are familiar in modern compositions with portraits made up of many different traits and painted with artistic detail. The art of the primitive story-tellers is very different. True it is based on the actual conditions of primitive ages in one respect; the men of antiquity were in general more simple than the many-sided men of modern times. Yet it would be an error to suppose that men in these early days were as simple as they are represented to be in the legends; compare in evidence of this the character sketches of a somewhat maturer art in the Second Book of Samuel. With this example in mind we shall recognize also that there is some other ground for the brevity of the legends in Genesis than the abbreviation of the real which is inevitable in every artistic reproduction of life.[3]

The simplification of characterization in the patriarchal narratives takes the form of a typical portrayal: those who stand before us are clearly drawn types rather than complicated individuals who would not be amenable to such portrayal. On the one hand this is evidence of a certain superficiality, of a need to preserve simplicity and to avoid more complicated situations than those which can be managed by a limited artistic grasp. On the other hand the method maintains the right proportions of characterization in a genre where everything else has to be subordinated to the action, and where an exhibiting of essential traits rather than an interior exploration of sentiment and motivation is necessary to preserve a proper artistic balance.

---

[1] *Legends*, p. 53.   [2] *ibid.*, p. 56.   [3] *Legends*, p. 54.

It is . . . a peculiar, popular conception of man that we meet in Genesis. This conception was unable to grasp and represent the many sides of man, much less all; it could see but a little. But so much the more need had it to catch the essential traits of the individual, wherefore it constructed types. Thus in the story of the flight of Hagar, Hagar is the type of the slave (xvi) who is too well treated, Sarah of the jealous wife, Abraham the type of the conciliatory husband. Rachel and Leah are types of the favourite and unloved wife; in the story of the migration of Abraham to Egypt or the story of Joseph, Pharaoh acts like the typical Oriental king in such cases; his courtiers are courtiers and nothing more; Abraham's servant, chap. xxiv, is an old and tried servant; Isaac, in the story of the deception, is a blind, old man and Rebecca a cunning, partial mother. Abraham in his migration and in chap. xxii is the type of the pious and obedient man.[1]

In this process of rationing traits to the several characters the general principle which is followed is that characterization is subordinate to the action of the story and that only those particular qualities of the person which are germane to the unfolding of the story are described.

In other literatures there are narratives in which the action is merely a garb or a thread, while the chief concern is the psychological study, the brilliant conversation or the idea; but not so with the primitive Hebrew legend.[2]

The story of the deception practised by Jacob tells how the latter, following his mother's counsel, induces his father to bless him instead of Esau; here Jacob is crafty, he practises deception; Esau is stupid, he lets himself be cheated; Isaac is easily deceived, he is blind; Rebeccah is cunning, she gives the deceitful advice and is partial to Jacob.[3]

Instead of interior or psychologizing portrayals of characters there is the device of representing the action of the story in such a way as to hint at the inner condition of the characters who act and are acted upon. This record must necessarily be lacking in explicitness and immediacy. It will illuminate only in so far as those who hear or read can transpose action into thoughts and feelings and this requires a special kind of intuition or power of translation.[4]

In the sight of the city of Sodom (xix 27 f.) Abraham had heard certain remarkable utterances from the three men; they had said that they were going down to Sodom to examine the guilt of the city. This strange remark he let run in his head; in the morning of the following day he arose and went to the same place to see whether anything had happened in

---

[1] *Legends*, p. 55.   [2] *ibid.*, p. 69.   [3] *Legends*, p. 57.   [4] *ibid.*, pp. 58-60.

Sodom during the night. And in fact he sees in the valley below a smoke, whence he must infer that something has taken place; but this smoke hides the region and he cannot make out what has happened. For the story-teller this scene is plainly not of interest because of the thing that happened, but because of the thoughts which Abraham must have thought, and yet he does not tell us what these thoughts were. He merely reports to us the outward incidents and we are obliged to supply the really important point ourselves.[1]

In many cases where a modern would undertake a psychological analysis the primitive story-teller represents an action. We are not told that Hagar was outraged at her treatment by Sarah, but that she ran away (Gen. 16.6); not that Laban's greed was awakened by the stranger's gold, but that he immediately invited him to the house (Gen. 24.30); not that the conflict between obedience and parental love within Abraham was finally resolved, but simply that he set out on his sad journey (Gen. 22.3); not that Tamar was steadfast in her loyalty to her dead husband, but simply that she took measures to have a child and to save his name from extinction (Gen. 38).[2]

This phenomenon can be described both negatively and positively. It may be ascribed to inarticulateness, to an incapacity for the description of the finer oscillations of moods and motives, to a lack of familiarity with the techniques for investigating the complex inner areas of conflict and uncertainty which are masked by the final simplicity and decisiveness of action.

This story-teller, then, has an eye for the soul-life of his hero, but he cannot conceive these inward processes with sufficient clearness to express them in definite words.[3]

The positive side is that economy and reserve in the matter of sentiment and rationalization may be appropriate to the setting in which the stories are told and heard, and may correspond to a deliberate artistic disinclination to explain too much or to impose too great a fixity of interpretation on the stories. Each telling of the stories is a performance and the *lacunae* are filled in by the interpretative contribution of the story-teller. In order that he may have full scope for his artistry in the 'theatre' where he does his story-telling, it is necessary that the spoken words themselves should not be too explicit or impose too great a fixity of interpretation.

---

[1] *ibid.*, p. 60.   [2] *Legends*, pp. 60 f.   [3] *ibid.*, p. 60.

But even where the story-teller said nothing about the soul-life of his heroes, his hearer did not fail entirely to catch an impression of it. We must recall at this point that we are dealing with orally recited stories. Between narrator and hearer there is another link than that of words; the tone of the voice talks, the expression of the face or the gestures of the narrator. Joy and grief, love, anger, jealousy, hatred, emotion, and all the other moods of his heroes, shared by the narrator, were thus imparted to his hearers without the utterance of a word.[1]

Even where the characters speak, they sometimes do so with a brevity and a measure of opaqueness which leaves us in doubt about what their words were intended to communicate, so that here again there is scope for liberty of interpretation.[2]

Although speech is used sparingly as a means of revealing thoughts and feelings, it is in places used tellingly.

Words are not, it is true, so vivid as actions, but to make up for this they can better reveal the inner life of the personages. The early story-tellers were masters in the art of finding words which suit the mood of the speakers; thus the malice of the cunning serpent is expressed in words, as well as the guilelessness of the childlike woman, Sarah's jealousy of her slave as well as the conciliatoriness of Abraham (xvi 6), the righteous wrath of Abimelech (xx 9), the caution of the shrewd Jacob (xxxii 9), and the bitter lament of Esau (xxvii 36) and of Laban (xxxi 43) when deceived by Jacob. Notable masterpieces of the portrayal of character in words are the temptation of the first couple and the conversation between Abraham and Isaac on the way to the mount of sacrifice.[3]

Nevertheless, the main impression which is to be gained from the stories is that of the laconicism of their creators. The characters fail to speak at places where speech seems to be demanded and where it might have appeared an artistic necessity to a modern writer.

We may well imagine that Joseph complained aloud when he was cast into the pit and carried away to Egypt (cp. also xlii 21) . . . that Hagar left Abraham's house weeping and complaining that Abraham had put her away (xxi 14); but there is nothing of the kind . . . Not a word does Rebeccah say in chapter xxvi . . . nor Abraham in chapter xviii when a son is promised him, or when he is commanded to sacrifice Isaac; neither Hagar when she sees her child dying, nor later when God heard the weeping of Ishmael. One who has examined these references might easily conclude that the personages of Genesis were intended to be portrayed as taciturn and even secretive; he would find the only talkative individual to be God.[4]

The reason for this reserve is to be sought in the subordination

[1] *Legends*, p. 62.   [2] *ibid.*, p. 66.   [3] *Legends*, p. 63.   [4] *ibid.*, pp. 63 f.

of speech to the action of the stories, and it will be found that such speech as is allowed to the characters is necessary to the progress and intelligibility of the action. In these cases the function of speech is not to throw light on the nature of the person who speaks, but to maintain the interest and impetus of the story and to confer plausibility and intelligibility on it.

Abraham begs his wife to declare herself his sister; and thus it comes about that she was taken into the harem of Pharaoh (xii 11 ff.). Abraham gave Lot the choice of going to the east or the west; hence Lot chose the plain of Jordan. At Sarah's request Abraham takes Hagar as a concubine and at her request he gives her up again. In these cases the words are not idle; on the contrary they are necessary to suggest an inner motive for the action to follow.[1]

The bearer of the decisive words in the stories of blessing and cursing is God rather than man.

This explains why God is so often represented as speaking in Genesis; for speech is really the chief medium through which God influences the action in these legends.[2]

There is a tendency in Gunkel to describe negatively those literary complexes which are more extensive than the brief, individual patriarchal story. Thus he speaks of the discord which results when an attempt is made to combine stories each of which is dominated by a single mood. What is produced on this view is not a larger, more complex artistic entity, but rather the marring of the simple perfection which each story possesses in itself and which is displayed for so long as the independence of the little entity is not blurred. Hence Gunkel adopts an evaluative rather than a purely descriptive attitude to the combination of stories into cycles.

In order to judge of the artistic quality of these compositions, we must first of all examine the joints or edges of the older stories. Usually the narrator makes the transition by means of very simple devices from one of the stories to the other.[3]

This suggests that the combining of the stories is no better than a piece of semi-skilled literary joinery, and certainly not an activity to which a high artistic value should be accorded.[4]

Allied to this attitude there is also in Gunkel a preference for the brevity of what he takes to be the oldest form of the patriarchal story over against the diffuse style of the later forms. He is

---

[1] *Legends*, p. 65.
[2] *ibid.*, p. 65.
[3] *Legends*, p. 81; cf. *Genesis* (*3*), pp. xxxi ff.
[4] *Genesis* (*3*), p. xxxii.

temperamentally and aesthetically disposed to the laconicism and reserve of the old style over against the artificiality and more ample sentiment of the later stories.

The art of story-telling, which in olden times was in such high perfection, degenerated in later times, and the latest, in particular, care more for the thought than for the narrative.[1]

We do not always agree with this taste of the later time; for instance, the story of Joseph approaches the danger line of becoming uninteresting from excessive detail.[2]

Yet his attitude to those stories which are more involved in their construction and in which speeches and psychological exploration take precedence over action is ambiguous. He praises the fast-moving quality of the short stories, where action is always in the foreground and character has to be inferred from action, but he recognizes that the more leisurely pace of the longer narratives and the increased interest in characterization reflect a more mature aesthetic sensibility.[3] He acknowledges that the Joseph story is a feat of composition, but finds that it is in danger of becoming tedious.[4] Such narratives are far removed from the brevity of the old type and are characteristic examples of the diffuse style. They are fragile, sentimental, tearful and soft-hearted, whereas the older stories strike more powerful notes. The Joseph stories show a more feminine taste than 'the pearls of Genesis'.[5]

Gunkel compares the more developed stories unfavourably with the brief stories in three respects: (a) The combining of the stories spoils the artistic quality of each individual story, (b) The diffuse style and the more elaborate devices of story-telling are dramatically less effective than the terse style which subordinates everything to the action, (c) The more ample sentiment of the later stories verges on sentimentality and is less pleasing than the reserve of the older stories. Gunkel, however, does not stop at this and the balance which we have seen operative elsewhere in his thinking comes into play here. He cannot say everything at once and he is capable of adopting a more constructive attitude to cycles of stories and to changes in style than the above points taken by themselves would suggest. Nevertheless, there is some conflict between his predilection for the independent story and the laconic style, and a purely descriptive treatment of the history of the genre. He is

[1] *Legends*, p. 100.   [2] *Legends*, p. 85; cf. *Genesis* (*3*), pp. xxxiii f.
[3] *Genesis* (*3*), p. xxxiv.   [4] *Genesis* (*3*), p. 396.
[5] *Genesis* (*3*), p. 398.

entitled to his aesthetic preferences and value judgements, but it
may be that they interfere more than they ought with his function
as a literary historian.

Against this negative estimate of the diffuse style one has to put
his statement that the longer narratives as compared with the
shorter ones are 'more considerable works of art'.[1] Of the Jacob-
Esau-Laban cycle he says that a plausible reason is given why
Jacob goes to Laban (he is fleeing for his life from Esau), but that
in other respects the original stories lie side by side unblended.[2]
In *Genesis* (*3*), however, he describes the Jacob-Esau-Laban cycle
as 'an artistic composition' (*künstlerische Komposition*) rather than
a loose compilation from the hands of redactors.[3] In his article on
'Jacob' he still regards the individual story as the principal aesthetic unit,[4] and in discussing the use of the Jacob-Esau cycle as a
frame for the Jacob-Laban cycle observes that the edges of the
individual stories are still visible.[5] Of the Jacob-Laban cycle he
says that it is put together out of several individual stories, the
kernel being a short story which tells how Jacob came to Laban,
fell in love with Rachel, and won her and her father's sympathy
when he took her part against the boorish shepherds and watered
her flocks[6] (Gen. 29). Although Gunkel still regards the Jacob-
Esau-Laban cycle as the result of an aggregation of originally
independent artistic entities, he does now appear to acknowledge
that skill and even creativity are involved in the making of the
larger entity, and that it is not to be regarded simply as a piece of
joinery. His remarks on the Abraham-Lot cycle in *Genesis* (*1*) are
more negative in character. The journey to Sodom by the three
men after they leave Abraham at Hebron is not a very convincing
link between the Abraham story and the Lot story, nor is it obvious why Abraham should accompany the men to the gates of
Sodom and return there the following morning. There is

no attempt at an inner harmonization of the different legends, but the
narrator has exerted himself all the more to devise artificial links of
connexion. . . . In this we receive most clearly the impression of conscious
art which is trying to make from originally disconnected elements a more
plausible unity.[7]

[1] *Legends*, p. 80.
[2] *ibid.*, p. 81.
[3] *Genesis* (*3*), p. 292.
[4] 'Jacob', *Preuss. Jahrb.* 176, 3 (1919), p. 343.
[5] 'Jacob', p. 351.
[6] *ibid.*, p. 353.   [7] *Legends*, p. 82.

With regard to the Joseph story, already in *Genesis* (*1*) Gunkel says:

In the Joseph legend we have an instance of a much more intimate blending of parts than the frames of these other stories, a whole series of different adventures harmonized and interwoven.[1]

In *Genesis* (*3*), where he still regards the component parts of the Joseph story as originally independent artistic unities, he describes the whole as a saga cycle with a more rigorous degree of composition than the other cycles. Compared with the individual items of the Abraham-Lot cycle, which are like pearls arranged on a string, the Joseph story is a well organized whole. Whereas in the other saga cycles the individual stories can be clearly distinguished from one another, in the Joseph story joins can be recognized in only a few places. It is the best specimen of composition in the book of Genesis, and such a highly developed craft of compounding material is the end and not the beginning of a process of development.[2] The distinctiveness of the Joseph story is such that he is disposed to describe it as *Novelle* rather than *Sage*,[3] and the full implications of this nomenclature are worked out in his subsequent article.[4] The Joseph story is no longer described as a combination of originally independent *Sagen*, but as a new genre – a *Novelle*. The components of the Joseph story are the raw material of what was *ab initio* a complex, architectonic achievement, and the work was composed by a significant artist (*Künstler*). The individual stories are not aggregated but are rather organized around a nucleus and as such form a continuous narrative and constitute a manifest unity. From the outset they are no more than parts of a greater whole.[5]

Associated with this final estimate of the Joseph story is a recognition that a literary work which awakens many moods or strikes many notes does not necessarily end up in confusion or discord. Implicit in this is the admission that an author who can explore emotional conflicts or vagaries of mood in his characters is attempting something which is artistically more complicated than the short story with a unitary mood; also that the existence of such a genre is indicative of audiences or readers who demand more

[1] *Legends*, p. 82.
[2] *Genesis* (*3*), p. 396.
[3] *ibid.*, p. 397.
[4] 'Die Komposition der Joseph-Geschichten', *ZDMG* lxxvi (1922), pp. 55-71.
[5] *ibid.*, pp. 66 f.

complicated cathartic procedures and who appreciate the more exacting emotional tug of war which is offered to them. Hence Gunkel remarks that the author of the Joseph story knows how to awaken in his hearers a complex of different moods: anxiety for Joseph, indignation at his brothers, abhorrence of the intriguing Egyptian wife, joy at Joseph's elevation and compassion for the aged Jacob.[1]

Gunkel comments on the striking contrast between the epic diffuseness of the Joseph story and the brevity of the older stories. We find it in an abundance of long speeches, of soliloquies, of detailed descriptions of situations, of expositions of the thoughts of personages. The narrator is fond of repeating in the form of a speech what he has already told.[2]

Nor is this increase of eloquence in the characters and the liking for episodic distractions solely confined to the Joseph stories

for we find the same qualities, though less pronounced, in the stories of the wooing of Rebeccah, of Abraham at the court of Abimelech (Genesis xx), in some features of the story of Jacob (notably the meeting of Jacob and Esau); and the stories of the sacrifice of Isaac and various features of the story of Abraham and Lot also furnish parallels.[3]

Gunkel has a preference for the brief, swift-moving, dramatically tense older stories, but he recognizes that the later style represents a more complicated kind of story-telling and reflects more sophisticated tastes. It has arisen out of a desire for new and less obvious aesthetic enjoyments in connexion with story-telling, and the subordination of everything else to the action is no longer an artistic objective. The hearer or the reader expects subtlety and complication and does not wish to be carried along at speed in order to reach a conclusion by the shortest route. He is stimulated and intrigued by delays and suspensions and the conclusion when it is reached is all the more pleasurable because on the way he has had the opportunity of listening to the speeches of the characters or of enjoying episodic by-paths which are off the main route of the narrative.

Very evidently we have to do here with a distinct art of story-telling, the development of a new taste. The new art is not satisfied like its predecessor with telling the legend in the briefest possible way and with suppressing so far as possible all incidental details; but it aims to make the legend richer and to develop its beauties, even when they are quite incidental. It endeavours to keep situations which are felt to be attractive and inter-

---

[1] *Genesis* (3), p. 397.   [2] *Legends*, p. 82.   [3] *Legends*, p. 82.

esting before the eye of the hearers as long as possible. Thus, for instance, the distress of Joseph's brethren as they stand before their brother is portrayed at length; there is evident intent to delay the narrative, so that the hearer may have the time to get the full flavour of the charm of the situation.[1]

Joseph does not reveal his identity at his first meeting with his brothers, but postpones the outcome by demanding that Benjamin be brought to him, and Jacob's unwillingness to let Benjamin go prolongs the delay. In the story of the sacrifice of Isaac there is a deliberate slackening of pace, through the spinning out of detail, just before the appearance of God, as a means of heightening the tension and intensifying the cathartic effect of the final happy ending.[2]

A particular device for the prolonging of the story is the repetition of the same scene with variations.

Joseph's brethren must meet him in Egypt twice; twice he hides valuables in their grain sacks in order to embarrass them (xlii 25 f.; xliv 2 ff.); twice they bargain over Joseph's cup, with the steward and with Joseph himself (xliv 13 ff., 25 ff.) and so on.[3]

There is now a tendency for the action to be subordinated to the speeches – the reverse of the old stories – and even for the order of events to be disturbed in order to enhance the informative effect of the speeches, as in the story of Abraham's meeting with Abimelech in chapter 20.

Here, quite in opposition to the regular rule of the ancient style, the events are not told in the order in which they occurred, but a series of occurrences are suppressed at the beginning in order to bring them in later in the succeeding speeches (vv. 9-16). Thus the narrator has attempted to make the speeches more interesting even at the expense of the incidents to be narrated.[4]

The importance thus assumed by speech over against action has to be related to a new inner area of thoughts and feelings which deeper and more extensive descriptive passages try to capture. Although Gunkel is not altogether enamoured of this taste of a later time, he acknowledges that it is evidence of a newly discovered faculty.[5] He admires the strength, simplicity and decisiveness of the old style which stops short at the description of overt action and does not venture into the maze of motivation and sentiment,

---

[1] *Legends*, pp. 82 f   [2] *ibid.*, p. 83.
[3] *ibid.*, p. 83.   [4] *Legends*, p. 84.
[5] *ibid.*, p. 85.

but he is aware that an attempt to portray the flux of feelings and thoughts is a more ambitious artistic venture and a more profound human achievement.

While the earlier time can express its inner life only in brief and broken words, the new generation has learned to observe itself more closely and to express itself more completely. With this there has come an increase of interest in the soul-life of the individual. Psychological problems are now treated with fondness and skill. Thus in the story of the sacrifice of Isaac there was created the perfection of the character study.[1]

The narrator of the Joseph story is a master of the art of portrait painting 'by means of many small touches'.[2] Particularly successful is his description of the emotional storm aroused within Joseph at the sight of Benjamin (43.30) or the texture of Jacob's sentiment when he hears that Joseph is still alive (45.26). In *Genesis* (*1*) Gunkel describes these pieces as *Romance* and transitional forms, such as the Jacob-Laban story or the Rebecca story, are said to be 'sagas touched with romance' or 'romances based on saga themes'.[3] In *Genesis* (*3*), where he makes the distinction in terms of *Sage* and *Novelle*,[4] he observes that the characterization of Joseph is more complex and manifold than anything found in the earlier stories. The older story-tellers contented themselves with the portrayal of one or two traits of the hero, but in the case of Joseph a richly colourful portrait is drawn. He is clever, good-looking, favoured by God, inspired, a favourite son of a beloved wife, god-fearing, chaste, noble, attached to his father and brothers. The older art did not portray ideal figures, but rather credible types of human beings. Joseph is drawn as a paradigm of piety, morality and ability.[5]

It is perhaps just to say that Gunkel undervalues the artistic achievement of the new style, and that he concentrates his analysis too much on the Joseph stories. According to his own premise (which, as we shall see, is not entirely consistent with his later views about the origins of the patriarchal stories) the decisive speech in the original, short story is attributed to God. We may say, therefore, that this is consistent with the theory to which he is attracted in *Genesis* (*1*) that the patriarchal stories are derived from

---

[1] *Legends*, p. 85.   [2] *ibid.*, p. 85.

[3] *ibid.*, p. 86 (I have substituted 'sagas' and 'saga' for 'legends' and 'legendary').

[4] Above, p. 39.

[5] *Genesis* (*3*), pp. 396 f.

myth. Where God intervenes and speaks the decisive word as a matter of course, the atmosphere of the story is mythological, and, in this context, it is difficult or impossible for the other characters to shake off an aspect of sub-humanity. In other words, in a world where God interferes regularly and takes all the responsibility, the literary probing of the ingredients of humanity is hindered or even inhibited. There is a sense in which man is still in tutelage; he is not sufficiently alone and the proportions of his humanity cannot be investigated and assessed. Thus the elements of secularity and worldliness in the Jacob-Laban story represent a measure of literary emancipation over against the bondage of stories where God is the decisive speaker. One must therefore praise the new style for the opportunity which it affords to literary art to portray a more emancipated human being in the mystery and fine gradations of his humanity. There is progress here from mythology and sub-humanity to a study of man in his freedom, inner uncertainties and conflicts; in his efforts to understand himself and to make public in speech the inner flux of feeling and thought, he is a rich subject for literary art.

III

Klatt[1] has illustrated nicely the change in Gunkel's opinions about the origins of the patriarchal stories which took place between 1901 and 1910. This affected particularly his estimate of the historicity of the stories and his earlier understanding of their aetiological function. His view in Genesis (2) (1902) is that the original nature of the narratives does not appear from the shape which they now assume in the book of Genesis.

The sagas themselves are, in the last analysis, not capable of elucidation by us.[2]

The obscure elements in the extant stories, which Gunkel supposes to represent traces of their original character, are termed *novellistisch*.[3] In *Genesis* (*3*) he remarks that the saga material in the patriarchal narratives is, for the most part, neither historical nor aetiological in origin. Before they were appropriated by Israel and acquired new functions, the stories had already been circulating for a long time and were originally examples of imaginative story-telling. He remarks:

In the commentary such obscure pieces are, for want of a better expres-

---

[1] *op. cit.*, pp. 129-138.   [2] *Genesis* (*2*), p. x.   [3] *Genesis* (*2*), p. xxviii.

sion, called *novellistisch*, perhaps the expression *märchenhaft* is prefer-able.[1]

He adds in a note[2] that he has deliberately avoided the statement that the patriarchal narratives are *Märchen*, because they have a tighter construction than *Märchen* and the distinctive phantasy of *Märchen* is absent from them. Klatt explains the difference of terminology as between Introduction and Commentary in *Genesis* (*3*) by the circumstance that the introduction was written subsequently to the detailed exegesis of the commentary. It is clear from the evidence of *Genesis* (*2*) that *novellistisch* represents an earlier and more agnostic phase of Gunkel's thinking than does *märchenhaft*, so that Klatt's point could be put rather differently by saying that Gunkel's detailed exegesis tended to lag behind his changing opin-ions about the origins of the patriarchal narratives, and this is noted by Klatt in another connexion. In a letter to his publisher, dated 4th December, 1918, concerning a new edition of *SAT*, Gunkel says:

Very many alterations will be necessary, since I, in the meantime, so far as research into Genesis goes, have arrived at a new exegesis. It is a great joy to me that I in person can set this keystone to my researches.[3]

Klatt explains that the new exegesis refers to the application of the *Märchen* concept to the stories of Genesis and remarks:

He was so taken up with his work on the Psalms that neither in *SAT* nor *HK* was he able to get down to the new work which he had in mind.[4]

In an article published in 1910 Hugo Gressmann[5] argued that the patriarchal narratives derive from *Märchen* and indicated his indebtedness to Wilhelm Wundt.[6] Gressmann maintained that the patriarchs are neither gods nor personifications of tribes; they bear personal names, but they are not historical individuals. Their names are the popular, personal names of their time, just as Hansel and Gretel were, or else they are paradigmatic names with a special suitability to the type of story in which they appear. The patriarchal stories derive from *Märchen* and *Märchen* cannot by any amount of apologetic skill be transformed into historiography.[7] The transition from *Märchen* to *Sage* is seen in the *Ortssage* in

---

[1] *Genesis* (*3*), p. xxvi.   [2] *Genesis* (*3*), p. xxvi, n. 2.
[3] *op. cit.*, p. 134.   [4] *ibid.*, p. 134.
[5] H. Gressmann, 'Sage und Geschichte in den Patriarchenerzählungen', *ZAW* 30 (1910), pp. 1-34.
[6] W. Wundt, *Völkerpsychologie*, 2 Band, III *Mythus und Religion* (1909).
[7] *op. cit.*, p. 9.

which the ownerless material of *Märchen* is attached to a person and a place (Abraham at Hebron, Lot at Sodom), but the contents of such *Ortssage* are strongly *Märchen*-like in character and are virtually uninfluenced by Old Testament religion.[1] The derivation from *Märchen* severs the patriarchal *Sage* from higher mythology and so the patriarchs are not to be thought of as demoted gods. *Märchen*, however, had connexions with lower mythology, with daimons and sprites, and traces of this are to be found in the portrayal of Esau and in the Penuel story.

Since the patriarchal narratives are basically *Märchen*, aetiologies which explain the history and relationships of tribes or which represent the patriarchs as eponyms are secondary developments and do not constitute the foundations of the patriarchal stories. Nevertheless, Gressmann's position is not altogether clear. He appears to say that there is no aetiological element in the Sodom story[2] and the aetiology which he offers of the Penuel story is a strange one: it explains why Israelites do not eat the thigh muscle; they refrain because it is subject to damage and the eating of a damaged muscle may cause lameness.[3]

Different from the *Ortssage* is the *Kultursage* (the Jacob-Laban story; the Isaac stories about disputes over wells) which have an indirect historical value, although the patriarchs who figure in them are characters in a story and not historical persons.[4] *Kultursagen* reflect the cultural complexion and historical conditions of the age and society out of which they come. The patriarchal *Kultursagen* reflect semi-nomadic conditions of life, for the most part in the wilderness of Judaea and the Negeb. The Joseph story is neither mythology nor tribal history; it is *Novelle* and is developed from a *Glücksmärchen*. To begin with the story was about a Hebrew youth called Joseph who was sold into Egypt as a slave and who there had adventures of all kinds in the style of the *Märchen*. In another article which appeared thirteen years later[5] Gressmann's position is much less clear. He has not resiled from his view that the Joseph story is fundamentally *Novelle*, but he

---

[1] *ibid.*, pp. 11 ff.
[2] *ibid.*, p. 13.
[3] *ibid.*, p. 20.
[4] *ibid.*, pp. 25 ff.
[5] H. Gressmann, 'Ursprung und Entwicklung der Joseph-Sage'. *EUCHAR-ISTERION. Studien zur Religion und Literatur des Alten und Neuen Testaments.* Hermann Gunkel zum 60 Geburtstage (*FRLANT* N.F., 19, I, 1923), pp. 1-55.

now holds that Joseph is an historical individual, the creator or *Ahnherr* of the tribe of Joseph. In addition he finds many elements of tribal history in the Joseph story and he correlates different features in it with particular historical moments or with cultural changes in the life of the Israelite tribes.[1]

Klatt supposes that Gressmann was a decisive influence on Gunkel,[2] although he notes that this is not the impression which Gunkel himself gives. In his article on 'Joseph' Gunkel says:

Searching after the original meaning of the Joseph story I had begun to seek out parallels in other nations and literatures. It was in this way, at first without any theory and subject to no influence, that I stumbled on the *Märchen*.[3]

Klatt, perhaps, does not allow enough weight to this statement. He notes that Gressmann himself gave the credit to Wundt for the *Märchen* theory, and he assumes that the dedication of Gunkel's *Das Märchen im Alten Testament* (1917) to Gressmann is meant to be an acknowledgement of Gunkel's debt to his friend in this particular area of study. It is not altogether clear why Klatt is persuaded that Gunkel only reluctantly adopted the theory that the patriarchal narratives were derived from *Märchen* and then subsequently developed it enthusiastically. According to Klatt evidence for this is supplied by discrepancies in Gunkel's exposition:

But then towards the end of the first World War he suddenly, under what impetus it cannot be shown with certainty, became convinced of the rightness of the application of the *Märchen* concept to the Old Testament.[4]

With regard to discrepancies in Gunkel's exposition the reason which Klatt gives in another place,[5] namely, that Gunkel did not have time to work out the full implications of his changing opinions for his detailed exegesis, is more cogent than the suggestion of reluctance. As for the suddenness of Gunkel's capitulation towards the end of the first World War (presumably Klatt has *Das Märchen im Alten Testament* in mind), it does not seem right to say that Gunkel became convinced of the rightness of the application of the *Märchen* concept to the patriarchal stories. Gunkel's reserve or reluctance is connected with the extant form of the patriarchal narratives. They are not now *Märchen*, but in so far as they have

---

[1] Below, pp. 101 ff.   [2] *op. cit.*, p. 136.
[3] *op. cit.*, p. 56.   [4] *op. cit.*, p. 137.
[5] Above, p. 44.

elements which are *novellistisch* or *märchenhaft* there are indications that they may be derived from *Märchen*. His position in this regard does not change quickly. The beginnings of it can be seen in *Genesis (2)* (1902), it is clearly stated in *Genesis (3)* and it has not changed significantly in *Das Märchen im Alten Testament* (1917). The progress which was made from 1910 onwards was of a different kind. The assumption that the patriarchal narratives are derived from *Märchen* is already influential in *Genesis (3)*; the subsequent task of drawing out the implications of this assumption and reconstructing the original form of the patriarchal stories is done most fully for the Jacob and Joseph stories. However, it should be noted that the order of development of the Jacob stories which is given in *Genesis (3)*[1] is the scaffolding of the detailed reconstruction in the 'Jacob' article, and Klatt[2] has noticed that in *Genesis (3)*[3] Gunkel speaks of the close resemblance of the Joseph story to *Märchen*. From all this it is evident that Gunkel had already taken the decisive step in 1910 and that thereafter it was a question of finding time to work out in detail the 'original' forms of the patriarchal narratives. Hence there is no reason to suppose that Gunkel's recollection was mistaken when he said in 1922 that it was the scrutiny of the Joseph stories which had suggested to him that the patriarchal narratives might be derived from *Märchen*.

The changes in *Genesis (3)* imply a literary history of the patriarchal narratives which is significantly different from and irreconcilable with the history of the genre given in *Genesis (1)*. The tentative but influential supposition that the stories were derived from myths is now given up. In *Genesis (1)* this was regarded as an attractive hypothesis which might one day be demonstrated, but now it is dismissed as 'no more than a pure conjecture'.[4] The patriarchs are not demoted gods[5] and the patriarchal stories are not Canaanite.[6] Gunkel now says that the stories about Abraham, Isaac and Jacob do not originate in Canaan, but are brought there by the Israelites. The setting of the patriarchal narratives is not the settled areas of Canaan, but the southern and eastern

---

[1] *Genesis (3)*, pp. 291-293. The outline of the Abraham story in *Genesis (3)* (pp. 199-201) also assumes a derivation from *Märchen*.

[2] *op. cit.*, p. 137.

[3] *Genesis (3)*, p. 399.

[4] *Genesis (3)*, p. 284 (cf. lxxviii f.).

[5] Cf. *Legends*, pp. 119 f. with *Genesis (3)*, pp. lxxvi ff.

[6] Cf. *Legends*, pp. 91-93.

fringes of that land, and the cultural context of the earliest form of the stories is a pre-sedentary one. The oldest stories of the patriarchs envisage them not as farmers but as nomads, particularly as shepherds.[1] The patriarchal narratives are essentially of Old Hebrew origin with a few additions from the historical period of Israel, while the Joseph story looks towards Egypt. Canaan exerted no influence on the patriarchal stories, for Israel was too proud to have taken her founding fathers from Canaan; she had too clear an awareness that she did not belong originally to Canaan and that her ethnic relationships lay outside it for this appropriation to have taken place.[2]

The detailed consequences of this new evaluation of the patriarchal narratives can be seen in the 'Jacob' article which appeared in 1919. Gunkel still emphasizes that the individual story is the principal aesthetic unit,[3] and, in discussing the use of the Jacob-Esau story as a frame for the Jacob-Laban story, he remarks that the edges of the individual stories are still visible.[4] He supposes that the narratives about the sale of the birthright and the obtaining of the blessing by deceit are the kernel of the Jacob-Esau cycle and suggests that their relationship may be marked by the device of near homonymy ($b^e k \bar{o} r \bar{a}$ and $b^e r \bar{a} k \bar{a}$). On the sale of the birthright he observes that the opposition of two different professions (hunter and shepherd) and also the representation that the two contestants are brothers is a very common Märchen setting. Such a hunter-shepherd Märchen could only originate in a community where hunters and shepherds lived side by side. It is told from the point of view of the shepherds who relate with enjoyment how the hunter is having to give place to them. The hunter lives from hand to mouth and if he comes home without a catch he has to go hungry. The shepherd possesses property and has accumulated stocks of food in his flocks and herds. Consequently shrewdness and calculation are part of the shepherd's style of life which contains elements of foresight and planning foreign to the existence of the hunter.[5]

The blessing like the birthright ensures precedence, and this story, with its theme of the triumph of brain over brawn, stands

[1] *Genesis* (*3*), p. lix.
[2] *Genesis* (*3*), p. lxi.
[3] *op. cit.*, p. 343.
[4] *ibid.*, p. 351.
[5] *ibid.*, pp. 358 f.

on the highest level of *Märchen*. Here the shepherd – the kids which are the instruments of deception are supplied from the flock – outwits the hunter. The hunter is as hairy as a billy-goat and has so strong a smell that it adheres even to his good clothes. The shepherd is more cultivated – a smoother man who pays attention to his appearance. Esau who runs about wild is his father's favourite, but the mother prefers the smoother Jacob who stays with the flocks. The hunter's game tastes better than the flesh of the shepherd's domesticated animals, but the art of cooking serves to conceal the difference. The hunter is of a violent disposition and would not hesitate to kill the brother who has deceived him, whereas the shepherd gains his ends by guile.[1]

Concerning the Jacob-Laban cycle Gunkel says that it is put together from several different stories, the kernel being a short story which tells how Jacob came to Laban, fell in love with Rachel, and won her and her father's sympathy when he took her part against the boorish shepherds and watered her flock. The Jacob-Laban cycle is a contest *Märchen* between an older and a younger shepherd. Jacob and Laban are related as son-in-law and father-in-law and the quarrel between them arises out of this relationship. The narrative is sympathetic to Jacob who is at first outwitted by Laban over the matter of Rachel, but who uses his skill as a shepherd to build up wealth in livestock, and successfully escapes with Rachel and with his property, despite Laban's unwillingness to let him go. Hence in the battle of wits the younger man eventually emerges victorious.[2] Laban is an Aramaean and Jacob a young man in foreign parts seeking his fortune; there is no original kinship between the two of them and this is supplied secondarily in order to link the Jacob-Esau cycle with the Jacob-Laban cycle. Laban is the brother of Rebecca who advises Jacob to flee to his uncle (Gen. 27.42-45), and Jacob, when he reaches Laban, tells him that he is Rebecca's son (Gen. 29.11-13). Hence the motif of the 'journey' (a young man journeying in foreign parts in search of his fortune), which serves to connect the two narrative cycles, belongs originally to the Jacob-Laban story and this is a *Märchen* to which the name of Jacob is only secondarily attracted. Its theme is that of the young shepherd who leaves home in search of his fortune, who falls in love in a strange land, and who uses

---

[1] *ibid.*, pp. 360 f.
[2] *ibid.*, pp. 353 f., 361.

his wits to overcome all the pitfalls which the girl's father prepares for him.[1]

The second part of the Jacob-Esau story, set in east Jordan, is not composed of ancient sagas. It has an *ad hoc* inventive character and was devised by story-tellers in order to satisfy the desire of their audiences for a prolongation of the story of Jacob, and also in order to complete the framework for the Jacob-Laban story. The main connecting motif here, as also between the first part of the Jacob-Esau cycle and the Jacob-Laban cycle, is Jacob's cunning, but Esau is no longer simply a hunter – he is now a leader of a guerilla band of four hundred men (Gen. 32.6). Jacob needs all his cunning in order to escape the depredations of Esau thirsting for revenge, encumbered as he is with his livestock and family. His cunning is exemplified in the division of his flocks and herds into two camps (Gen. 32.7 f.), in so locating his family as to give them the best chance of escape (Gen. 33.1-3), and in making his present to Esau in five instalments, so that it may appear the more impressive (Gen. 32.13-21). The element of artifice in all this is seen in the fact that the episodes are spun out of the place-name Mahanaim ('two camps'), while, at the same time, there is a deliberate word-play on *mah^{a}neh* 'camp' and *minhā* 'gift'. Again in the Penuel episode it is the name which has given a direction to the imagination of the story-tellers. The Penuel story (Gen. 32.23-33) has hardly anything in common with the other Jacob stories, for here Jacob is brave rather than crafty, and it can be concluded that this story had no original connexion with Jacob. The places which feature in the second part of the Jacob-Esau cycle are determined by the assumption that they would have lain on the route which Jacob would most probably have taken on his journey home.[2]

Gunkel's position is now clearly that the patriarchal narratives are *Märchen* which have subsequently acquired historical connexions in so far as the patriarchs and other, originally *Märchen*, characters (Esau, Laban, Lot) are 'nationalized' as eponyms.[3] The characterizations of Jacob and Esau in the patriarchal narratives do not reflect the nature of the historical relations between Israel and Edom. Jacob gains his ends by guile, while Israel overcame

[1] *ibid.*, p. 355.
[2] *ibid.*, pp. 352 f.
[3] *ibid.*, p. 361.

Edom by force. Edom had a reputation for wisdom and had achieved the status of a monarchy before Israel, while Esau is depicted as dull-witted and a primitive. The equation of Esau with Edom (cf. Gen. 25.23-25) stems from the period after David's subjugation of Edom (i.e., after 980 B.C.), and, in this connexion, Jacob's acquisition of the birthright and the blessing are interpreted nationally. Edom has lost her seniority and superiority and is subject to the once inferior Israel. Laban is also originally a *Märchen* figure, a typically crafty Aramaean who subsequently acquires the status of an eponym in the period before the Aramaean wars (860-770 B.C.). Hence the transformation of these *Märchen* figures into eponyms belongs to the first period of the monarchy. The most primitive Jacob stories are much older, since they come out of a community in which hunter and shepherd co-existed. The unity of Israel under the first kings and the new sense of self-identity encouraged by military victory and political advance led to the selection of the best loved figures of *Märchen* as eponyms. The impetus for the transformation of Jacob into a national figure was the attraction which his traits had for the Israelite community, and the circumstance that they could so completely identify themselves with him.[1]

The attraction of notices and stories about sanctuaries to Jacob is subsequent to the equation of Jacob with Israel. This implies that the cultic aetiologies are not of the essence of the patriarchal narratives which only acquire an aetiological dimension subsequent to the equation of Jacob with Israel. These notices and stories concerning Shechem and Bethel (Gen. 28.10-22; 33.18-20; 35.1-8) and Penuel (Gen. 32.23-33) are attached to Jacob-Israel in order to establish that he founded or, at least, named these sanctuaries. They are all local traditions which in form and content have only a loose connexion with the Jacob narrative cycle. The aetiological features of the Penuel story are explicable with reference to the name 'Israel' rather than the name 'Jacob'. Jacob/Israel who strives with God is brave rather than crafty, and it is because of the nature of the injury which he suffered that Israelites do not eat the sinew of the hip. The name Penuel, which suggests a place of theophany, is explained in terms of Jacob/Israel's struggle with a night-demon and it is the kind of tale which arises from a bad dream or nightmare. In the case of Bethel the foundation of the

[1] *ibid.*, pp. 358-360, 362.

sanctuary is ascribed to Jacob *qua* Israel, so that he might be represented as the founder of the sanctuary of the people who bore his name.[1]

Finally the notices about the births of Jacob's 'sons' (who are Israelite tribes) are only connected with Jacob as a consequence of his having become Israel and so the 'father' of these tribes. These birth stories represent the ultimate stage of the composition of the Jacob cycle and were incorporated by means of an insertion in the Laban story (Gen. 30.1-24). They were invented by narrators who in what followed had stories to tell about Simeon and Levi, Reuben and Judah (Gen. 34; 35.22; 38). These stories are the only original, tribal-historical elements which survive Gunkel's analysis. The colourless and artificial character of the birth stories, which are largely taken up with the aetiologies of the names of Jacob's 'sons', is an indication that they do not rest on old saga traditions.[2]

An important consequence of this account of the history of the genre is the diminished importance now attached to aetiology over against Gunkel's position in *Genesis* (1). This change is connected with his acceptance of Wundt's theory that the oldest human stories are *Märchen* and not myths.[3] If the oldest stories are *Märchen* and, if the patriarchal stories are derived from this genre, the aetiological elements in them can no longer be regarded as primary. They arise at a point where Jacob (and the other patriarchs) acquire an all-Israelite status, or, in other words, where the originally *Märchen* figures acquire historical attachments. It is when Jacob becomes Israel that ethnological and cultic aetiologies are attracted to him, and similarly the aetiological attachments to Laban and Lot have also to be correlated with their acquisition of national status.

The effect of the reconstruction of the Abraham cycle in terms of the new theory is somewhat more confusing. The original form of the story now postulated by Gunkel is similar to that conjectured by Gressmann.[4] It concerns three gods who were hospitably received by a childless couple to whom they promised a son. Gunkel supposes that the story was not originally located at Hebron and

[1] *ibid.*, pp. 348-350.
[2] *ibid.*, pp. 345, 347 f.
[3] *ibid.*, p. 341.
[4] 'Sage und Geschichte', pp. 11 f.

that the cultural incompatibility of 'tent' and 'tree' (Gen. 18.1 and 2) is an indication that this story too originated outside the arable areas of Canaan. It was once a story about a shepherd who was visited by three gods; it originated in the pre-Yahwistic period and was later related to Israel and to Yahweh, the three men then being represented as messengers of Yahweh.[1] But even so there are special difficulties attaching to the attempt to relate what is regarded as the kernel of the Abraham story to a specifically no-madic context. It can be argued that the Isaac and Jacob stories directly reflect the concerns of shepherds, but a story about a man who is visited by three gods does not have direct cultural links with nomadic or semi-nomadic life on the fringes of Canaan. It does not deal with disputes over wells nor is it a contest *Märchen*. It is rather a story with a high mythological content and one whose foreignness and wide distribution are asserted by Gunkel both in *Genesis* (*1*) and *Genesis* (*3*).[2] The estimate of the Abraham story which still prevails in *Genesis* (*3*) is in some ways more suited to the theory of *Genesis* (*1*) that the patriarchal narratives derive from myths than to the new theory of *Genesis* (*3*).

In the case of the Jacob story, on the other hand, the logic of the new theory is fully worked out and the aspect of international culture which was associated with the stories in *Genesis* (*1*) is re-moved. Instead of an international genre with widely disseminated motifs we have shepherds' tales intrinsically related to simple con-ditions of life which are local and particular, and which therefore, are neither international nor of high cultural prestige. From this point of view the high cultural context in which the discussion about the origins of the patriarchal narratives was set in *Genesis* (*1*) has been abandoned and instead it is precisely the localization, the limited cultural horizons and the particularity of nomadic condi-tions of life which are employed to explain the features of these stories for which original *Märchen* are postulated. The Joseph story is a somewhat different matter, because Gunkel's final view of it allows both for foreignness and erudition. The Joseph story marks the emergence of a new genre – the *Novelle* – which is an architectonic achievement of a different kind from the saga cycle, and in which *Märchen* components, some of them foreign, are no more than raw material in the hands of the creator of a new and complex artistic unity.

[1] *Genesis* (*3*), p. 200.   [2] *Legends*, p. 95; cf. *Genesis* (*3*), pp. lxiii, 200.

As I have already indicated, another of the effects of the new theory is to establish the secondary nature of the aetiological functions of the stories. In *Genesis* (*1*) Gunkel says that while the stories are not deliberately didactic and do not instruct in a pedestrian way, they, nevertheless have a point (i.e., an aetiological point) and 'are not free inventions of the imagination'.[1] This lends a certain educational seriousness to them, for they are told in order to answer questions which betray a genuine scientific curiosity and so they can be regarded as the beginnings of science. But according to Gunkel's later understanding of the matter, the stories are precisely free inventions of the imagination and the aetiological functions are secondary accretions.[2] Already in *Genesis* (*1*) Gunkel observes that the aetiological principle of interpretation is inapplicable to large parts of the Joseph story and that the 'deceptions and tricks', which are the chief feature of the Jacob-Laban cycle, 'cannot be understood from the standpoint of either history or aetiology'.[3] He supposes in *Genesis* (*1*)[4] and also in *Genesis* (*3*)[5] that the account of Joseph's agrarian policy is an aetiology: it explains why Egyptian peasants have to give up a fifth of their produce, while the fields of the priests are exempt. In *Genesis* (*3*) he says that the story of Joseph's agrarian policy, contrary to nearly all the other Joseph stories, is aetiological in character and may be based on an Egyptian model.

Subsequent to the adoption of the theory that the patriarchal narratives are derived from *Märchen* the position is that the ethnographic or ethnological and cultic aetiologies, which had been regarded by Gunkel as of the essence of the genre in *Genesis* (*1*), are now understood as functions attached to the stories as a consequence of their 'nationalization'. The rewriting of the section 'Arten der Sagen der Genesis'[6] shows that Gunkel does not always entirely succeed in breaking free from the assumptions of *Genesis* (*1*) and in accommodating his views on aetiology to the new theory that the patriarchal stories are derived from *Märchen*. The general implications of the new theory are that all the stories are originally located outside the sphere of Canaanite sanctuaries and that con-

[1] *Legends*, p. 74.
[2] *Genesis* (*3*), p. xxvi.
[3] *Legends*, p. 36.
[4] *ibid.*, p. 26.
[5] *Genesis* (*3*), p. 400.
[6] *Genesis* (*3*), pp. xiii-xxvi.

sequently the cultic aetiologies belong to a late stage of the development of the stories. Further, the patriarchs are all originally characters of *Märchen* and the achievement by them of representative Israelite status is prior to the cultic aetiologies in which they appear. In other words the ethnological aetiologies are prior to the cultic aetiologies.[1] Hence the decisive speech of God, which in *Genesis* (*1*) was singled out as a feature of the 'original' short story, is now associated with a function which is an aspect of a late Israelite development of the 'original' *Märchen*. The idea that the decisive speaking of God was an original feature of the genre, agreeable to the theory that the patriarchal narratives were derived from myths, now appears in a different light when the narratives are derived from *Märchen*.

Gunkel's final account of the origins of the patriarchal narratives has some similarity to Gressmann's contention that they began as art for art's sake. In so far, however, as they are related to contest *Märchen* (so the Jacob-Esau and the Jacob-Laban stories), they not only entertain but also have the function of defining the ethos of a group, of developing its faculty of self-identification and of undertaking a kind of social criticism or satire of a competing group. When we have made due allowance for this functional element it is broadly true that, according to Gunkel, the genre is to begin with innocent of ulterior motives and is no more than a good story created to satisfy an artistic urge and to give pleasure to those who hear it. Subsequently (as Gunkel will have it) the patriarchal story loses its self-determination and aesthetic autonomy and acquires extra-aesthetic functions; the story which came into being only to entertain is subordinated to other ends – is made to serve God and the community and to satisfy intellectual curiosity.

There is, as I have already noted,[2] a dichotomy between Gunkel's aesthetic appreciation of the genre and his religious or theological estimate of it. Klatt[3] remarks that Gunkel attaches higher aesthetic merit to the short, laconic story than to the more discursive style of story-telling, and yet holds that the ethical content of the earlier, shorter stories is inferior to that of the later ones. There is a discrepancy or even incompatibility between aesthetic and religious value judgements and they work against one another in

[1] Above, p. 51.
[2] Above, pp. 26 f.
[3] *op. cit.*, p. 121.

such a way that they cannot be reconciled. The aesthetic estimate is self-contained, and the religious and ethical estimates are separate and contrary to the aesthetic estimate, so that there are two independent appraisals which lead to opposite results and which cannot be integrated.

Gunkel's statement of this position in *Genesis (1)* is to some extent influenced by the theory that the stories are derived from myths, and that the earlier the story the more probable it is that there will be a mythological residue in it and that it will reflect a primitive level of morality. Such a passage as the following in *Genesis (1)* appears without alteration in *Genesis (3)*:

> The great age of the legends is seen . . . by the primitive vigour of many touches that reveal to us the religion and the morality of the earliest times, as, for instance, the many mythological traces, such as the story of marriages with angels, of Jacob's wrestling with God, and the many stories of deceit and fraud on the part of the patriarchs and so on.[1]

The new theory that the patriarchal narratives are derived from *Märchen* does make a difference to this view of the matter, and so there is evidence here that *Genesis (3)* is still, in some respects, transitional and that Gunkel has not yet had time to assimilate all the implications of a new theory. Thus, if the stories are to be derived from *Märchen*, the Penuel episode (Jacob's wrestling with God) is part of a late inner-Israelite development of the Jacob story.[2] Nevertheless, even according to the new theory, the concept of a gradual religious and ethical refinement of stories whose original purpose is entertainment rather than edification remains intact. Indeed, Gunkel's point would seem to be that the lack of religiosity and moral tone in the stories is of the essence of their aesthetic excellence. It is because the characters are not pious, because they are worldly rascals who scheme for their own ends, that the stories are entertaining to those who listen to them. Apart from the Joseph story there is not, according to Gunkel, any evidence of a desire to portray ideal characters or to construct models of piety and high morality. The aim of the story-tellers is rather to fashion credible types whose motives are as mixed as those of most men and whose worldliness, self-seeking and cunning are there to be recognized as truly human traits, to give amusement and enjoyment and not to awaken criticism or censure.

Many of the legends of the patriarchs are filled with a pure enjoyment of

[1] *Legends*, p. 88; *Genesis (3)*, p. lvi.   [2] 'Jacob', pp. 349 ff.

the characters of the patriarchs. Consequently many things in these characters which are to us offensive caused no hesitation in the time which first told the stories, but were, on the contrary, a source of pleasure or of inspiration.[1]

The olden time undoubtedly took delight in the patriarchs; it did not consider them saints, but told of them quite frankly all sorts of things that were far from ideal.[2]

Hence a primary aesthetic excellence belongs to the stories when they are innocent of religious and ethical seriousness, and subsequent attention to these concerns must necessarily work to the detriment of the stories. There is a kind of hierarchy of artistic merit and those who make the stories into vehicles of edification are 'remodellers and collectors',[3] but not creators. Their vocation to edify and instruct, to inculcate piety and expurgate the scandalous, makes them enemies of art. They put the original, imaginative product in chains; they corrupt the intention of the 'creators', because they are instructors and moralists without poetry in their souls. Gunkel supplies examples of this:

The earlier times knew also legends of the patriarchs which were altogether of profane character, such as the legends of the separation of Abraham and Lot, or that of Jacob and Laban. In later tradition religious elements made their way even into these legends and gave them a religious colouring. For instance, objection was taken to the notion that Canaan belonged to Abraham simply because Lot did not choose it and an addition supplied to the effect that God himself after Lot's withdrawal personally promised the land to Abraham (xiii 14-17). Similarly later narrators hesitated to say that Jacob had run away from Laban and accordingly interpolated the explanation that God had revealed the plan to him (xxxi 3).[4]

Despite Gunkel's great aesthetic sensibility he himself is eventually caught between his aesthetic judgement and his religious seriousness. The 'remodellers and collectors' are aesthetic vandals and enemies of art, and yet we find in Gunkel such statements as these:

The most important feature of this study is the history of religion.[5]

But, despite these instances, we must not surrender our gratification of the gradual improvement in ethical judgement which we can see in Genesis.[6]

---

[1] *Legends*, pp. 111 f.; *Genesis* (3), p. lxxii.

[2] *Legends*, p. 113; *Genesis* (3), p. lxxiii.

[3] *Legends*, pp. 137 ff.

[4] *Legends*, p. 111; *Genesis* (3), p. lxxii. Also *Legends*, pp. 112 f.; *Genesis* (3), pp. lxxii f.; *Legends*, pp. 114 f.; *Genesis* (3), pp. lxxiii f.

[5] *Legends*, p. 103; *Genesis* (3), p. lxvii.   [6] *Legends*, p. 115.

Here then is a history of the patriarchal narratives from another angle. The original, secular story, which is unconcerned with piety and morality, which is worldly and whose characters can be rascals, is transformed into an edifying tale of high moral tone peopled by pious characters. The entertaining story is changed into a sacred story.

Here the formerly popular saga is on the point of becoming 'legend', that is a characteristically 'sacred' or 'priestly' narrative. Whether the phenomenon was connected with the fact that the legends were at that time making their way into certain definite 'sacred' or 'priestly' circles we are unable to say.[1]

This process constitutes the *Vergeistlichung* of the patriarchal narratives.[2]

Gunkel's final reconstruction of the patriarchal narratives assumes that they were originally *Märchen* and Klatt[3] doubts whether the 'original' stories, as reconstructed by Gunkel, ever existed in Israel. Klatt acknowledges that Gunkel tries to meet this criticism by his observation[4] that the spirit of biblical religion is antipathetic to the 'floating' character of *Märchen* material and its disengagement from specific localization. Gunkel's view is that the extant patriarchal narratives are *Sagen* rather than *Märchen* because they do have local attachments. Klatt, however, like Eissfeldt,[5] would appear to be saying that not only are the stories not *now Märchen*, but that it is a mistake to attempt to derive them from *Märchen*.

The bearing of the derivation of the patriarchal narratives from *Märchen* on the historicity of the narratives has been considered in the Introduction. The very different impression of the patriarchal narratives to be gathered from the history of the tradition which is given by Martin Noth will be the main concern of Chapter iii. It will be sufficient to say in this place that Noth's account rests on an assumption about genre taken from Albrecht Alt which is different from that of Gunkel. Alt indicates the un-

---

[1] *Legends*, p. 111; *Genesis* (3), p. lxxii. The final sentence, 'Whether the . . . say', does not appear in *Genesis* (3).

[2] Cf. W. Klatt, *op. cit.*, p. 152.

[3] *ibid.*, p. 137.

[4] *Märchen*, pp. 12 f.

[5] O. Eissfeldt, 'Die Bedeutung der Märchenforschung für die Religionswissenschaft, besonders für die Wissenschaft vom Alten Testament', *Zeitschrift für Missionskunde und Religionswissenschaft*, 33 (1918), pp. 65-71, 81-85; *KS* i (1962), pp. 23-32.

tenability of the theory that the patriarchs were originally gods and also of the supposition that they are personifications of tribes.[1] He dissents from Gunkel's view that they are figures of fiction, and, in the place which he accords to aetiology, he is nearer to the earlier than to the later Gunkel. He holds that Jacob, Esau and Ishmael were all eponyms from the outset and that these narratives are therefore essentially (in the terminology of the earlier Gunkel) 'ethnological aetiologies'.[2] Alt's distinctive understanding of the genre derives from his view that the patriarchs are founders of cults. If this is so, the narratives in respect of genre are cultic history. All that can be said about the patriarchs, however, is that they were founders of semi-nomadic clan cults which were brought into Canaan and attached to Canaanite sanctuaries by their descendants. Hence the patriarchs themselves had no direct historical connexion with Canaanite sanctuaries or with El worship,[3] since the sanctuaries in question did not come within the orbit of Israel until after the settlement. Any representations of the patriarchal narratives which have a *prima facie* pre-settlement character must therefore necessarily be anachronistic.[4]

According to the later Gunkel the patriarchal narratives are derived from *Märchen*, while, according to Noth, who builds on Alt's work, the narratives are developed from a kernel of cultic history. The significantly different history of the genre given by Noth rests ultimately on Alt's 'god of the fathers' hypothesis. According to this view the patriarchal stories are not to be derived from myth or *Märchen* but from a pre-Yahwistic clan cult to which Alt gave the name 'god of the fathers'. The patriarchal narratives have a cultic origin and it is the promise of posterity and land, constitutive of this type of cult,[5] which is the primary theme of the stories. The entire subsequent, elaborate development of the narratives grows out of the credal significance which this patriarchal type of cult comes to possess for Israel.

Abraham, Isaac and Jacob were all founders of 'god of the fathers' cults and when the semi-nomads, to whose conditions of life this type of cult corresponds, settled in Canaan, the cults of

[1] 'Der Gott der Väter', *BWANT*, III Folge, Heft 12 (1929); R. A. Wilson (translator), 'The God of the Fathers', *Essays on Old Testament History and Religion* (1966), p. 46.

[2] *ibid.*, p. 55, n. 160, 161.

[3] *ibid.*, p. 9, n. 19; p. 29.

[4] *ibid.*, pp. 48 f.   [5] Cf. below, p. 116, n. 4.

the founders were attached to one or other of the ancient Canaanite sanctuaries. The Israelites who settled in mid-Palestine and whose principal sanctuary was Shechem appropriated the cult of the 'ābīr of Jacob, which had become attached to that sanctuary, and it was in this way that a patriarchal, pre-Yahwistic cult was incorporated into the Israelite creed. The patriarchal article of that creed 'A wandering Aramaean was my father' or 'An Aramaean in danger of perishing was my father' (Deut. 26.5) is set in the context of the fulfilment of Yahweh's promise to settle Israel in the land of Canaan, and this is an indication that the occupation of Canaan has been understood as the fulfilment of the promise of posterity and land which was constitutive of the cult of the god of Jacob. It is also an indication that the consequent, rich development of the patriarchal stories in the context of the Pentateuch was the result of an all-Israelite appropriation of the cult of the god of Jacob.[1]

According to this view of the matter the patriarchal narratives have a cultic origin and they are originally dominated by a credal concern. It can be said generally of Noth's history of the genre that it is one of gradual disengagement from credal concern and political or social function, until a condition of literary autonomy is eventually achieved. Such a history of the genre takes exactly the opposite direction to that of Gunkel. Gunkel's view is that the stories are originally art created for enjoyment and, more or less innocent of function. They are an end in themselves and only subsequently are they burdened with ulterior motives. Noth, on the other hand, maintains that it is at the earliest stage of the history of the genre that stories or notices are vehicles of theological claims, especially the claim to rightful possession of the land of Canaan. The history of the genre is then a history of the gradual slackening of the, at first, dominant credal function. In the east-Jordan Jacob-Laban stories, in which sanctuaries no longer feature, and where the credal importance of promise of land no longer answers to political and social priorities, the stories have a more secular aspect and reflect the concerns of east-Jordan Ephraimite colonists from west-Jordan who have to find a *modus vivendi* with their Aramaean neighbours. Finally there are examples of stories, belonging to a late stage of the history of the tradition, which exist only for their own sake. What we therefore have in

[1] For a detailed account, see Chapter iii.

Noth's account is a history of gradual literary emancipation until the story is finally set free from all credal, political and social subservience and from aetiological function.[1] In terms of Gunkel's *Märchen* theory the cultic aetiologies belong to a late stage of the history of the genre, whereas in terms of Noth's starting-point in cultic history they are of the very essence of the genre. It is, according to Noth, at a late stage in the history of the genre that the artist is free to exercise his imagination and to give full play to the freedom of inventiveness and device. He is no longer answerable either to creed or to society in general. He is a master of his house and creates a story as a work of art in order to give pleasure to others.[2]

IV

Westermann[3] locates the original forms of the patriarchal narratives in the sphere of the family and argues that these stories reflect a state of affairs where everything that happens belongs to the circle of the family which, therefore, comprehends the totality of man's experience. The narratives are originally anchored to a stage in the history of civilization where the family is the only social unit – where there is no institution corresponding to a state issuing claims for wider, political forms of loyalty to its citizens. The patriarchal narratives so described do not possess any particular historicity. They have a certain paradigmatic or standardized aspect; they deal with experiences and concerns in which all families participate at a particular level of culture, rather than recording what is special to a particular family.[4]

Westermann distinguishes between *Väter* and *Erzväter*: the stories as *Vätergeschichten* are, according to his account, necessarily general and representative. They tell us about a style of family life in which all families participate at a particular stage in the history of civilization. But the *Erzvätergeschichten*, the stories about Abraham, Isaac and Jacob as founding fathers of Israel, have an aspect of particularity and historical uniqueness. Westermann's account of the origins of the genre cannot be regarded as a quest after the historical patriarchs, because the patriarchs only emerge at the

[1] Below, pp. 112 ff.
[2] Below, pp. 123 ff.
[3] C. Westermann, 'Arten der Erzählung in der Genesis'. *Forschung am alten Testament* (1964), pp. 9-91.
[4] *ibid.*, pp. 35 ff.

point where the stories cease to be family stories and become Israelite ones in an all-Israelite credal context (i.e., in the context of a *Heilsgeschichte*).[1] For so long as they are family narratives nothing, so far as I can see, of a particular historical character is attributed to them. When Westermann says that family history is the totality of history for those whose lives are reflected in these stories, he does not mean that it is impossible to locate the stories chronologically and culturally in the wider framework of Ancient Near Eastern history, although he himself makes no attempt to establish such historical correlations. There is, at any rate, a world of difference between what Westermann is doing and the efforts of others to locate the patriarchs as historical individuals in a second millennium B.C., Ancient Near Eastern context.

What is the nature of the connexion between the patriarchal narratives as *Vätergeschichten* and as *Erzvätergeschichten*? A consideration of this question suggests that Westermann's work may be regarded in some sense as a development of the positions of Alt and Noth. According to Alt and Noth the kernel of the patriarchal stories is a particular type of cult, and it was the movement of the adherents of this cult into Canaan which brought about the integration of the promise of the 'god of the fathers' cult with the Promise of Canaan to the Israelites. Westermann's view, on the other hand, is that the original forms of the patriarchal narratives originate not inside Canaan as a growth from a credal kernel, but as family narratives at a stage which is chronologically and culturally earlier than the settlement of the Israelites in Canaan. The themes of these narratives and the concerns which find expression in them were such that they were capable of reinterpretation in relation to Abraham, Isaac and Jacob in their roles as *Erzväter*. In particular the aspect of Promise belongs to the stories in their family setting: the combination of promise of posterity and promise of land is not original – these are rather to be regarded as alternative themes of Promise. As in the case of Alt and Noth two dimensions of Promise serve more than any other feature to connect the two spheres in which the stories operate, the family sphere where they are *Vätergeschichten* and the Israelite sphere where they are *Erzvätergeschichten*. About the God (or gods) who issues the promises and effects deliverance in the *Vätergeschichten* Westermann does not appear to say anything; he does not com-

[1] *ibid.*, pp. 36, 61.

ment on the religion of the patriarchal narratives *qua Vätergeschichten*.[1]

So far as he is dealing with the genre of the patriarchal narratives his position appears to have similarities with that of Gressmann and Gunkel, both of whom maintained that the stories originated on the fringes of Palestine and reflected semi-nomadic conditions of life. Certainly Westermann does not relate the stories to *Märchen*, but, otherwise, it is not clear what status he accords to them. Is he saying that the *Vätergeschichten* are family records? I am not certain about this, but his *Gattungsforschung* suggests to me that he regards the patriarchal narratives as a kind of literature which reflects typical situations in the family at a time when life within the family is exhaustive of social experience, rather than that the stories are records of the experiences of particular families.

The position with Alt and Noth is that we cannot rediscover the historical patriarchs; that the terminus of research into patriarchal origins is a type of cult named after its founder. We cannot reach back to Abraham, but only to the god of Abraham, and similarly with Isaac and Jacob. Noth's account does explain how it comes about that Jacob, Isaac and Abraham are connected genealogically and become the subjects of a connected story – they were all founders of the same type of cult and the Promise of this cult was integrated with the Promise of an Israelite creed.[2] So far as I can see there is a less intrinsic theological connexion, according to Westermann, between the Abraham, Isaac and Jacob of the *Vätergeschichten* and the patriarchs of the *Erzvätergeschichten*. All we can say is that there were themes in these family histories which could be reinterpreted in terms of Israelite credal affirmations and the *Väter* were transformed into *Erzväter*. Moreover Noth undertakes to explain the historical circumstances in which the second dimension of Promise emerged, but Westermann is silent about the historical circumstances in which this pre-Israelite literature was appropriated by Israel and integrated with the Promise embedded in her creed.

There is a paradoxical character to Westermann's work. He is arguing that the patriarchal narratives antedate the settlement of the Israelites in Palestine and is countering the assertion of Noth that they reflect historical conditions subsequent to the settlement.

---

[1] *ibid.*, pp. 19-34.
[2] Below, Chapter iii.

From this point of view he would seem to be urging that the patriarchal narratives give us access to the prehistory of Israel. But, on the other hand, he does not use the stories to fill out this prehistory nor does his description of them as *Vätergeschichten* suggest that they can be so used. The end result is that the stories are much more in a historical vacuum than they are in Noth's work, for Noth allows them a secondary historical significance and relates them precisely to historical events and conditions in Canaan. According to Noth the stories can be related particularly to Israel's history in Canaan; according to Westermann they mirror typical family concerns at a given cultural stage, but they do not relate particularly to historical events.

With regard to aetiology Westermann asserts that no story is merely aetiological.[1] If, says Westermann, a story merely satisfies intellectual curiosity, it will lack 'suspense' and this 'suspense' is always present in the *Vätergeschichten*. But the fact that a story answers a question does not necessarily have significant artistic consequences for the story itself. The term 'aetiological story' indicates that we have both an aetiology and a story, so that the aetiology is not a 'scientific answer'. The aetiology does not necessarily restrict the imagination or fetter artistic resourcefulness, but rather challenges the imagination to find ways and means of answering the question by telling a good story.

This is not to say that Westermann is wrong in arguing that the aetiological elements in the patriarchal narratives are often secondary. Gunkel also had necessarily come to this conclusion once he traced the origins of the patriarchal narratives to the conditions of semi-nomadic life, since he regarded aetiology as a mark of a certain sophistication or, at any rate, not as a feature of a semi-nomadic tale derived from a *Märchen*. Thus Westermann holds that the aetiological interest though strong is not primary in the story about the sacrifice of Isaac.[2] More primary than the desire to explain how animal sacrifice was substituted for the sacrifice of the first-born son is a story characterized by 'suspense' about a child who was to be sacrificed and who was saved in the nick of time. Again in respect of Gen. 26 he argues that the aetiological motif in the names of wells is subsidiary to the motif of strife between semi-nomads over wells.[3]

[1] *op. cit.*, pp. 40 ff.   [2] *ibid.*, p. 71.
[3] *ibid.*, p. 67.

We have seen in this chapter that Gunkel's view of the genre of the patriarchal narratives undergoes a fundamental change between *Genesis* (*1*) and *Genesis* (*3*), and that in accord with the later opinion that the stories are developed from *Märchen* the aetiological elements in them are held to be secondary, functional accretions. In this respect Gunkel's history of the genre is diametrically opposed to that of Noth for whom the cultic aetiologies, associated with the West Jordan Jacob, belong to the earliest stage of that history. According to the later Gunkel the stories are developed from *Märchen*, while according to Noth they grow from a credal kernel, so that the genre at its inception is cultic history. Gunkel envisages the first stage as one of stories told for entertainment and the history of the genre as the subsequent acquisition of different functions expressed by aetiologies of different kinds and associated with a *Vergeistlichung* which supplies a moral content and tone not original to the stories. Noth's history of genre, whose implications for his history of tradition are worked out in chapter three, postulates a reverse process, whereby the patriarchal narratives are progressively emancipated from functions, credal, social and political, and achieve in the latest stages of their history a literary autonomy. Westermann agrees with Gunkel that the aetiological functions of the narratives are secondary, but he describes them as family histories coming from a culture in which experience within the family was exhaustive of social experience. The tribal-historical interpretation of the patriarchal narratives, which should be regarded as vestigial in *Genesis* (*1*) and whose application is minimized by the later Gunkel and by Noth, is the subject of special consideration in the next chapter.

Finally, Gunkel's devotion to aesthetic analysis and his ambition to speak like Herder with a tongue of fire is relatively independent of his shifting opinions as to the origins of the patriarchal narratives and represents an interest and capacity which sets him apart from the normal preoccupations of Old Testament scholars. One aspect of this is his contention that the narratives are little works of art which are performed before audiences and recreated at every performance. In this connexion Gunkel emphasizes that the stories have a 'popular' setting, that they are the cultural property of the group and that in performing them before an audience the story-teller employs a whole armoury of extra-literary devices.[1]

[1] This idea has been taken up in a quite independent and different way by

Schökel as an approach to Old Testament literature in general. For Schökel the thought that every reading of the scriptures is a 'performance' is related to the context of public worship and liturgical action. The hermeneutical possibilities of the scriptures are realized in liturgical 'performance' and every 'performance' involves revivification and the possibility of new dimensions of significance (L. A. Schökel, *The Inspired Word*, 1967, pp. 255 ff.; this is an English translation of *La Palabra Inspirada*, 1966).

CHAPTER II

The Narratives as Tribal History

I

The view that the patriarchal narratives are tribal history under the guise of the history of individuals is present in *Genesis* (*1*) and betrays the influence on Gunkel of Cornill, Guthe and Steuernagel.[1] In Guthe elaborate rules are formulated to transpose into tribal-historical terms husband, son, daughter and slave-girl.[2] Gunkel gives up a tribal-historical interpretation of the patriarchal narratives in *Genesis* (*2*) (1902), but in *Genesis* (1) he maintains it with two reservations: (*a*) All of the patriarchs may not originally represent tribes. (*b*) Sagas which originally had no connexion with tribal history have assumed a tribal-historical form in the extant narratives as a consequence of having been attracted to the patriarchs.[3] Thus Jacob was not originally Israel nor Esau Edom.[4] Abraham and Isaac were not from the outset fathers of Israel.[5] Gunkel also asserts in *Genesis* (*1*) that the women who appear in the patriarchal stories are to be interpreted as tribes.[6] Incompatible with this view that the patriarchal narratives give us access to pre-settlement tribal history is his contention in *Genesis* (*1*) that the patriarchs are Canaanite and that the stories about them were appropriated by Israel subsequent to the Settlement in Canaan.[7] On these premises Israelite tribal history can be distilled from the patriarchal narratives only in the cases of Dinah, Simeon and Levi (Gen. 34), Reuben (35.22) and Judah (38). These references are to Israelite tribes in Canaan in the earlier part of the period of the Judges.[8] Bare genealogies are not a nucleus of tribal history, but are late additions by 'Collectors' and chapter 49, which presupposes the Davidic entity 'Israel', is also late.[9]

---

[1] Cf. H. Weidmann, *op. cit.*, pp. 41 ff.
[2] H. Guthe, *Geschichte des Volkes Israel* (*3*) (1914), pp. 4 f.
[3] *Legends*, p. 20.
[4] *ibid.*, pp. 23 f.
[5] *ibid.*, p. 95.
[6] *ibid.*, p. 118.
[7] *ibid.*, pp. 88-90, 93.
[8] *Legends*, pp. 92, 136 f.
[9] *Legends*, p. 132.

When we come to the 'Jacob' article (1919) we find that the
Märchen theory has dissolved the historicity of the patriarchal
narratives and that the only elements of tribal history which remain
relate to the 'sons' of Jacob. The genealogical scheme is a way of
representing tribal history and Jacob is the 'father' of the twelve
tribes in virtue of his identification with Israel. It was congenial to
the thought of ancient Israel to give expression to a sense of corporate identity by representing national structure in terms of
family structure.[1] Hence the notice about Reuben (Gen. 35.22;
49.4) indicates that this tribe lost the leadership which it once held
among the tribes and entirely disappeared. This, however, is, in
Gunkel's terms, an 'ethnological' and not an 'ethnographic' aetiology.[2] That is to say, the story which explains the demise of
Reuben, his seduction of Bilhah, is literary invention and not historical incident. The same is true of the other tribal-historical
aetiologies. The disappearance of Levi as a secular tribe and the
scattering of Simeon is explained in terms of Shechem's seduction
of Dinah and the precipitate revenge taken by Simeon and Levi
against the wiser counsels of their father[3] (Gen. 34). Finally, the
fictional content of chapter 38 serves to record the tribal history of
Judah and its associates, how certain clans disappeared (the deaths
of Er and Onan) and new clans emerged (the births of Perez and
Zerah).

[1] 'Jacob', p. 340.
[2] *Legends*, pp. 25-27.
[3] Cf. G. E. Wright, *Shechem: The Biography of a Biblical City* (1965).
Wright holds that the story in Gen. 34 reflects an attack on Shechem by the
Israelite tribes of Simeon and Levi in the Amarna period (pp. 139 f.) His conviction that the tradition is old rests on the assumption that Levi was a secular
tribe at the time of the attack, but had been set aside for priestly duties as early
as the twelfth or eleventh centuries B.C. (pp. 131 f.). This view of Levi is contested by E. Nielsen, *Shechem: a traditio-historical Investigation* (1959). Nielsen
agrees that the portrayal of a Simeonite raid on Shechem would fit well into the
earliest history of that tribe so far as this can be reconstructed and that the events
related of Simeon in Gen. 34 belong to the earliest history of Israel (pp. 259-264).
He maintains, however, that there never was a secular tribe of Levi and that the
reason for the association of Simeon and Levi in Gen. 49.5 ff. may be that both
are regarded as 'scattered tribes'. Both tribes in different ways were extremists
and it is this which explains their juxtaposition in Gen. 34. There is here,
according to Nielsen, the implication of an adverse estimate of their extremism
by other Israelite tribes. Simeon's lack of moderation was shown by the attack
on Shechem, whereas Levi's extremism takes the form of a rigorous opposition
to the Canaanite cult and so to such centres as Shiloh, Bethel and Jerusalem.
As an alternative hypothesis Nielsen suggests that the Simeonites may have

What is told of Tamar in detail rests on the same basic motif as the story of Ruth and is in its origin not historical but fictional.[1]

Similarly in the case of the Joseph story we have a complex of *Märchen* motifs and the composition is 'Israelitized' in so far as the youngest, cleverest son is identified with the tribe of Joseph and the other brothers with certain of the Israelite tribes. The only historical recollection preserved is that Joseph which was the youngest of the tribes became the most dominant among them.[2]

Nor is the Jacob-Laban pact, according to Gunkel, a primary tribal-historical datum (Gen. 31.43-54). Laban is a *Märchen* figure and only subsequently an Aramaean eponym and the treaty as depicted by E (vv. 43-50) is a private one between two *Märchen* characters. Its transformation into a political pact in J (vv. 51-54) is a consequence of the acquisition of national status by Jacob and Laban.[3]

II

The most influential and thoughtful contemporary exponent of the view that the patriarchal narratives are tribal history is Otto Eissfeldt. Eissfeldt rejects Gunkel's theory that the stories originate as a kind of imaginative literature and that the patriarchs are the products of creative story-telling. He holds that the narratives are essentially tribal history and that the representation of this history through individuals is related to a way of perceiving the corporate which has reality and appropriateness for ancient men. The communication of tribal history through family history is a poetic vision of the solidarity of the group and the genealogical list an expression of or participation in this solidarity.[4]

The patriarchal narratives are then essentially tribal history and this is characteristically contained in genealogical lists.[5] The history of the genre can be most broadly expressed as a movement from tribal-historical notices to 'human' stories, and in connexion with

---

been 'inspired' by Levite priests or even accompanied by them on the occasion of their raid on Shechem (pp. 280-283).

[1] 'Jacob', p. 346.

[2] *ibid.*, p. 346.

[3] *ibid.*, p. 355.

[4] 'Die Bedeutung der Märchenforschung', *KS* i, p. 31; 'Stammessage und Menschheitserzählung in der Genesis', *Sitzungsberichte der sächsischen Akademie der Wissenschaften zu Leipzig*, Phil.-Hist. Klasse, Band 110, Heft 4 (1965), pp. 5-26, especially p. 6.

[5] This is contrary of Gunkel's view, above p. 68.

this process of narrative enrichment of the original notices or other forms of tribal history the question of historicity or non-historicity ceases to be significant. The narratives now move in the sphere of creative literature, and 'truth' as it is conveyed by the imagination is compatible with free invention and, indeed, can only be achieved when prosaic ideas of historicity are transcended. The 'truth' lies in the creation of truly human situations and characterizations, in the catching and communicating of the subtleties of inter-personal relationships, especially within the intense social life of the family. In so far as the patriarchal narratives describe and explore these elemental areas of human intercourse, they are released from all temporal and local limitations and lose their relevance as specific accounts about historical groups in given temporal and spatial contexts. They are emancipated into the realm of universal human-ity and in so far as they register quintessential experiences they have a quality of timelessness and are true of men in any time and at any place. With this development of the patriarchal stories from tribal history to imaginative literature is associated the utilization of literary material of different kinds. This thesis is most fully expressed in 'Stammessage und Menschheitserzählung'.

Bare tribal history with a minimum of narrative embellishment is preserved in the account of the expulsion of the children of Keturah (Gen. 25.1-6). This reflects a historical circumstance and explains why Israel, represented by Isaac, the 'son' of Sarah, pos-sesses Canaan, while those represented as 'sons' of Keturah, that is, Midian, have their beat and pastures in the steppe east of the settled regions of trans-Jordan. The 'sons' of Keturah are historical entities (the tribes of the Syrian-Arabian desert), but Keturah her-self is probably a product of narrative invention. This is in line with Eissfeldt's estimate of all the women who appear in the tribal histories (Sarah, Hagar, Milcah, Reumah, Rebecca, Leah, Rachel, Zilpah, Bilhah). Other possibilities which he considers but dis-counts are that the women were once goddesses and have been demoted to matriarchs, or that they embody reminiscences of his-torical individuals. He favours the conclusion that the introduction of wives and mothers belongs to the fictional elements which enrich the tribal histories. The concept, considered valid in Israel and elsewhere in the ancient world, that groups and societies derive from one tribal father and that a chain of births can represent the history of these groups, makes it natural to assign to the father one or more wives, in which case the difference of status between a chief wife and a subordinate wife may reflect differences in status between tribes. Thus Sarah is the mother of Israel, but a subsidiary wife (Keturah) is the mother of the six desert tribes.[1]

The Hagar stories (Gen. 16.4-14; 25.18; 21.8-21) deal with a similar theme and explain how it comes about that Sarah's son, Isaac, possesses Palestine, while the twelve desert tribes descended from Hagar's son, Ishmael, have their beat and pasture in the Sinai peninsula and on the east side of the gulf of Akaba. In this instance, however, there has been a considerable narrative development on the tribal-historical base and this process can be traced in the differences between chapters 16 and 21, for in the latter the aspect of tribal history has yielded to the creation of a human story which evokes pity and compassion. The centre of interest is no longer the child in Hagar's womb whose birth is an event of tribal history, but the mother with her child in the desert in the extremity of her distress.[2]

The short notice about the birth of Nahor's twelve sons (Gen. 22.20-24) compared with the extensive narrative concerning the birth of the twelve sons of Jacob (Gen. 29.29-30.24) illustrates the evolution from tribal history to human story. In the Nahor list tribal history is more prominent than fiction and the nomadic Aramaean tribes north-east of Palestine, who are derived from Nahor, are historical entities, while Nahor himself is either to be understood as a group of tribes or as a geographical location. The wife and concubine are probably literary inventions, and the derivation of Tebah, Gaham, Tahash and Maacah from Reumah, the concubine, may indicate that they were tribes of lesser status than the 'sons' of Milcah.[3]

In the account of the birth of Jacob's sons the element of tribal history is overshadowed by a rich narrative growth, and a delight in investigating the characters in themselves and in their inter-relations takes control. The two chief wives (Leah and Rachel) compete for the favour of their husband, making accomplices of their slave-girls, Zilpah and Bilhah, and mastering their husband rather than being mastered by him. The etymological aetiologies associated with the names of the twelve sons are pure invention

---

[1] 'Stammessage und Menschheitserzählung', pp. 6 f.
[2] *op. cit.*, pp. 8 f.
[3] *ibid.*, pp. 9 f.

and no tribal history is contained in them. Eissfeldt is disinclined to distil any tribal history from the genealogical structure and does not assume that the 'sons' of Zilpah (Gad and Asher) and Bilhah (Dan and Naphtali) represent tribes of subordinate status. The juxtaposition of Dan and Naphtali is to be explained by the circumstance that they occupied contiguous areas after the migration of Dan to northern Palestine, and Gad and Asher are linked for purely etymological reasons – both names mean 'luck'.

All the women are probably literary creations, but the Leah and Rachel groups of tribes represent two different areas of settlement of Jacob tribes, one in southern Palestine and the other in central Palestine and trans-Jordan. Issachar and Zebulon, whom Leah is said to have borne after a time of barrenness, may have been associated with the Leah group because they were originally settled in the same area before they moved further north. This, however, is uncertain and all that is certainly indicated is that Issachar and Zebulon were neighbouring tribes. On the story of the birth of Benjamin (Gen. 35.16-20) Eissfeldt is non-committal as to whether this is to be assessed as history or literature. It may be a literary device to increase the suspense of the story and to introduce variety, since all the other sons of Jacob are said to have been born in Mesopotamia. Or it may reflect the historical fact that Benjamin was disengaged from the House of Joseph coalition and achieved full tribal status for the first time in Palestine. At any rate it is certain that the grave of Rachel, which had the status of a holy place, was located in the tribal territory of Benjamin, for this is attested by Gen. 35.20, I Sam. 10.2 and Jer. 31.15.[1]

The process of development from tribal history to human story is also illustrated by the Joseph narrative in which Eissfeldt identified two strands, one Palestinian and the other Egyptian. The former consists basically of tribal history and the latter is a narrative with the artistic construction of a *Novelle*. The tribal history is contained in Gen. 35.21-22a (the short notice that Reuben lay with Bilhah, his father's concubine), 34.1-31, 35.5 (the folly of Simeon and Levi at Shechem), 38 (the secession of Judah), 49.2-7, 26 and Deut. 33.7 (sayings of Jacob about Reuben, Simeon, Levi and Joseph, and the saying of Moses about Judah). Eissfeldt argues that these sayings reflect inter-tribal relations in the pre-settlement

---

[1] 'Jakob-Lea und Jakob-Rahel', *Festschrift für Hans Wilhelm Hertzberg zum 70 Geburtstag am 16 Januar, 1965*, pp. 50-55; *KS* iv (1968), pp. 170-175.

period in Palestine, namely, the passing of precedence from the four tribes, Reuben, Simeon, Levi and Judah (the four oldest 'sons') to Joseph. The positive saying concerning Joseph (Gen. 49.26) contrasts with the negative sayings attached to the four oldest sons, and the setting of all these sayings is Palestine and not Egypt. These notices and sagas of the older Palestinian strand are not homogeneous with the Egyptian story which is contained in Gen. 37; 39-48; 50, and which is introduced by chapters 33-36. In the later narrative everything hinges on Joseph and a thematic and structural unity is achieved. The older sagas, on the other hand, are, more or less, unconnected with each other: details are given about the deeds of Reuben, Simeon and Levi, but these tribes are connected only in the series of sayings which allude to them and group them together (Gen. 49.2-7). Certainly greater scope is afforded to literary invention in the older strand of the Joseph story than in the account of the expulsion of the 'sons' of Keturah or the list of Nahor's 'sons', but despite this narrative expansion the tribal-historical nucleus is intact. In chapter 34 there is the recollection of a treaty concluded between the tribes Simeon and Levi, who were settled beside Shechem, and the inhabitants of that city – a treaty which broke up in a blood bath. Chapter 38 touches on the relations of Judah with certain sub-tribes: it reflects the decline of the sub-tribes Er, Onan and Shelah over against Perez and Zerah who had maintained their position. The transition from 'tribal-historical' to 'human' in Gen. 38 is marked by the decisive part which is played by marriages, births and deaths – events which have a human universality and are not temporally or spatially specific.[1]

The Egyptian strand of the Joseph story (Gen. 37; 39-48; 50) has a general, human character and contains only a few tribal-historical elements. The sojourn of first Joseph and then his father and brothers in Egypt reflects the historical fact that the fore-runners of a part of the later Israel spent twenty years or so in Egypt, although the details are no longer recoverable. The adoption of Manasseh and Ephraim by Jacob is to be related to the disappearance of the secular tribe of Levi and a concern to preserve the number of twelve tribes. The account of Jacob's blessing of Manasseh and Ephraim seeks to explain how it came about that precedence passed from Manasseh to the hitherto subordinate

[1] 'Stammessage und Menschheitserzählung', pp. 18 f.

Ephraim (Gen. 41.50-52; 48.1-20). Otherwise the Joseph story set in Egypt has no specific tribal-historical content, but deals with men as they have always been and will always be. This is true not only of the stories which have the flavour of Egyptian *Märchen*, and are at least partially dependent on them (the seductive wife of Potiphar and Joseph's chastity, chapter 39; his renown as an inter-preter of dreams and his subsequent preferment, 40-41), but also of his sale into Egypt at the instance of his brothers, the confronta-tion with his brothers (42-45) and his loving concern for his aged father (46-48).

Especially inter-personal relations which give to family life its peculiar quality of intensity are portrayed and probed – relations between father and sons, between brother and brothers. Jacob cannot conceal his particularly tender regard for Rachel's children and this has inevitable repercussions within the closely bound circle of his family, where relations are intense and are swept by powerful and conflicting emotions. The brothers cannot contain their jeal-ousy, and yet Reuben and Judah are torn between hatred and brotherly affection. Joseph himself is especially close to Benjamin, Rachel's other son, and he too when he is in a position to exact revenge for the wrong done to him oscillates between the delight experienced in settling a score and a tenderness for the old home and for family ties which rises like a flood and swamps him.[1]

This account of the history of the genre is supplemented by Eissfeldt's article on 'Genesis'[2] in *The Interpreters' Dictionary of the Bible*, particularly in respect of aetiology. Eissfeldt recognizes aetiologies in the case of Galed ('cairn of witness', 31.46-48), Suc-coth ('booths', 33.17), and an element of etymological aetiology in Penuel (32.31).[3] The narratives which are attached to sanctuaries are partly if not wholly foundation aetiologies, that is, they explain the circumstances in which an El cult was established at a parti-cular place, typically in connexion with a theophany; or they ex-plain the existence of particular ritual features of a cult. The sanc-tuary stories comprise: (*a*) Abraham and Melchizedek at Jerusalem (Gen. 14), (*b*) Hagar at Beer Lahai Roi (16; 21.8-21), (*c*) The sacri-

---

[1] *op. cit.*, pp. 19 f.; also 'Achronische, Anachronische und Synchronische Elemente in der Genesis', Jaarbericht van het Vooraziatisch-Egyptisch Genoot-schap, *Ex Oriente Lux* 17 (1963), pp. 148-164; *KS* iv, pp. 153-169.

[2] *The Interpreters' Dictionary of the Bible*, vol. ii (1962), pp. 366-380.

[3] 'Genesis', p. 376; also 'Jakobs Begegnung mit El und Moses Begegnung mit Jahwe', *OLZ* 58 (1963), Sp. 325-331; *KS* iv, pp. 92-98, especially pp. 96 f.

fice of Isaac (22.1-19), (d) Jacob at Bethel (28; 35.9-13, 15), (e) Jacob at Penuel (32.23-33), (f) The burial of gods by Jacob at Shechem and the building of an altar at Bethel (35.1-4, 6b-7), (g) Abraham, Isaac and Jacob at Beersheba (21.22-32; 26.12-33; 46.1-4). The fact that the blessing bestowed on Abraham is repeated for Isaac and Jacob at Beersheba leads Eissfeldt to suppose that Beersheba has a special religious significance and is the place to which chapter 15 should be attached. This goes with the assumption that 21.33, with its reference to Beersheba, originally stood at the end of chapter 15. Eissfeldt's account is not altogether clear, but he says that these sanctuary stories, at least in part, existed as Canaanite aetiologies prior to any association of them with the patriarchs. In so far as this is so they are from the point of view of history of genre Canaanite cultic aetiologies which have been 'taken over' by the Israelites when they settled in that land. Eissfeldt also holds, however, that

the cult legends like the other literary genres have been made subservient to the tribal and national sagas which are the essence of Genesis.

Hence he asserts that the sanctuary legends give us access to pre-settlement history and to the religion of the patriarchs, whether it is tribal history, as with Isaac and Jacob, or the history and religion of an individual, as with Abraham. Thus he says that the religious significance of Mamre and Hebron goes back to the pre-Israelite period (Gen. 17 and 18) and that the god El Shaddai, worshipped by the patriarchs, is to be located there.[1]

Eissfeldt also touches on the theme of the narrative expansion or 'humanizing' of tribal history in his article 'Genesis'. In the story of Jacob's unsuccessful attempt to precede Esau at birth, and in the similar but successful determination of Perez, the basis of tribal history is clearly recognizable (Gen. 25.26; 38.27-30). This reflects Israel's will to dominate or take precedence over Edom and similarly with the sub-tribes Perez and Zerah. The basis of tribal history is more obscured in the story of Esau's sale of his birthright (Gen. 25.29-34) by a narrative motif – two types of brothers, the older one who is slow and ponderous, and the younger one who is shrewd, intellectually nimble and competent. This motif is also influential in the story of Jacob's ruse to gain Esau's blessing (25.27-28; 27) and has its richest development in the Joseph story (37; 39-48; 50), where the able younger brother

[1] 'Genesis', pp. 376 f.

eventually turns the tables on his older brothers and has them at his mercy. The obscuring of tribal history through the exercise of the craft and devices of story-telling has not proceeded so far in chapter 34, where the tribal-historical basis – a treaty of trade and friendship between two groups of people and its disintegration in bloodshed – is still clearly recognizable. But the aspect of tribal history, communicated through a representation of family history, has been superseded by a delight in the drawing of human characters and the subtle interplay of family relationships. The brothers are hot with impatience to avenge the dishonour done to their sister, and the father, who can see further into the consequences of an instinctive act of reprisal, is appalled at what they have done.[1]

Again the contrast between tribal history and its narrative embellishment is seen in the comparison of the marriage notices of Abraham (25.1-6) and Nahor (22.20-24) with the long story about the wooing of Rebecca (24) or the story of Jacob's quest for Leah and Rachel (29). Deep human feelings may be injected not only into tribal history but also into what is basically a cultic aetiology. Thus 22.1-19 is originally an explanation of the circumstances in which human sacrifice was replaced by animal sacrifice, but the cult legend has been made subservient to literary and theological goals. The literary effect is achieved here not so much by a detailed dissection of Abraham's feelings as by an almost wordless allusiveness which indicates without description the tensions that build up within him as he approaches the place of sacrifice with Isaac. The theology relates, on the one hand, to the steadfastness of God's Promise which endures, however problematical it may become, and, on the other hand, to the status of Abraham as a paradigm of obedience.

The foregoing exposition will have shown that questions about the historicity of the patriarchal narratives cannot be separated from the question about history of genre. Eissfeldt's views on historicity (also his views on the religion of the patriarchs)[2] follow from his account of history of genre. The historicity of the patriarchal stories is dealt with particularly in two articles already cited,[3] but one or two others have to be considered also. The article

---

[1] 'Genesis', pp. 377 f.; 'Achronische, Anachronische und Synchronische Elemente in der Genesis', pp. 159 ff.

[2] Below, chapter iv.

[3] 'Achronische, Anachronische und Synchronische Elemente in der Genesis' and 'Jakob-Lea und Jakob-Rahel'.

'Jakob-Lea und Jakob-Rahel' bears on what has already been said about the history of the genre, but it may now be considered particularly in connexion with the nature of the historicity which Eissfeldt claims for the patriarchal narratives. Jacob and his twelve sons are historical entities, but they are personifications of tribes, not historical individuals. The explanations which are given of the names of Jacob's sons[1] have no relationship to tribal history and contain no allusions to the areas of settlement or destinies of the tribes. They have the narrative intention of expressing the emotions which were uppermost in the minds of Leah and Rachel in the presence of the children brought into the world by them and their slave-girls.[2]

In the case of Benjamin the father's as well as the mother's emotions are registered. The purely narrative interest of describing the emotions of fathers and mothers contrasts with the tribal-historical references in the series of sayings about the twelve 'sons' of Jacob contained in chapter 49. In the extant series the sayings about Judah, Zebulon, Issachar, Dan, Gad, Asher, Naphtali and Benjamin (49.8-20, 27) reflect post-settlement conditions,[3] but pre-settlement tribal relationships are reflected in 49.3-7 (Reuben, Simeon and Levi), in Deut. 33.7 (Judah) and in Gen. 49.22-26 (Joseph). Reuben, Simeon, Levi and Judah, on the one hand, and Joseph, on the other, are two groups of Jacob tribes settled in southern and central Palestine respectively in the pre-Mosaic era, the central Palestinian group also having a foothold in trans-Jordan. This view is reinforced by the division of the Joseph story into an older Palestinian and a later Egyptian strand.[4] The older Palestinian strand reflects a shift in power and precedence from the older 'sons' of Jacob to the youngest 'son' Joseph, and in Gen. 49.27 Benjamin is associated with Joseph as a younger child of Rachel.

Hence the Jacob-Esau narrative and the Jacob-Laban narrative both contain a nucleus of pre-settlement tribal history. The Jacob of the Jacob-Esau story is the group of tribes settled in southern Palestine, and Esau is also a tribal entity – the Edomites on the other side of the Jordan. The Jacob of the Jacob-Laban narrative

[1] Gen. 29.32-35; 30.1-24; 35.18.
[2] 'Jakob-Lea und Jakob-Rahel', p. 157.
[3] Cf. 'Achronische, Anachronische und Synchronische Elemente in der Genesis', pp. 161 f.
[4] Above, pp. 72 ff.

is the group of tribes in central Palestine and trans-Jordan, and the story mirrors their relations with the Aramaeans who are in the adjacent area of trans-Jordan and extend far to the north east. The kernel of the south Palestinian material consists of the stories of the births of Esau and Jacob (25.21-26, 29-34), and of Jacob's deception of Isaac and appropriation of the blessing (25.27 f.; 27.1-40). These stories are set in and around Beersheba, while the central Palestinian Jacob is chiefly connected with Bethel (28.10-22 35.1-15), Penuel (32.23-33), Mahanaim (32.3), Succoth and Shechem (33.17-20), and Galed, where he made his pact with Laban (31.44-32.1). On the level of tribal history there is no connexion between the Jacob-Esau cycle and the Jacob-Laban cycle. The link is a secondary one of a purely literary kind and it is effected through the device of the 'Journey', whereby the south Palestinian Jacob travels east of the Jordan as far as Mesopotamia.[1]

This construction placed on the series of sayings about Jacob's 'sons', along with the explanation which is given of the Jacob-Esau and Jacob-Laban cycles as essentially tribal history, is associated with the assumed, older, Palestinian form of the Joseph story and its concern with the transfer of power and leadership from the four older sons to Joseph (Gen. 34; 35.21-22a; 38). In chapters 29 and 30 the setting of the births of Jacob's 'sons' has been transferred from Palestine to Mesopotamia, just as in the later Joseph story the setting has been transferred from Palestine to Egypt. The birth story of Benjamin, which is set in Palestine, was probably originally the birth story of Joseph, and has been transferred secondarily to Benjamin. This would mean that Joseph was originally the youngest son and the only child of Rachel and that the representation of Benjamin as the youngest son is either pure literary elaboration or reflects further circumstances of tribal history.[2]

In another article[3] Eissfeldt deals with those elements of the patriarchal narratives which are non-historical or unhistorical, and most of these have been noticed in connexion with the exposition of the history of the genre. These elements are the *Märchen* of Egyptian provenance in the Joseph story, fictional embroideries of tribal history, such as the story about Reuben and the mandrakes (30.14-18, 22-24) and narrative themes such as the wife-sister

---

[1] 'Jakob-Lea und Jakob-Rahel', pp. 172-174.   [2] *ibid.*, pp. 174 ff.

[3] 'Achronische, Anachronische und Synchronische Elemente in der Genesis', pp. 157 f.

motif (12; 20; 26) which have no historical basis. A more general indication of Eissfeldt's approach to the historicity of the patriarchal narratives is his statement that a mixture of anachronistic and synchronistic elements is characteristic of them. By this he means that history is always written with a modernizing tendency – that the past is always seen through the eyes of the present and that consequently there is an anachronistic aspect to the portrayal of past events.

The traditional material, of which there is a large quantity, grew in compass from generation to generation and in the process, partly unconsciously, partly deliberately, was accommodated to the changing circumstances.

This process, however, did not involve invention of new narratives or the obliteration of an authentic recollection of the past.

Narratives which originally reflect circumstances or events from before the period of the settlement are expanded by features which represent the contributions of later times, as, for example, the Jacob-Esau story whose basis (*Grundlage*) touches on the period before the settlement, but which has been modified in the light of the circumstances of Israel's relations with Edom in the periods of David and Solomon.[1]

This appears to be a modification of an earlier position, for Eissfeldt[2] had previously maintained that the cultural history which is mirrored in the patriarchal narratives is that of the periods of the authors of the documentary sources. The histories contained in these sources (J1, J2, E and P) locate in the past, either naïvely or deliberately, concepts, customs and legal principles which are current in their own times. Since each of the sources reflects the cultural conditions of the period to which it belongs, and since the relative chronology of the sources is firmly established, the cultural history of Israel can be plotted by a right use of the sources. The premises of this argument may be restated as follows: every age, more or less, gives up the sense of historical distance; recollections of earlier events are retained, but the distance of the cultural circumstances of the past from those of the present is forgotten. Hence for every age previous representations appear to be intolerably antiquated and there is an incentive to reconstruct the past in terms which are acceptable to the present.

An example of how these principles apply is given in respect of

---

[1] *ibid.*, pp. 161 f.
[2] 'Die Schichten des Hexateuch als vornehmste Quelle für den Aufriss einer israelitisch-jüdischen Kulturgeschichte', *Pr.M* 23 (1919), pp. 173-185, *KS* i (1962), pp. 33-43.

the Abraham and Jacob narratives. According to J (29.1 ff.) Abraham's place of origin and the place where Jacob settles is 'the land of the eastern tribes' (NEB), that is, the Syrian-Arabian steppe east of Palestine. According to E, Abraham's place of origin and the place where Jacob settles is Harran (29.4). According to P (11.31) Abraham's original home was Ur Kasdim. E and P are influenced by the desire to derive Abraham from the great world and are moved by the consideration that the universal power of their God is more impressively demonstrated the more distant the region out of which he led Abraham into the land of Canaan. With regard to Laban's pursuit of Jacob (31), the Mount Gilead reference is borrowed by E from J, but Mount Gilead is six hundred kilometres as the crow flies from Harran and sagas do not deal with such distances. According to J, Laban lives in the Syrian-Arabian steppe and this makes the seven days' journey credible (31.23). The statement that Laban overtook Jacob at Mount Gilead is retained by E, but the reference to a journey of seven days is dropped. P's dependence on E is shown by the circumstance that while he represents that Abraham stems from Ur Kasdim, he retains Harran as an intermediate stage between Ur Kasdim and Canaan.[1]

Eissfeldt's view here is that the age of the material in the patriarchal narratives must first be determined by a comparison of the sources. He also holds that the history written by the authors of the sources reflects the cultural conditions of the age in which they write, but this does not entirely preclude the possibility of an authentic recollection of the events and circumstances of a historical period earlier than those of the authors of the sources.

A more recent view of the kind of historicity possessed by the patriarchal narratives has clear affinities with the positions of the earlier Eissfeldt.[2] Mazar's general view is that the historical circumstances reflected in the patriarchal narratives are those of the post-settlement period and that Genesis was given its original written form in the period of the establishment of David's empire.[3] He questions the use which has been made of second millennium B.C. archives to elucidate the patriarchal narratives and the propriety of postulating a 'patriarchal period' so as to elucidate the

[1] *KS* i, pp. 37-43.

[2] B. Mazar, 'The Historical Background of the Book of Genesis', *JNES* 28 (1969), pp. 73-83.

[3] He also associates Genesis with the 'Solomonic Enlightenment'; cf. G. von Rad, below, p. 243.

emergence of the patriarchs against the background of general history in the second millennium B.C. He urges that the historical and cultural circumstances reflected in the patriarchal narratives are rather those of the end of the period of the Judges and the beginning of the period of the monarchy.[1] Consequently he argues that the portrayals of the patriarchs in the Negeb, at Beersheba and Gerar agree with the conditions which existed when David and his men resided in the Western Negeb in the territory of Achish, king of the Philistines, and under his jurisdiction. In particular, this is illustrated by the relations between Abimelech, king of the Philistines, and Isaac's group in Gen. 26, and the lapse in the title of Ps. 34, 'To David when he feigned madness before Abimelech' (instead of Achish) is significant. At times disputes broke out among these Israelite shepherds and the Philistines over wells

and occasionally they moved southward with their flocks to the expanses of the Negev, reaching Kadesh-Barnea and Beer-lahai-roi on the road to Shur. When there was a severe drought they went down as far as the Nile delta with Pharaoh's consent.[2]

Similarly Mazar holds that references to the Aramaeans and Ishmaelites in the patriarchal narratives reflect the historical circumstances of the last quarter of the eleventh century B.C. The Aramaeans do not appear on the stage of history before the end of the twelfth century B.C. and in the course of the eleventh century they gain a foothold in the Euphrates crescent and adjoining areas of Mesopotamia. The references to Aramaeans, to Padan-aram, Aram-naharaim and Harran in the patriarchal stories reflect the historical circumstances which obtained towards the end of the eleventh century B.C. These Aramaeans were principally shepherds whose main area of settlement was Harran in Aram-naharaim, but whose pasture-lands spread as far as eastern trans-Jordan. The account in Gen. 31.45-54 reflects the relations between Israel and these Aramaeans before the outbreak of David's war against the kingdom of Aram-Zobah and her allies in trans-Jordan.[3] The Ishmaelites were camel nomads whose religious centre was Beer-lahai-roi and who did not appear on the fringe of Palestine earlier than the eleventh century B.C. The characterization of Ishmael as a wild ass of a man, his hand against everyone and everyone's hand against him (Gen. 16.12), is to be correlated with the pressure

[1] *op. cit.*, pp. 73-77.   [2] *ibid.*, p. 77.
[3] *ibid.*, pp. 78 f.

exerted by the Hagarites against the borders of Israelite settlements in trans-Jordan in the reign of Saul (I Chron. 5).[1]

On the migrations of the patriarchs Mazar observes that all the
places associated with them fall within the principal areas of
Israelite settlement in Canaan – Judah, Mount Ephraim and
Gilead. Most of them are known as cultic centres, or as important
centres of the Israelite tribes or as both, during the period of the
Judges and the beginning of the Monarchy.[2]

The position of the later Eissfeldt is shown by his statement in
'Genesis' (1962) that the anachronisms in the patriarchal narratives
(features relating to the periods of the Judges and the Monarchy)
have been blended with reliable, historical recollections of the
characters, conditions and events of the prehistorical Israel before
the time of Moses.[3] Moreover, what Eissfeldt had to say in
'Achronische, Anachronische und Synchronische Elemente in der
Genesis' exhibits a positive attitude to the prehistory of Israel.
Thus he notes certain anachronistic features which reflect post-
settlement circumstances[4] and then he details aspects of historical
portrayal which touch on the conditions of the pre-Israelite or
pre-Mosaic Palestinian scene: (*a*) The patriarchs are represented
as strangers who do not conquer or possess the land and this contrasts with the representation of the status of the Israelite tribes
in Palestine in the books of Joshua, Judges and Samuel. Abraham
has to buy a grave (23) and Jacob a sanctuary (33.19-20), and the
relationships which are depicted between the patriarchs and the
Canaanites indicate that the latter are in possession of the land and
have the power to give rights and privileges to the patriarchs or to
withhold these from them. The patriarchs are ass nomads or ass
semi-nomads who are shadow-possessors of Palestine (on the analogy of the English idiom 'shadow-cabinet') in virtue of the Promise.
(*b*) The relations which obtain between these Israelites and the
Ishmaelites and Keturites of the Sinai peninsula and Arabian
desert reach back into the period before the settlement. Similarly
Esau in Seir, Lot in the territory later settled by the Ammonites
and Moabites, and Laban in the north-east of trans-Jordan and
in Mesopotamia are 'shadow-possessors' (Deut. 2.10-12, 20-23) of

---

[1] *ibid.*, p. 79.
[2] *ibid.*, p. 81.
[3] 'Genesis', p. 379.
[4] Above, pp. 76 ff.

the areas where their descendants settled and belong as the Israelite patriarchs do to the period before the settlement. At this point Eissfeldt restates the principles governing his assessment of the historicity of the patriarchal narratives. The popular recollection of past periods is often in error in the definition of the exact period with which it deals, but the sequence of events and the groups and persons who participated in them are as a rule correctly maintained. Hence there are no reasons for rejecting the representation that Esau and Lot as well as Nahor, Bethuel and Laban belong to more or less the same period as the Israelite patriarchs.[1]

This would seem to indicate a change of mind about the assessment of the Mesopotamian connexions of Laban as compared with the view of the earlier Eissfeldt (1919) that there is no historical connexion between Laban and Harran, that the link was established by E for theological reasons and that sagas deal in smaller distances. It can be said with more certainty that Eissfeldt's appraisal of the historicity of the Mesopotamian connexions of Abraham has changed. According to the 1919 article Ur Kasdim is the creation of P who is motivated by a desire to widen further the horizons of the Abraham story, Harran (E) being retained as an intermediate stage of Abraham's journey to Canaan.[2] In 'Genesis' (1961), on the other hand, he says:

The tradition that Abraham came from Harran to Canaan in the period before Moses is thus probably correct, and, even the report, in other respects very questionable, that Abraham's father had sojourned in Ur Kasdim may have preserved correctly the recollection that for a time this place or its environs was the home of a group of nomads or semi-nomads related to Abraham.[3]

It will be noted that Eissfeldt here applies a tribal-historical interpretation to Abraham's father, as he also does to Isaac and Jacob, while he reserves a special interpretation for Abraham, namely, that he was a historical individual.

Abraham, according to Eissfeldt, was probably a nomadic or semi-nomadic sheikh with a considerable following and the genealogical scheme Abraham-Isaac-Jacob is as unhistorical as the representation that the twelve tribes of Israel were sons of Jacob. The latter is a case of tribal history in the guise of family history

[1] 'Achronische, Anachronische und Synchronische Elemente in der Genesis', pp. 162-164.
[2] Above, pp. 79 ff.
[3] 'Genesis', p. 379.

and similarly Abraham was not really the father of a historical person, Isaac, nor the grandfather of another historical individual, Jacob, so that the genealogical scheme has to be explained differently. Not unrelated to the special historical status which Eissfeldt assigns to Abraham is his attitude to the narratives in chapters 14 and 19 in which Abraham appears. He classifies these chapters tentatively as achronistic and describes 14 as an unrealistic composition from biblical and extra-biblical sources. Of chapter 19 he says that it is an aetiology of the barrenness of the Dead Sea area, but he finds in both narratives, along with a strong admixture of fictional elements, recollections of actual events in the first half of the second millennium B.C.[1] Later in the same article he considers more closely the residue of historicity in chapters 14 and 19 and describes 14, which equates Kadesh with En-Mishpat (14.7) and locates it in the neighbourhood of Amalekite territory (cf. Ex. 17.8-16) as derived from a well-informed extra-Israelite source. He also notes that Hoba (Gen. 14.15), which is situated north of Damascus, is mentioned in the El Amarna letters. From these indications of reliability he is encouraged to suppose that the account of the four kings may have historical value, and he suggests that we should understand the situation as one where resistance to an attempt at commercial exploitation moved the four kings to undertake a punitive expedition. If what is described is this rather than a major military campaign, the incredibility of the representation that great kings were ranged against city states is in some measure removed. Eissfeldt does not say explicitly whether or not he maintains that there is an original, historical connexion between Abraham and the events recorded in 14.1-17.[2]

With respect to 14.18-24 he says that we have no reason to doubt that an El Elyon cult existed in Jerusalem in the middle of the second millennium B.C. and he would appear to assert that there was a historical encounter between Abraham and the priest-king of the Jerusalem temple, Melchizedek. Certainly he is not satisfied with the interpretation of 14.18-24 as a cultic aetiology, which is associated with David's appropriation of the Jebusite, Jerusalem cult of El Elyon, and whose function is to equate this deity with Yahweh and to establish that Abraham had connexions with that

[1] 'Achronische, Anachronische und Synchronische Elemente in der Genesis', pp. 160 f.

[2] ibid., pp. 166 f.

cult and rendered a tithe to its priest-king. He argues that the reference to the tithe is not necessarily a mark of lateness (it is not to be understood as a retrojection of Amos 4.4) and his view is that Isaac and Jacob (interpreted as tribes) were El worshippers at Canaanite sanctuaries in the second millennium B.C. and that therefore the encounter of Abraham (a historical individual) with Melchizedek, priest of El Elyon, may be regarded as historical.[1]

In the Sodom story (chapter 19) he recognizes aetiological traits and explains the pillar of salt reference as the aetiology of a peculiar rock formation, but he is not disposed to accept a thoroughgoing aetiological interpretation of the chapter. If this were carried through to its logical conclusion, the story that the area was once a fertile one would have to be regarded as pure literary invention. Eissfeldt supposes rather that we have the reminiscence of a catastrophe which overtook the southern part of the area of the Dead Sea in the middle of the second millennium B.C., and that this historical recollection has been mixed with elements of saga and myth. He also holds that the connexion of Abraham with the Sodom story is primary and historical. Abraham, camping near Hebron, heard of the catastrophe and saw it. An explanation of chapter 19 which assumes a historical relationship between Abraham's group and Lot's group and the onset of a catastrophe about the middle of the second millennium B.C. is more natural than the supposition that Abraham and Lot are only connected by secondary literary or traditio-historical processes.[2]

III

The foundation of Eissfeldt's subtle and complicated argument is his treatment of the series of sayings about the twelve 'sons' of Jacob (Gen. 49). There is no disagreement about the fact that these twelve 'sons' are historical entities in so far as they correspond with the twelve tribes of Israel who were settled in various areas of Canaan at the beginning of the period of the Judges. We can say therefore with certainty that tribal history is being portrayed as family history and that the historical circumstances which are reflected in the genealogical scheme of Jacob and his twelve sons are those of the period after the settlement. It is true that we are left with a problem about the status of Jacob.[3] If his 'sons' are

---

[1] *ibid.*, pp. 165-167.   [2] *ibid.*, pp. 168 f.
[3] Below, pp. 116 ff.

tribes, it cannot be supposed that he is really the father of twelve sons, and he cannot be interpreted as an historical individual, if we maintain, as we must, a tribal-historical interpretation for his 'sons'.[1]

Eissfeldt, for his part, agrees that the sayings about Judah, Issachar, Dan, Gad, Asher, Naphtali and Benjamin in Gen. 49 mirror the historical circumstances of these tribes after the settlement, but he supposes that pre-settlement circumstances are reflected in the sayings about Reuben, Simeon and Levi in Gen. 49 and in the saying about Judah in the Blessing of Moses (Deut. 33.7). The saying about Reuben has to be correlated with the notice in 35.22 that Reuben lay with Bilhah, his father's concubine, and those about Simeon and Levi with the account of the revenge which they exacted on Shechem after the outrage done to their sister Dinah (Gen. 34). The saying about Judah in Deut. 33.7 can similarly be correlated with the narrative in Gen. 38 which indicates that Judah was associated with Canaanite communities. Eissfeldt holds that there were several waves of immigration of Israelite tribes into Canaan, and it is reasonable to affirm, as he does, that the historical circumstances reflected in the sayings about Reuben, Simeon, Levi and Judah are earlier than those reflected in the sayings about the other tribes. He does, however, underestimate the importance of the observation that the framework in which these sayings appear in Gen. 49 (the twelve 'sons' of Jacob) represents a post-settlement situation.

At this point it becomes crucial to ask in relation to Eissfeldt's argument whether it is possible to disengage any elements from this genealogical representation of the post-settlement structure of the Israelite tribes and to use them in order to reconstruct pre-settlement tribal history. This may well be possible in the case of the tribes Reuben, Simeon, Levi and Judah, but is it possible in the case of Jacob (Leah and Rachel)? Eissfeldt can only effect the transition from the post-settlement Jacob, who is integrated in a genealogy with his wives, concubines and twelve 'sons', to a pre-settlement Jacob, who is a group of tribes, by assuming that Leah and Rachel mirror pre-settlement historical circumstances, namely a Jacob group of tribes in southern Palestine and another in Central Palestine and trans-Jordan. Eissfeldt's general view is that the women in the genealogies which he interprets as tribal history are

[1] Above, pp. 11-13.

the products of literary elaboration, and this contradicts the assumption that Leah and Rachel can have the pre-settlement historical significance which he attaches to them. In that case the transition from the post-settlement Jacob who is the 'father' of twelve tribes to the pre-settlement Jacob who is the father of the Leah and Rachel tribes (that is, who is elucidated as a group of tribes) cannot be made.

Further, by emphasizing the circumstance that the Joseph saying is integrated in the genealogy of the twelve 'sons' of Jacob, the point can be made that this saying is more probably focused on a post-settlement situation than a pre-settlement one, and that the contrast between Joseph and the Leah tribes (even if Eissfeldt is right in his view that the sayings about these latter tribes touch on an earlier historical period) relates to the post-settlement precedence and power of the House of Joseph. Thus Eissfeldt's argument that the Joseph story belongs primarily to Palestine and that the Egyptian Joseph is a subsequent elaboration is correct, but the Palestinian Joseph is the post-settlement group of Joseph tribes and the *Novelle* about the Egyptian Joseph is a venture into imaginative literature in praise of the hegemony of the House of Joseph. Even if it were true that Egypt was chosen as the place of Joseph's success because the tribe or elements of it had once been in Egypt, the story of Joseph in Egypt can hardly be regarded as historical recollection.

That the Joseph story has a tribal-historical reference has recently been queried by Whybray[1] and Redford[2]. Whybray argues that a work which is described as 'a novel through and through' has to be created as an artistic whole in one piece and that it does not make much sense to speak of earlier versions of a novel. The Joseph story is a kind of wisdom literature which could not have come into existence earlier than the period of the Israelite monarchy, and so there is an incompatibility between the definition of the Joseph story as a novel and the supposition that the documentary sources J and E have variant accounts which rest on earlier versions of the story. If the extant Joseph story were indeed a conflation of two independent versions of that story, it is impossible to believe that this would have produced artistic enrichment. On the contrary it

[1] R. N. Whybray, 'The Joseph Story and Pentateuchal Criticism', *VT* xviii (1968), pp. 522-528.
[2] D. B. Redford, *A Study of the Biblical Story of Joseph*, *VTS* xx (1970).

would inevitably have produced a botch of the artistic unity possessed by the story in either of its postulated forms.

Even if this reasoning were thought to be sound, it does not follow that the Joseph story *qua* novel has to be entirely dissociated from tribal history. Since Jacob and his sons appear in the Joseph novel, and since they also appear in a genealogical scheme where the 'sons' are Israelite tribes, there is at least a case for investigating the possibility of reconstructing a history of the Joseph traditions from Palestinian tribal history to a novel set mainly in Egypt in which a character called Joseph is the hero. What Whybray's argument amounts to is that there is no possibility of constructing in relation to the Joseph story a history of genre (Eissfeldt) or a history of tradition (Noth) which would begin with a tribal-historical nucleus.[1]

Redford also postulates the complete separation of the Joseph story from tribal history, despite his awareness that the genealogical scheme of Jacob and his 'sons', which is elsewhere a device for communicating tribal history, is present in the Joseph story. According to Redford the story is late and it belongs to a period which is remote from the age when the Jacob genealogy had tribal-historical significance. It is used by the author of the Joseph story merely as the scaffolding for an imaginative work. If the story can be said to reflect any set of historical circumstances, these are perhaps exilic:

Do we hear a faint echo of the Exile in the story of a boy, sold as a slave into a foreign land, whither shortly his clan journeys to join him, themselves to enter into a state of servitude to a foreign crown?[2]

The background of the composition is determined through a detailed examination of the Egyptian colouring[3] and the conclusions are reinforced by an argument from silence which cannot be regarded as having much weight:

We can only conclude that the reason why the historical books and the Prophets say nothing of the Joseph romance is because the narrative was

---

[1] For Noth's position, with which Whybray indicates his disagreement, see below, pp. 146-150; cf. B. Mazar, *op. cit.*, pp. 82 f. Mazar observes that there is no basis for the hypothesis that the Joseph story is based on an historical event in the Hyksos or Amarna periods. The traditions and motifs which go to make up the story were developed on Mount Ephraim. The sophisticated, literary form of the story is not earlier than the beginning of the monarchy.

[2] D. B. Redford, *op. cit.*, p. 250.

[3] *ibid.*, pp. 187-243.

not yet in existence when they were written. In other words, the chronological limits assigned above to the background, c. 650-425 B.C., are probably quite valid for the date of composition as well.[1]

Redford argues that in the 'original' Reuben version of the
Joseph story no connexion was established between the story and
the Exodus, and that this link was first made by the Judah expansion of the Joseph story. One of the points which he makes is that
according to one Jacob tradition (Gen. 50.11-14) the patriarch
lived out his life, died and was buried on Palestinian soil, while
according to another (Deut. 26.5) he descended into Egypt with
a small group. He continues:

This lack of unanimity in the tradition regarding the death of Jacob and
the nature of the Descent probably explains why the writer of the original
Joseph story could flaunt what was later considered to be an unshakable
tradition, viz. that upon the Israelites' descent into Egypt under Jacob
they stayed there several centuries, and to bring his characters back to the
Land of Promise after the famine was over.[2]

But Redford is making an illegitimate use of Gen. 50.11-14 when
he says of it: 'One persistent tradition made Jacob live out his life,
die and be buried on Palestinian soil'.[3] All that is shown by this
passage is that there are two Jacob grave traditions: according to
one he was buried beside the Jordan, since the funeral rites at 'the
threshing floor of Atad' cannot be separated from the place of
burial; according to the version of P he was buried in the family
grave at Machpelah near Hebron. Since 50.11-14 is set in the context of the transportation of Jacob's corpse from Egypt to Palestine,
there is no sense in which it is a tradition that Jacob lived out his
life and died in Palestine. A conclusion drawn on traditio-historical
grounds that the Joseph story begins in Palestine and that the
Egyptian Joseph is a secondary literary elaboration requires a
different process of argumentation.

Redford appears to assume that Jacob is an individual character
and that only the name Israel has a corporate status. He says:

The earliest version of the Biblical Joseph story that can be detected is
that in which the role of the helpful brother is filled by Reuben alone and
in which the father is called Jacob. The choice of these names is understandable; Reuben is the oldest brother and Jacob is the original name of
the patriarch. The writer was ignorant of, or, at least, unimpressed by,

[1] *ibid.*, p. 250.
[2] *ibid.*, p. 251.
[3] *ibid.*, p. 250.

the attempt to personify Jacob as the 'pre-historic' embodiment of a political organization 'Israel' by giving him that name. He was writing a simple, entertaining story, not a piece of politico-historical propaganda.[1]

The use of 'Israel' as the patriarch's name is, according to Redford, a feature of the Judah expansion of the Joseph story. The assumption which Redford appears to make in the passage which I have quoted is that 'Jacob' has no corporate reference until he is renamed 'Israel'. Rather the renaming of Jacob as Israel must be correlated with the genealogical scheme of Jacob and his twelve 'sons', where the 'sons' are Israelite tribes and where the 'father' must necessarily be a larger corporate entity.

Redford leaves some important questions unanswered. Why is it precisely Joseph who appears as the hero of this story? Why is it Judah who replaces Reuben? Are there not more particular reasons for the choice of Joseph and the displacement of Reuben by Judah than those which Redford has given? This line of thought would lead to the conclusion that while Redford is right in the kind of literary criticism which he applies to the Joseph story (in appraising it as imaginative literature rather than as historiography), he is wrong in detaching it so completely from the tribal history which is communicated by the genealogical model of Jacob and his sons. If the Joseph of the Joseph story has some connexion with the Israelite tribe Joseph, it would seem right to relate the story to the period when the tribe of Joseph exercised hegemony among the Israelite tribes, or, at least, to postulate in a more general way that the extended portrayal of the Egyptian Joseph cannot be entirely disengaged from a nucleus of Palestinian tribal history. It is also tempting to correlate the displacement of Reuben by Judah with specific historical circumstances and these would have to be the dominance achieved by Judah as a consequence of David's rise to power and his Jerusalem establishment.

If doubt is cast on the conclusion that there was a group of Jacob tribes in southern Palestine and another in Central Palestine and trans-Jordan, this has consequences for Eissfeldt's account of the history of the genre. If it cannot be demonstrated that there was such a group of Jacob tribes in southern Palestine, it may be doubted whether the Jacob of the Jacob-Esau story was originally a tribal entity and whether this narrative, as Eissfeldt maintains, derives from a nucleus of tribal history. It is arguable that the

[1] *ibid.*, p. 178.

Jacob-Esau story is not about relations between different tribes or tribal groups, but mirrors rather processes of cultural change within the one group. It has also been noticed that the slow-witted hunter, Esau, is not an appropriate representative of Edom, a community which had kingship before Israel and which had an international reputation for wisdom.[1] Eissfeldt partly answers these objections by his stipulation that the narrative is about the pre-Israelites and the pre-Edomites, but he supposes, nevertheless, that the extant story reflects the historical circumstances of David's reign, when Edom was subjugated by Israel. There is no doubt that both Jacob and Esau have been 'nationalized', but what is indicated by this is not a story that is basically tribal history, but rather a subsequent development of the Jacob-Esau story which presupposes the post-settlement status of Jacob as 'father' of the twelve tribes, that is, as 'Israel'. The story is basically about a conflict of occupations and it is told from the side of the shepherd for whose sharp wits and resourcefulness the ponderous and simple-minded hunter is no match.

Both Gunkel and Eissfeldt agree that, in so far as Jacob is Israel and Esau Edom, the story reflects the ascendancy achieved by Israel over Edom in the reign of David. The differences between the two scholars emerge when questions are asked about the earlier form of the Jacob-Esau story. Gunkel's view is that the story is originally a contest *Märchen*,[2] whether a form of professional self-assertion – an entertainment which shepherds enjoy at the expense of hunters – or a more serious mirroring of processes of cultural change within a community. For Eissfeldt the fully developed Israelite/Edomite opposition rests on an earlier tribal-historical base, related to pre-settlement historical circumstances and connected with a confrontation between a group of Jacob tribes in southern Palestine and a group which eventually became Edom, both groups having the character of shadow-possessors of their respective territories. Noth like Gunkel argues that the identification of Esau with Edom is secondary, but he has his own particular, cultic-historical explanation of Jacob[3] and does not give to the equation of Esau with Edom the historical significance attached to it by Gunkel and Eissfeldt. He says that it is a secondary com-

---

[1] Above, p. 51.
[2] Above, pp. 48 ff.
[3] Above, pp. 60 ff.

bination whose basis has still to be discovered.[1] He does, however, take up Eissfeldt's idea of confrontation and contiguity and suggests that the east Jordan Esau was too far removed from the sphere of concern of Israelite tribes in the south of Palestine, and that the Edomites with whom they were in contact seemed to them to be an appropriate new incorporation of Esau.[2]

All this underlines the tentativeness and uncertainty of the historical correlations and political affiliations which are read into features of the patriarchal narratives. Thus for Noth the genealogical scheme of the twelve 'sons' of Jacob is to be correlated with a twelve-tribe amphictyony in the earliest period of the settlement in Canaan,[3] whereas for Mowinckel it is to be linked to the insertion of Judah into a reconstructed genealogy after David's rise to power.[4] The story about the blessing of Ephraim and Manasseh is related by Noth to an Ephraimite expression of an ongoing rivalry between the two tribes,[5] whereas Gressmann explains it in terms of an historical moment in the reign of Jereboam I, when hegemony passed from Manasseh to Ephraim.[6]

Eissfeldt's categorizing of the patriarchal narratives as essentially tribal history is incomplete and unclear in other respects. For example, the Abraham-Keturah and the Abraham-Hagar genealogies would appear to be more correctly described (even on Eissfeldt's own account of them) as ethnological aetiologies (Gunkel's terminology) than as tribal histories. With regard to the Abraham-Keturah list, it is doubtful whether Eissfeldt is right in assuming that the 'concubines' (Gen. 25.6) include Keturah and that consequently one can speak of an expulsion of Keturah's 'sons'. This point, however, need not be laboured, since the main issue can be raised independently of it. In so far as Eissfeldt says that the Abraham-Keturah and Abraham-Hagar genealogies explain why there are desert tribes which follow a nomadic way of life, his emphasis is on an aetiological interpretation and he misjudges the influence of the aetiological element in his own account. The tribal-historical nucleus is discoverable only if it is assumed that there is an original historical connexion between Abraham and

---

[1] M. Noth, *Überlieferungsgeschichte des Pentateuch* (1948), p. 104.
[2] *ibid.*, p. 210.
[3] Below, pp. 112 ff.
[4] Below, pp. 98 f.
[5] *Überlieferungsgeschichte*, p. 92, n. 249.
[6] Below, p. 102.

the Keturites or Abraham and the Ishmaelites. This is difficult to sustain, although it is made easier for Eissfeldt by the fact that he is not impressed by the traditio-historical approach in general and, in particular, by the argument that Ishmael is connected primarily with Isaac and only secondarily with Abraham. Another problem arises from the status which Eissfeldt accords to Abraham, who, as an historical individual, is outside the framework of his otherwise comprehensive tribal-historical interpretation of the patriarchal narratives. Consistency requires that if Jacob, as the 'husband' of Leah and Rachel and the 'father' of the Leah and Rachel tribes, is interpreted as a group of tribes, Abraham also, as the 'husband' of Keturah and Hagar and the 'father' of the Keturites and Ishmaelites, should be interpreted as a group of tribes and not as an historical individual.

The problem of the Nahor-Milcah-Reumah genealogy (22.20-24) is somewhat different, since Abraham is only indirectly involved as the brother of Nahor. The claim that this is essentially tribal history is more easily reconciled with the attitude of the later Eissfeldt to the Mesopotamian connexions of the patriarchal narratives than with the arguments of the earlier Eissfeldt that the Mesopotamian references are to be connected with processes of secondary elaboration whose motivation is either literary or theological. Thus Abraham and Laban are said to have had their home in an area east of the Jordan much nearer to Canaan than to Harran or Ur Kasdim; the 'sons' of Jacob are said to have been born in Palestine not in Mesopotamia. Eissfeldt is influenced here (as also in his view that the Joseph story had an original Palestinian setting and was subsequently expanded into an Egyptian story) by his application of a saga law, namely, that the horizons of the saga are restricted and that the distances involved are not too great. It is then a just conclusion, even in terms of Eissfeldt's own arguments, that the connecting of Abraham with a Nahor-Milcah-Reumah genealogy presupposes a secondary, unhistorical, Mesopotamian expansion of the patriarchal stories and therefore cannot be defined as essential tribal history. More generally, all three genealogies (Abraham-Keturah, Abraham-Hagar, Abraham-Nahor-Milcah-Reumah), together with the representation that Abraham was the uncle of Lot, should be regarded as late, unhistorical magnifications of the status of Abraham with whom all the surrounding peoples are connected. It does not follow that there is no truth in the general proposition that the proto-Israelites were Aramaeans.[1] This, however, cannot be used to show that specific observations on the history of genre and history of tradition of the patriarchal narratives are erroneous, nor can it establish that Abraham *qua* historical individual originated in Mesopotamia. The statement that the proto-Israelites were Aramaeans is compatible with the view that the primary setting of the patriarchal narratives is Palestine and that the Mesopotamian references reflect historical circumstances only in the tenuous sense in which the Joseph story may be said to reflect historical circumstances.[2]

Abraham is a special problem and the defects of Eissfeldt's interpretation of the patriarchal narratives centre in him. It has been indicated above that the dissociation of Abraham from the general tribal-historical interpretation adopted by Eissfeldt is difficult to justify, and his view of Abraham as an historical individual and Lot as a personification of the proto-Ammonites influences his exposition of chapters 14 and 19. With regard to 14.1-17 Eissfeldt is not uninfluenced by the arguments that this is a late *midrash* whose motive is to glorify Abraham by placing him on the same plane of international history as the great kings of antiquity. He is, however, impressed by the accuracy of the notice in 14.7 and concludes that we have in this account an authentic recollection of historical events.[3] The nettle which has to be grasped, however, is whether Abraham can credibly be connected with this encounter between four great kings and five rulers of city states, and on this point Eissfeldt is not altogether explicit. Even if it is held that we have here a reliable report from an extra-Israelite source of a military engagement in the second millennium B.C., it would be right, in my view, to argue that the connexion of Abraham with these events is not an original, historical one, but is to be elucidated as a late traditio-historical development.[4] Hence it is the combination of the postulated extra-Israelite source with the figure of Abraham which is the really significant aspect of the structure of the passage and on which interpretation must focus.[5]

[1] Above, p. 4, n. 2.

[2] Above, p. 87.

[3] Above, pp. 84 f.

[4] Below pp. 95 f.

[5] This point is well made by R. de Vaux, *Histoire Ancienne D'Israël*, pp. 208-212. De Vaux argues that even if the names of the four kings in Gen. 14 have been extracted from an extra-biblical source, it cannot be supposed that this

Eissfeldt's argument that a straightforward historical explanation of Abraham's association with Lot and with the disaster which overtook Sodom carries more weight than a traditio-historical explanation[1] begs the question, because it starts from the premise that both Abraham and Lot are historical entities; that Abraham is an historical individual and Lot a group of tribes. Chapter 19 is particularly susceptible of a thoroughgoing aetiological interpretation and it is not clear why Eissfeldt interprets the pillar of salt aetiologically and the story about the destruction of Sodom historically. The argument that the primary phenomena here are not historical but geological and physical and that the story is entirely an *aition* of the barrenness of the Dead Sea area is in my view difficult to withstand, and Eissfeldt's conclusion that the narrative rests on an historical catastrophe which overtook the area in the second millennium B.C. is a lapse of judgement. If chapter 19 is aetiological, it has no original historical connexion with Abraham, and the formation of the Abraham-Lot cycle is then susceptible of a traditio-historical but not of an historical explanation.

Finally, something may be said specifically from the side of history of genre about the sanctuary stories. In respect of these stories Eissfeldt leaves two possibilities open: they are originally Canaanite stories concerned with the foundation of sanctuaries on which patriarchal (tribal) history has been superimposed; or that sanctuaries like Shechem (33.18-20) and Bethel (28.10-22) were proto-Israelite foundations on 'virgin soil' and that the patriarchs in these cases were cult founders.[2] That these stories or notices about Shechem, Bethel, Beersheba, Hebron (Mamre) and Jeru-

---

source established a connexion between the four kings and the five cities of the Dead Sea, much less between the four kings and Abraham. The names of the kings are such as historical individuals could have possessed at the beginning of the second millennium B.C., but enough is known of the history of that period to enable us to say with certainty that the five cities of the Dead Sea could not have been vassals of Elam and that Elam could not have headed a coalition which united the great powers of the Ancient East. Cf. M. Noth, 'Der Beitrag der Archäologie zur Geschichte Israels', p. 271. Noth observes that only here is Abraham rooted in Ancient Near Eastern History. The chapter is enigmatic and one for which there is no convincing interpretation. Also B. Mazar, *op. cit.*, p. 74 who holds that the historical situation which is reflected by Gen. 14 is the one subsequent to David's capture of Jerusalem. See below, p. 96.

[1] Above, p. 85.

[2] 'Achronische, Anachronische und Synchronische Elemente in der Genesis', p. 166.

salem were derived from foundation legends of Canaanite sanctuaries is difficult to demonstrate. Whatever else may be said of them
they have this in common that they are devices for legitimating the
integration of the El cult practised at ancient Canaanite sanctuaries
with Yahwism. The legitimating device is the representation that
the patriarchs worshipped at these sanctuaries a God who can be
regarded as an adumbration of Yahweh. Eissfeldt's assumption
that the patriarchs may have founded sanctuaries in Canaan is
bound up with his view of patriarchal religion and will be discussed
in chapter iv.[1] In the case of 14.18-24 it seems to me unlikely that
the passage in the form in which we have it can testify to the
existence of the cult of El Elyon in Jerusalem in the second millennium B.C. This supposition is associated with Eissfeldt's view
that Abraham was an historical individual who had an encounter
with a priest-king of Jerusalem at that period. The story in 14.18-24
reflects only the historical circumstances of David's reign, his capture of Jerusalem and his integration of the Jebusite cult of El
Elyon with Yahwism. This is legitimated by representing that
Abraham had once given a tithe to Melchizedek who had blessed
him in the name of El Elyon who, as creator of heaven and earth,
is none other than Yahweh. This equation is made explicitly in
v. 22, where Abraham, in refusing any share of the booty, swears
by YHWH El Elyon.[2]

IV

The work of two other scholars may be conveniently considered
at this point. Mowinckel's[3] treatment of the Jacob genealogy is a
blend of mythology and tribal history, and Gressmann has interpreted Joseph as both a historical individual and a tribe. The
mythological elements in Mowinckel's treatment of the Jacob
genealogy represent a resurgence of a way of interpreting the
patriarchal narratives which was in vogue before Gunkel[4] but
which has for a long time seemed dead. Rachel ('ewe') is a fertility
goddess whose grave near Ramah is a sanctuary of her cult, and
Leah ('wild cow' or 'coiled serpent') is also a fertility goddess whose
home is Mesopotamia. Sarah and Milcah are to be associated with

[1] Below, pp. 195 ff.

[2] Cf. J. A. Emerton, 'The Riddle of Genesis xiv', *VT* xxi (1971), pp. 437 f.

[3] S. Mowinckel, 'Rahelstämme und Leastämme', *Von Ugarit nach Qumran*,
BZAW 77 (1958), pp. 129-150.

[4] Above, pp. 17 ff.

goddesses of Harran and Laban bears the name of a moon god. Bilhah and Zilpah may also be fertility goddesses with traits which derive from the reverse, destructive aspect of the cult.[1] Joseph too is an apotheosized tribal eponym to whom worship is made and whose grave is a shrine, but, since he has a type of personal name (Joseph is an abbreviated form of Joseph-El), he was probably originally a chieftain and the founder of the tribe which bears his name.[2] The women in the patriarchal narratives, it appears, are originally deities, but it is not obvious why tribal history, which is represented, as Mowinckel explains, 'in accord with the ancient Hebrew and probably general Semitic conception that every sociological and ethnic whole is a community of blood deriving from a single father',[3] should become so mixed up with mythology.

Mowinckel argues that the renaming of Jacob as Israel is recognizable as a folk-lore feature and that the conclusion which must be drawn is that Jacob and Israel were originally different persons. There are no traditions about Israel and the renaming in Gen. 32.23-33 is a subsidiary aetiology, explaining the identification of Jacob and Israel, alongside the two main aetiological preoccupations of the passage. The first of these is concerned to explain how Penuel acquired its sanctity and the second how a cult taboo associated with Penuel arose. On the other hand, there are rich Jacob traditions attached to localities in central Palestine and trans-Jordan. Israel is none other than the *heros eponymos* of the twelve tribe amphictyony which is a Davidic creation, and the ample Jacob traditions were attracted to Israel just because there were no Israel traditions. Mowinckel offers no elucidation of the figure 'Jacob' as such, but he holds that there were tribes settled in Palestine, represented as 'sons' of Jacob, in the period before the incursion of the 'Israelites' under Joshua. He draws a sharp distinction between 'Israelites' who come from the Sinai peninsula and the 'sons' of Jacob who are 'patriarchal Hebrews' from Mesopotamia. Among the tribes settled in Canaan prior to the incursion of the 'Israelites' under Joshua and reckoned as 'sons' of Jacob only Simeon and Levi (Gen. 34), who came from the Sinai peninsula and entered Canaan from the south, are 'Israelites'. The others (Reuben, Joseph, Benjamin and perhaps Gad) are 'patriarchal Hebrews'.[4]

---

[1] 'Rahelstämme und Leastämme', p. 133.   [2] *ibid.*, p. 144.
[3] *ibid.*, p. 129.   [4] *ibid.*, pp. 131 f., 146 f.

Mowinckel maintains that the ten tribes mentioned in the Song of Deborah (Judg. 5) can be regarded as a ten tribe amphictyony (Ephraim, Benjamin, Machir, Zebulon, Issachar, Reuben, Gilead, Dan, Asher, Naphtali).[1] The account in Judg. 5 comprises those tribes which responded and those which did not respond, and it is intended to be exhaustive. Hence we can conclude that there was a system or grouping of ten tribes at this period. The different conclusions of Noth and Mowinckel largely hinge on the circumstance that Mowinckel makes this the starting-point of his reconstruction and minimizes the value of Num. 1.5-15, 26.5-51 and Gen. 49. According to Mowinckel, Judah, which is not mentioned in the Song of Deborah, was not a member of any amphictyonic grouping until a place was found for it in the reconstituted twelve tribe amphictyony which is a Davidic creation and the ideological expression of the greater Israel brought into existence by him. Eleven would have been an 'unsymbolic' number as thirteen would also have been, and in order to achieve the number twelve Simeon and Levi, which had ceased to be effective tribes prior to the period reflected by the Song of Deborah, and which are not mentioned there, were reinstated, and Ephraim and Manasseh were unified as Joseph. The lists in Gen. 49, Num. 1 and 26 and the birth stories in Gen. 29.29-30.24 are consequently all post-Davidic. Levi was never at any time a member tribe of an amphictyony and Noth's view that Gad replaced Levi as the third in the series in Num. 26.15 is erroneous. Rather Gad, as probably a 'son' of Jacob in the period before the incursion under Joshua and as a 'patriarchal Hebrew' tribe, has preserved here its original place in the series.[2]

One of Mowinckel's arguments which must be regarded as less than satisfactory concerns the precedence of Ephraim over Manasseh. Num. 1.10 and Deut. 33.17 indicate this precedence, whereas Num. 26.28 ff. places Manasseh before Ephraim and this accords with the references in the Joseph story itself (Gen. 46.19 f. and 48.8-22). According to Mowinckel the history of Ephraim has to be carried back into the 'pre-Israelite' period and Manasseh originated as a consequence of the northwards expansion of the tribe of Ephraim. But the aetiology in Gen. 48 does not have any

[1] Cf. M. Noth, *Das System der Zwölf Stämme Israels*, BWANT 4 Folge, Heft 1 (1930), pp. 5 ff.

[2] 'Rahelstämme und Leastämme', pp. 137-142.

point if Ephraim had an original precedence over Manasseh. The aetiology indicates a shift in power and explains this by the circumstance that Jacob in blessing Joseph's sons placed his right hand on the head of the younger and his left hand on the head of the older. Nor is the form of the aetiology adequately explained by Mowinckel's assumption that the precedence of Manasseh over Ephraim in Gen. 46.19 f., 48.8-22 and Num. 26 reflects the anti-Samaritan tendency of P,[1] for the aetiology in Gen. 48 does not glorify Manasseh at the expense of Ephraim. Rather it explains why Ephraim has outstripped Manasseh. The concern of the aetiology is to explain why there has been a transfer of power from Manasseh to Ephraim and this cannot be reconciled with Mowinckel's account of the tribal history in respect of Ephraim and Manasseh.

This brings us to the main issue – whether it is possible to get behind the Jacob/Israel genealogy and to construct an earlier pre-Israelite scheme involving 'sons' of Leah and 'sons' of Rachel.[2] If one admits, as Mowinckel does, that Israel is the *heros eponymos* of the twelve tribes, it has to be acknowledged that the genealogy of the twelve 'sons' of Jacob originated at the same time as this Israel.[3] This implies that whatever tribal history is reflected in stories about the 'sons' of Jacob is post-Israelite (that is, post-settlement) tribal history. Hence the list of ten tribes in the Song of Deborah (where there is no genealogical structure) does not provide the material for a Jacob genealogy which is anterior to the Jacob/Israel genealogy. Thus the absence of Simeon from Judg. 5 and its presence in Num. 26 does not prove that the latter is post-Davidic and that Simeon is an element of an artificial reconstruction. In the particular case of Ephraim and Manasseh the tribal relationships which are indicated by Gen. 48 are post-settlement and there are no adequate sources for the tribal history of 'sons' of Jacob (present in Canaan as 'patriarchal Hebrews') prior to the formation of the entity 'Israel'. The fact that Ephraim's precedence is asserted in Judg. 8.1 ff. and 12.1 ff. and that Ephraim is the first-mentioned tribe in the Song of Deborah (Judg. 5.14) does not preclude the possibility that Gen. 48 is connected with a shift in power from Manasseh to Ephraim at an earlier stage in the post-settlement

[1] *ibid.*, pp. 141 f.
[2] *ibid.*, pp. 136, 143.
[3] So M. Noth, *Das System*, pp. 3 f.; cf. above pp. 85 ff.

period.[1] Or one may settle for a more general explanation, and Noth[2] has suggested that the assertion of Ephraim's precedence in Judg. 8.1 ff. and 12.1 ff. and her position as first-mentioned tribe in the Song of Deborah (Judg. 5.14) set against the original precedence of Manasseh, as represented by Num. 26.28 ff., Gen. 46.19 f. and Gen. 48.8-22, may be indicative of an ongoing tribal rivalry.

The basic weakness of Mowinckel's reconstruction is connected with his differentiation between 'patriarchal Hebrews' and 'Israelites', which can only be maintained if there is a pre-settlement genealogical structure of 'sons' of Leah and 'sons' of Rachel. The Israelites who came into Canaan under Joshua are generally held to have been the bearers of Yahwism (Josh. 24) and it is therefore to be expected that they would have occupied a dominant position in any coalition of tribes which they entered. Mowinckel's view is that these tribes settled in an area already occupied by 'sons' of Joseph (Ephraim and Manasseh) and that they identified themselves so completely with the Joseph tribes as to become indistinguishable from them. But if the Joseph tribes were in fact those who were led into Canaan by Joshua (as seems more probable) all of their tribal history in a Canaanite context is post-settlement. The tradition that Joseph was buried near Shechem (Josh. 24.32) may indicate that the Joseph story was originally set in Palestine and that the Egyptian Joseph belongs to a stage of secondary expansion, but it does not demonstrate that there were 'pre-Israelite' Joseph tribes settled in central Palestine as Mowinckel appears to argue.[3] That there were tribes settled in Palestine before the incursion under Joshua is clear (Reuben, Simeon, Levi and probably Gad, according to Mowinckel), but only Benjamin has arguably a genealogical link with Jacob which is anterior to the Jacob/Israel genealogy. Thus Mowinckel notes[4] that Rachel's grave is located in Benjamite territory according to I Sam. 10.2 and Jer. 31.15 and that it has been secondarily transferred to the area of the Joseph tribes (Gen. 35.19). This suggests that originally Rachel was the 'mother' of Benjamin, who was her only 'son', since she died at his birth, and it is possible that the tribe Benjamin may

[1] 'Rahelstämme und Leastämme', pp. 140 f. According to Mowinckel Gen. 48 is post-Solomonic.

[2] M. Noth, *Überlieferungsgeschichte des Pentateuch*, p. 92, n. 249.

[3] 'Rahelstämme und Leastämme', pp. 243 f.

[4] *ibid.*, p. 133.

have been represented as a 'son' of Jacob and Rachel prior to the relationship established between Joseph and Benjamin in the Jacob/Israel genealogy.[1]

In 'Sage und Geschichte' (1910) Gressmann says that the Joseph story is neither mythology nor tribal history; it is *Novelle* and its forerunner is the *Glücksmärchen*.[2] At the outset the story was about a Hebrew youth called Joseph who was sold into Egypt as a slave and who there had adventures of all kinds after the manner of the *Märchen*. In 'Ursprung und Entwicklung' (1923) his position is much less clear. He has not resiled from his view that the Joseph story is fundamentally *Novelle*, but he now maintains that Joseph was an historical person, the creator of the tribe of Joseph. In addition he finds many elements of tribal history in the Joseph story and he correlates different features of the story with particular historical moments or with cultural changes in the life of the Israelite tribes. With regard to the historical Joseph, Gressmann's argument is apparently a *non sequitur*: there was a tribe of Joseph in prehistorical times, therefore Joseph must have been an historical person.[3] He appears to be influenced by his observation that Joseph is a personal and not a tribal name, and his argument may be that the possession of a personal name by a tribe can only be explained on the assumption that it is the name of the creator of the tribe. How can the gap be bridged between Joseph as the hero of a *Novelle*, whose constituents are *Sagen* with *Märchen* features, and Joseph as an historical person? Gressmann argues that the notice about the settlement of Israelite tribes in Goshen (Gen. 47.27) is historical and not, like most of the story of Joseph in Egypt, literary invention. He does not say explicitly that Joseph was the leader of the tribes of Manasseh and Ephraim when they were in Goshen, but only if this is assumed can any geographical connexion be established between Joseph as the leader of a tribe and Joseph as the character of an adventure story set in Egypt. Further, Gressmann refers to the notice about the grave of Joseph in Canaan (Josh. 24.32), but it is not entirely clear whether he is speaking about Joseph as a tribal leader or Joseph as a character in a *Novelle*. If it is the first, the grave tradition might be supposed to indicate that Joseph came back to Canaan from Egypt with the

[1] Below, pp. 147 ff.
[2] Above, p. 45.
[3] 'Ursprung und Entwicklung der Joseph Sage', p. 5.

tribes which bore his name. If it is the second, the information would not relate to an historical Joseph, but to the final instalment of the *Novelle* according to which the bones of Joseph were brought to Canaan after his death.[1]

There are, however, also difficulties in correlating what is described as fundamentally a *Novelle* with a superstructure of tribal and cultural history. Certainly we know that there was a tribal entity called 'The House of Joseph' and that there were tribes called Reuben, Judah, Manasseh, Ephraim and Benjamin, and this creates a different situation from what obtains in other patriarchal stories. Abraham, Isaac and Jacob are not tribes, but the 'sons' of Jacob (however we interpret the genealogical model) are Israelite tribes. The striking thing, however, is that all the tribal history which Gressmann finds in the Joseph story relates to Israelite tribes in the context of Canaan, not in the context of Egypt (apart from his assumption that the tribes of Ephraim and Manasseh were once settled in Goshen). The substitution of Judah for Reuben (Gen. 37) reflects the passing of hegemony from Reuben to Judah during and subsequent to the reign of David. The intrusion of Benjamin into the Joseph story is a consequence of the close relations which had developed between the tribes of Joseph and Benjamin in Canaan.[2] And, most significantly, the blessing of Joseph's sons by Jacob (described by Gressmann as a piece of the Jacob saga) presupposes not an Egyptian setting but one at Shechem and is an aetiology which explains why power passed from Manasseh to Ephraim in the reign of Jeroboam I (922-901 B.C.).[3]

Gressmann argues to some effect that these pieces of tribal history, including the Goshen notice, produce artistic dislocation in the Joseph story and are thereby seen to be intrusive elements. It is not clear, however, that this can be combined with the other argument which Gressmann employs: the statement that Joseph, as a character in a *Novelle*, is from the outset a reflection of the tribe of Joseph is not easily reconciled with the other statement that the elements of tribal history in the Joseph *Novelle* are intrusive. Gressmann's position here differs significantly from his opinions about Joseph and the other patriarchs in 'Sage und

[1] *ibid.*, pp. 15 ff.
[2] *ibid.*, pp. 10-12.
[3] *ibid.*, pp. 7-10.

Geschichte'. We do not now have a Hansel and Gretel situation: Joseph is no longer simply a popular and paradigmatic name and the Joseph story is not about a Hebrew youth called Joseph who was sold into Egypt as a slave and who had all kinds of adventures in the style of the *Märchen*. The name Joseph, it is now maintained, is attached to a non-Israelite *Königsnovelle* as a reflection of the kingship of Gideon exercised in the tribe of Joseph.[1] It is doubtful whether Gressmann's argument can stand in the precise form which he has given it. If the story is fundamentally a *Novelle* and the historical correlations with the tribes are secondary, whether these are expressed as aetiologies or by the erection of characters into eponyms, the name borne by the hero of the *Novelle* cannot be explained by a direct connexion with historical circumstances in the tribe of Joseph, because this would make the Joseph story into tribal history *ab initio*.

It may be possible to make sense of all this in rather different terms. Discounting Gressmann's view that the notice about Goshen is evidence that the tribes Ephraim and Manasseh were in Egypt, we may say that in so far as the Joseph story is tribal history it is about the tribe of Joseph in central Palestine – its possession of Shechem, its relations with Benjamin and the shift in the balance of power as between Ephraim and Manasseh. The Joseph of the *Novelle* may be related to the tribe of Joseph, as Gressmann holds, but the Egyptian adventures belong to the sphere of free story-telling and are not tribal-historical in the same sense as the Palestinian material. Their intention is to glorify the tribe of Joseph and they do this with the use of saga and *Märchen* material, some of it of Egyptian provenance, in a spirit of literary inventiveness. They tell us nothing about the tribe of Joseph in Egypt or about an historical person called Joseph. If this is so, we must say that the Palestinian material constitutes the primary Joseph traditions and that the Egyptian adventures are imaginative and inventive. The tribal history can be described as secondary (so Gressmann) only in the sense that the Palestinian material is secondary in the literary context of the Egyptian adventures of Joseph, and that, where it intrudes in the *Novelle*, it dislocates the artistic unity of this work of imagination.[2]

What we have seen in this chapter, especially in the work of

[1] *ibid.*, pp. 10, 51 f.
[2] Cf. Noth on Joseph, below, pp. 146 ff.

Eissfeldt, but also with less clarity in Gressmann, is a combination of a basic tribal-historical interpretation of the patriarchal narratives with a postulated, rich literary development. We can say of Eissfeldt's approach that it furnishes a history of the genre which contrasts with that of Gunkel and Noth and which, while diverging fundamentally from Gunkel, seeks to do justice to his sensitive appreciation of the literary dimensions of the narratives. What Eissfeldt describes is a progress from tribal-historical notices to stories whose truth does not lie in their historicity or in their faithfulness to particular details, but in the authenticity of their humanity and the universality of their appeal. The fact that temporal particularity is no part of them is from this point of view an emancipation from historical imprisonment and a defence against obsolescence. These stories are not lost in antiquity, because we can enter into these situations and feel the poignancy and stress of these human relationships.

Thus we may say that, in the best sense of the word, Eissfeldt's interpretation is conservative – he conserves a kind of historical significance for the patriarchal narratives and yet he is sensitive to the claims of the area of literary investigation opened up by Gunkel. There are, however, critical difficulties which he does not adequately meet. Only in two places have we seen any interest in the patriarchs as historical individuals: Eissfeldt's treatment of Abraham contrasts with his tribal-historical interpretation of the other patriarchs and Gressmann maintains that Joseph was an historical individual.

CHAPTER III

The History of the Tradition

I

The concept of history of tradition in Gunkel is at least partly associated with the activities of professional story-tellers who combine originally independent stories about the same patriarch (Jacob), or even stories which are about different persons, as in the case of the Abraham-Lot cycle. There are two devices which they use in particular: one is the motif of the 'journey' which enables them to combine originally independent stories, as, for example, the Jacob-Esau and the Jacob-Laban stories; the other is the utilization of one story as a frame for another – the Jacob-Esau story is split into two and serves as a frame for the Jacob-Laban story.[1] Another aspect of history of tradition, as it relates to the activities of these postulated story-tellers, is the attachment of individual patriarchs to different places, and this is explained by Gunkel on the supposition that the stories travel with the story-tellers who practise their art at different places on the occasions of great pilgrimages to the tribal sanctuaries, and who adjust the setting of the story to the locality where they are telling it. Examples of this kind which he gives are the connexions of Abraham with Hebron, Beersheba, Bethel and Shechem; of Isaac with Beersheba and Lahai-Roi (Gen. 25.11); of Jacob with Penuel, Bethel and Shechem. He observes that although the meeting of Jacob and Esau is located at Mahanaim, the home of Esau is Edom (Gen. 32.3).[2]

The stage of oral tradition is one of 'remodelling' and by this Gunkel means the refinement of sentiment and the tendency to move away from economy of narrative to more involved literary processes which are a response to changing literary tastes. No new patriarchal narratives are formed after 1200 B.C. and the period of remodelling runs from then to 900 B.C. Thereafter the stories begin to be written down and this marks the end of the period of oral tradition.[3]

It is clear from Gunkel's article on 'Jacob' that, on his terms, a

[1] *Legends*, pp. 78-81.   [2] *Legends*, pp. 96 f.; *Genesis (3)*, pp. lxiii f.
[3] *Legends*, pp. 98 f., 137 f.; *Genesis (3)*, pp. lxxxviii ff.; cf. W. Klatt, *op. cit.*, p. 150.

distinction between history of genre and history of tradition is not easy to draw. History of tradition is more or less synonymous with history of composition.[1] The individual Jacob stories were in existence many centuries before J and E,[2] and the earliest, which is set in south Palestine, a meeting place of hunters and herdsmen,[3] is a contest *Märchen* involving a hunter and a shepherd. Jacob is a *Märchen* figure, a type of the shepherd who dominates the hunter and who bears a name which is an abbreviated form of Jacob-El. This would be a common name among shepherds at that time and it is found as a Canaanite place-name in a list of Thutmose III.[4] Hence we can say that this was a story to which shepherds listened with pleasure and through which they enjoyed a sense of superiority over the hunter.

The name of Jacob was attracted to another contest *Märchen* about a battle of wits between two shepherds, one of them a younger man who had left home to seek his fortune, and this motif of the 'journey' was linked to the flight of Jacob from the intended revenge of his brother Esau. The original presupposition of the Jacob-Laban story is that Laban is a near neighbour of the east-Jordan Jacob, and this state of affairs is preserved in E according to which Laban's territory is 'the land of the people of the east' (29.1), that is, the great steppe east of Damascus.[5] The locating of Laban in the more remote Harran, which is the work of J, reflects the eastward movement of the Aramaeans who took the story with them. The second part of the Jacob-Esau story has been supplied by professional story-tellers in order to satisfy the demands of their clients.[6] The nationalizing of Jacob and Esau has to be related to the period of Davidic expansion, when the older kingdom of Edom was overtaken by Israel and subdued by her. The subsequent attachment of local sanctuary legends to Jacob-Israel by J and E, along the line of Jacob's route on his return to Canaan,[7] serves to give a patriarchal foundation to the Yahwistic cult later practised at these sanctuaries.[8]

[1] 'Jacob', p. 344.
[2] *ibid.*, p. 343.
[3] *ibid.*, p. 352.
[4] *ibid.*, pp. 361 f.
[5] 'Jacob', pp. 354 f.
[6] *ibid.*, p. 351.
[7] *ibid.*, p. 348.
[8] *ibid.*, pp. 349 f.

If we take into account Gunkel's history of the genre of the patriarchal narratives,[1] his view of the history of the tradition subsequent to *Genesis* (*3*) (1910) becomes tolerably clear. There are two main cycles of patriarchal narratives, the Abraham cycle and the Jacob cycle. The Isaac stories (if chapter 24 is subtracted as a late development) are of small compass, but all three sets of narratives have this in common that they are first told beyond the boundaries of the arable land of Canaan on its southern and eastern edges. Thus the Abraham story is originally attached to Hebron and the Isaac story to Beersheba. These cycles of stories develop and are transmitted quite independently of one another, and their consolidation into a connected narrative is not so much a part of the history of tradition as a conflation resulting from the techniques of collectors. This is why, as I have already remarked, it is difficult to maintain a distinction between history of tradition and history of composition.

The history of the patriarchal stories, according to Gunkel, is not a unitary history embracing all the narratives, but separate and independent histories of the tradition of the important cycles of patriarchal stories. It is therefore possible and, from Gunkel's point of view, necessary, to deal with the history of the Jacob cycle from beginning to end, to do the same for the Abraham cycle, and then to ask how eventually they became related to one another. The most significant common factor is the cultural area in which (in and subsequent to *Genesis* (*3*)) all the patriarchal stories are assumed to take their rise. They reflect conditions of life on the edge of the arable land of Canaan and they are therefore tales about shepherds. The Jacob and Esau story reflects a conflict between shepherd and hunter arising out of social change. The Jacob-Laban story is also about Jacob, the expert shepherd, in his battle of wits with Laban. The two stories are connected by using the Jacob-Esau story as a frame for the Jacob-Laban story. The association of Jacob with ancient Canaanite sanctuaries west of the Jordan is a later stage of the tradition, and when Jacob is elevated to the rank of an Israelite eponym, this provides the impetus for further development. Jacob becomes the father of Israel and Esau the father of Edom and this stage has been reached by the early monarchy.[2] Similarly Abraham is the well-loved character of the story about a shepherd who lived at Hebron, and out of this

[1] Above, chapter i.   [2] Above, p. 106.

develops the Abraham-Lot cycle and the representation of Abraham as the father of Israel and Lot as the father of Moab.

One can see that a pattern of progress common to the Abraham and Jacob stories, and which would apply also to the Isaac story, is being postulated. The characters are all, in the semi-nomadic context in which the stories function, creations of a kind of story-telling which consists in the glorification of an occupation. They appear in tales which describe the prowess of shepherds. The beginning and the early stages of the tradition of these stories are therefore to be correlated with the semi-nomadic style of life. Where this correlation no longer holds, we have to reckon with subsequent stages of the tradition. Hence wherever the stories move into Canaan and the patriarchs are associated with the ancient sanctuaries of Canaan, we are confronted by later stages of the tradition. Another point is that there is no question of establishing any order of priority as between one cycle of stories and another. They develop concurrently and separately; they constitute parallel but independent histories of tradition which, however, come to the same kind of culmination, in so far as both Abraham and Jacob achieve a national status.

It is not obvious, however, that the history of the tradition of the patriarchal narratives, thus described, can elucidate the relations which obtain between Abraham, Isaac and Jacob in the book of Genesis. In so far as Gunkel deals with this, he does it through the role which he ascribes to the professional and peripatetic story-teller who, as a consequence of travelling between different sanctuaries where the separate narrative cycles had particular local attachments, established connecting links between one cycle and another. This has been done by utilizing a genealogical scheme, but what is not clear to me in Gunkel's account is why the genealogical relationships have been ordered in the way they have been. Why did Abraham end up as the senior patriarch, with Isaac in the middle and Jacob the junior?

According to Eissfeldt there is no important sense in which the patriarchal narratives can be said to have a history of tradition. 'History of tradition' and the techniques of the traditio-historical approach presuppose that the tradition possesses a structure, whether it is conceived organically and spoken of in figures of growth ('seed', 'kernel')[1] or whether it is thought of rather as an

[1] See Noth, below, pp. 112 ff., 155.

aggregation of smaller units (Gunkel). It might seem that there is some affinity between Eissfeldt and Gunkel in so far as Eissfeldt envisages the existence of cycles of narratives as well as individual narratives prior to the contributions made by the authors of the documentary sources.[1] One can, however, speak of a history of tradition in the case of Gunkel because his view of the documentary sources is that they are Collections, and Collectors are less than creative historians. Eissfeldt's understanding of the matter is quite different: those who are responsible for the documentary sources are authors, and the oldest of them, L (dated by Eissfeldt in the reign of David or Solomon[2]) fashions a new history from the creation of the world to the occupation of Canaan. The entire structure derives from his creativeness and the histories of J and E are on the same level of achievement. If this is so, no room is left for any significant structural exploration which goes beyond the sources, and this is the hinterland where the traditio-historical method operates. There is no structure preceding that which is imposed on the discrete and heterogeneous material by the earliest documentary source.[3]

Hence the only important literary task which remains after the sources have been identified and defined is a *Gattungsgeschichte* (history of genre) of the patriarchal narratives and this, as we have seen,[4] is undertaken by Eissfeldt. Further, only what can be demonstrated as old by a comparison of the documentary sources is a proper subject of *Gattungsgeschichte*.[5] The absence of a traditio-historical approach in Eissfeldt is shown by the circumstance that the question of the transfer of traditions from one patriarch to another is hardly raised at all. Shechem and Bethel traditions are not Jacob traditions which have been secondarily transferred to Abraham, and Beersheba traditions are not Isaac traditions secondarily attracted to Abraham. The association of Abraham with these sanctuaries is to be explained historically and not in terms of secondary traditio-historical processes.[6] Abraham, as an historical individual, participated in El worship at all these sanctuaries in

[1] 'Genesis', pp. 374 f.
[2] *ibid.*, p. 372.
[3] 'Die Schichten des Hexateuch', *KS* i, p. 37; 'Die kleinste literarische Einheit in den Erzählungsbüchern des alten Testaments', *Theologische Blätter* 6 (1927), pp. 333-337; *KS* i, pp. 143-149, especially p. 144.
[4] Above, pp. 69 ff.
[5] *KS* i, p. 35.
[6] Cf. 'Jahwe, der Gott der Väter', *KS* iv, pp. 83 f.

the second millennium B.C. The absence of traditio-historical influence is also seen in the fact that Eissfeldt is not impressed by
the possibility that in the course of the growth of the tradition
Abraham may have been drawn into contexts to which he did not
originally belong, so that a traditio-historical rather than a plain
historical elucidation is the correct one: the original connexion is
between the Ishmaelites and Isaac (however 'Isaac' is elucidated),
who had a common relationship with the sanctuary of Beer Lahai
Roi, and Abraham was only drawn into the story after the genealogical link between himself and Isaac had been established. Similarly the Abraham-Lot story is not susceptible of an historical
interpretation, whether the Sodom story or the account of the
journey of Abraham and his nephew from Mesopotamia to Canaan,
and the elucidation must be sought in traditio-historical terms. Or,
again, the account of Abraham's meeting with Melchizedek, the
priest-king of Jerusalem, and his relations with the cult of El-
Elyon, has to be understood against the background of the historical circumstances and cultic developments of David's reign – the
connexions of Hebron with David's rise to power, on the one
hand, and the ancient connexion of Abraham traditions with
Hebron on the other.

This aspect of the matter is developed by Clements who holds
that the promise of land to Abraham, associated with the El cult
of Mamre-Hebron, was taken over by the Calebites when they
settled in the Hebron area. Since they were Yahweh-worshipping,
it became a Yahwistic promise and was connected with the promise
of land in Canaan given to the Calebites by Moses (Num. 14.24).
Abraham, Isaac and Jacob were originally quite separate local
heroes, and the genealogical scheme Abraham-Isaac-Jacob was the
consequence of the transfer of Abraham traditions, now Yahwistic,
from a local Hebron setting into a larger Judaean context in connexion with the dominance of Judah in the Davidic-Solomonic
era. The blessings promised to Abraham are, according to the
theological understanding of J, fulfilled in the secure possession of
the Promised Land achieved by David, and in this connexion the
Abraham traditions from Hebron are transplanted in Jerusalem
in the context of palace and temple.[1]

[1] R. E. Clements, *Abraham and David*, pp. 33, 39, 47-60; 'Abraham', *Theologisches Wörterbuch zum alten Testament*, herausgegeben von G. J. Botterweck
und H. Ringgren (1970), Sp. 55 f.

As a final indication of the absence of a traditio-historical approach in Eissfeldt it may be noted that the account which he gives of the secondary linking of the Jacob-Esau and Jacob-Laban cycles is in source-critical terms – the two cycles are not yet joined in L but are in J and E.[1] Further, the sense in which Eissfeldt uses the word 'tradition' indicates the correctness of these observations. When he speaks about 'tradition' or 'traditions', he means 'material extant in the documentary sources which is historically reliable', and this is a different sense from what is intended by a 'history of tradition' of the patriarchal narratives.[2]

II

Alt's main contribution to the history of the tradition of the patriarchal narratives is his account of the circumstances which brought about the genealogical connexion of the originally separate cult founders, Abraham, Isaac and Jacob. He holds that Jacob stories are related to areas settled by the Joseph tribes and that the preservation of $'{}^a b\bar{\imath}r\ ya'{}^a q\bar{o}b$ in a saying about Joseph (Gen. 49.24) is no accident.[3] His view that the extension of the sphere of the Jacob stories to east Jordan is to be correlated with the colonization of that area by Joseph tribes[4] is subsequently developed by Noth.[5] Whereas Jacob has links with more than one sanctuary (Shechem, Bethel),[6] Isaac is localized at Beersheba, a sanctuary with a wide circle of worshippers, including those of the 'god of Abraham' from Hebron and those of the 'god of Jacob' from Shechem and Bethel. Such a sanctuary would afford opportunities for the growing together of the originally separate patriarchal cults and the relating of their founders genealogically.[7] It would also elucidate the secondary process by which Abraham became connected with

---

[1] 'Genesis', pp. 374 f.

[2] Cf. Eissfeldt's review of Noth's *Geschichte Israels*, 'Israel und seine Geschichte', *ThLZ* 76 (1951), Sp. 335-340; *KS* iii (1966), pp. 159-167, especially p. 163.

[3] A. Alt, 'Der Gott der Väter', *BWANT*, III Folge, Heft 12 (1929); 'The God of the Fathers', *Essays on Old Testament History and Religion*, translated by R. A. Wilson (1966), p. 51.

[4] *ibid.*, p. 52, n. 143.

[5] Below, pp. 123 ff.

[6] Mahanaim or Penuel is not, according to Alt (*ibid.*, pp. 50 f.), a great sanctuary with a resident El. Here there is no question of a local numen entering the story.

[7] 'The God of the Fathers', pp. 52 f.

the sanctuaries of Shechem and Bethel.[1] Unlike Noth, Alt supposes that Mamre was probably the place where the cult of the 'god of Abraham' was first localized and he suggests that the Machpelah grave tradition derives from the setting up of an outpost of the Mamre cult on the edge of Hebron.[2]

The journey of Jacob from Shechem to Bethel (Gen. 35.1 ff.) is, according to Alt, an aetiology of a pilgrimage from Shechem to Bethel which arose as a consequence of the elevation of Bethel to the status of a royal sanctuary by Jeroboam I after the division of the kingdom (I Kings 12.29; cf. v. 25 – Jeroboam had taken up residence at Shechem). The objects which are mentioned in Gen. 35.1 ff. would be on view at Shechem and Bethel (the oak under which the alien gods were buried, the altar which was built and the tree beside which Rebecca's nurse was buried), and these phenomena supply the aetiological impetus for the story of Jacob's journey.[3] The primary setting of the burying of foreign gods at Shechem is Josh. 24 and it is therefore a ritual which is originally associated with Joshua and which is secondarily attracted to Jacob in Gen. 35.1 ff.[4] The primary context which has to be assumed at Shechem is the Renewal of the Covenant Festival and the blessing and cursing of Deut. 27 and 28 belongs to the same setting. The burying of the alien gods is in effect a ritual repudiation of all gods other than Yahweh and this was an element of the Festival of the Renewal of the Covenant as it was celebrated at Shechem.

The view that the patriarchs are founders of cults and that consequently the nucleus of the patriarchal narratives is cultic history is taken by Noth from Alt and profoundly influences his history of the tradition of the patriarchal narratives.[5] A second decisive influence on Noth is von Rad, since the latter's conclusion that the kernel of the Hexateuch is credal[6] becomes the premise of Noth's history of the tradition of the Pentateuch.[7] The 'wandering

---

[1] *ibid.*, pp. 54 f.

[2] *ibid.*, p. 54.

[3] 'Die Wallfahrt von Sichem nach Bethel', In piam memoriam Alexander von Bulmerincq, *Abhandlungen der Herder-Gesellschaft und des Herder-Instituts zu Riga*, vi Band, Nr. 3 (1938), pp. 218-230; *KS* i, pp. 79-88, especially p. 84.

[4] *ibid.*, p. 83.

[5] Cf. above, pp. 59-61.

[6] G. von Rad, 'Das formgeschichtliche Problem des Hexateuchs', *BWANT* IV, 26 (1938); 'The Form-Critical Problem of the Hexateuch', *The Problem of the Hexateuch and Other Essays*, translated by E.W.T. Dicken (1966), pp. 1-78.

[7] M. Noth, *Überlieferungsgeschichte des Pentateuch* (1948).

Aramaean' (or, 'the Aramaean at the point of death') of the 'little creed' (Deut. 26.5-9) is Jacob and it is through Jacob that the patriarchs have been connected with what both von Rad and Noth acknowledge to be the leading themes of the Pentateuch – the exodus of Israel from Egypt, guidance through the desert and possession of the land of Canaan. Von Rad's view is that the treatment of the last of the themes, and so the conclusion of the story, is to be found in the book of Joshua and has original connexions with the sanctuary of Gilgal.[1] Hence von Rad's unit is the Hexateuch. Noth, on the other hand, does not accept that the settlement traditions have a special connexion with the sanctuary of Gilgal, since this depends on a use of the book of Joshua with which he disagrees:

This thesis depends on what seems to me the untenable literary-critical proposition that the old content of the book of Joshua, with its Benjamite narratives attached to Gilgal, constitutes a continuation and conclusion of the old Pentateuch material.[2]

The bringing of Israel out of Egypt and her possession of the land of Canaan are themes which originated as credal statements made by the tribal confederacy which is called Israel. According to Noth they take us back to a situation where these tribes worship Yahweh at a common sanctuary and recite a common creed, and they can take us back no further than this. The historical situation which corresponds to the credal use of these themes is the establishment of the Israelite tribes on the soil of Canaan and their worship of Yahweh at a central sanctuary.

We may want to ask how it came about that all of these tribes who subsequently became Israel were prepared to recite this creed, since they had not all been in Egypt and had had widely differing experiences in the process of settling down in Canaan. These are historical questions which it may be impossible to answer or to which only provisional, halting answers can be given. Noth makes a distinction between an historical answer and a traditio-historical answer. What is being attempted in the latter case is to locate the earliest stage of the tradition and then to plot its course. A traditio-historical enquiry is not an evaluation of possible historical sources; it is rather a consideration of what historical, cultural and religious

---

[1] 'The Form-Critical Problem of the Hexateuch', pp. 41 ff.
[2] *op. cit.*, p. 55, n. 170.

circumstances may be reflected by the differing stages of the tradition.

If this is so, the traditions do not necessarily give us the kind of information which they appear to impart. Thus the earliest stage of the tradition corresponds to the existence of the entity Israel as a tribal confederation on the soil of Canaan and at no subsequent point can the tradition inform us about any period of Israelite history prior to that which is reflected in the earliest stages of the tradition. This goes against the appearances, because there is a great expansion and elaboration of the credal nucleus into a complex narrative, as our extant Pentateuch testifies, and we appear to be informed about earlier historical experiences of the tribes.[1] This, however, from the traditio-historical point of view is a secondary expansion of the original, brief, credal themes which can never tell us any more about the ultimate historical connexions of the tradition than the original credal themes themselves.

Thus we have, according to Noth, a historical point to which we can attach the beginning of the tradition and that is the existence of the entity Israel in Canaan. If we accept this traditio-historical assumption, the study of the Pentateuch is then concerned with an analysis of the narrative elaboration of this creed which *ex hypothesi* takes place subsequent to the historical point to which the beginning of the tradition has been attached, that is, subsequent to the settlement of the Israelites in Canaan. Stories about the patriarchs or about Israel in Egypt or in the desert do not give the kind of historical information which they appear to give. In so far as they do reflect historical or cultural or religious conditions these belong to a later period of the history of Israel in Canaan than that which is reflected in the credal kernel of the Pentateuch. Hence Noth observes[2] that although the references to wandering in the wilderness appear to be temporally prior to the theme 'possession of Canaan', they are, from a traditio-historical point of view, an elaboration of the theme 'possession of Canaan'. Thus the theme 'wandering in the wilderness' or 'guidance through the desert' cannot give us reliable historical information about the Israelite tribes in the desert. It reflects rather the circumstances of the southern tribes who live on the edge of the desert and know the privations of such an existence.[3]

The theme 'exodus from Egypt' or 'deliverance from Egypt', to

---

[1] *ibid.*, p. 3.   [2] *ibid.*, pp. 62 f.   [3] Below, p. 116.

which Noth[1] gives first priority, may have arisen from experiences in which only a small number of those who subsequently became Israel participated. This is a historical question which cannot be answered with any certainty. Noth suggests that we should think in terms of family units smaller than tribes who were later interspersed throughout the Israelite tribes in Palestine and who were the bearers of the 'deliverance from Egypt' tradition. In this way he seeks to explain how this tradition acquired all-Israelite status. This, however, is a tentative, historical answer which may be wrong, but, even if it is wrong, the traditio-historical account itself is not affected. The acceptance of the traditio-historical position involves a certain historical agnosticism. We cannot say with certainty in what historical circumstances the 'deliverance from Egypt' theme established itself as a cardinal, all-Israelite credal assertion.

There is the same difficulty in discussing historically the theme 'possession of Canaan'.[2] Noth remarks that a great complexity and variety of experience attaches to the circumstances in which the tribes established themselves in Canaan, and that there must have been of necessity among the different tribes differing traditions of occupation. It is one particular tradition out of these many traditions which has achieved the status of an all-Israelite confession and has been accepted as such by all the tribes. This, according to Noth, is the tradition of occupation held by the central Palestinian tribes; the north and south Palestinian tribes reached the areas of their settlement by other and individual ways. The adoption of the central Palestinian tradition is a reflection of the dominance of these tribes and of the key position which they occupied among the Israelite tribes settled in Canaan. In particular, it is to be related to the circumstance that the first central sanctuary of the Israelite tribes was located in central Palestinian territory. There is, however, no immediate historical link between the 'deliverance from Egypt' theme and the 'possession of Canaan' theme. We are not to suppose that the central Palestinian tribes, whose traditions of settlement achieved all-Israelite status in connexion with the establishment of a central sanctuary in their territory at Shechem, were the tribes who had been in Egypt. We cannot relate the notices about the tribes who appear in the area of south trans-Jordan, who make a detour of Edom and who then proceed to their central

[1] *ibid.*, pp. 50-54.
[2] *ibid.*, pp. 54-58.

Palestinian area of settlement, to the tradition of the deliverance
of the Israelites from Egypt. The theme 'guidance through the
desert' is of no help in this respect, because it is of later origin (in
a traditio-historical sense) than the theme 'possession of Canaan'.[1]
There is no narrative connexion between 'deliverance from Egypt'
and 'possession of Canaan' and this circumstance speaks against
an historical connexion. The relation between the two in the creed
is not historically but traditio-historically conditioned. Fragments
of history are picked up, and, in a context of fulfilment in which
all the tribes participate, are seen as a history in which all the tribes
have shared, which has made them what they now are, and has
brought them to the place of fulfilment. The Israel which recites
the creed containing these great themes has transcended through
a common religious faith all the accidents of the diverse historical
origins of her constituent tribes, and has identified herself as the
Israel whose Fathers received the Promise, which was delivered
from Egypt and which has received the Land.

The reference to the patriarchs in the creed ('A wandering
Aramaean was my father' or 'An Aramaean at the point of death
was my father', Deut. 26.5) requires special treatment in so far as
its traditio-historical origins can be carried back further than the
remaining themes of the creed.[2] Unlike the other themes it is not
all-Israelite in character from the outset. It originates in a cult
which is not Yahwistic and which Alt has named 'the god of the
fathers'. Hence, according to Alt, and, in this respect, he is followed
by Noth, the patriarchal narratives are essentially cultic history.
All that we can say about the patriarchs is that they were founders
of semi-nomadic cults which were brought into Canaan and attached to Canaanite sanctuaries by their descendants. Hence the
patriarchs themselves had no direct connexion with Canaanite
sanctuaries or with El worship, since the sanctuaries in question
did not come within the orbit of Israel until after the settlement.
Where the representation of the patriarchal narratives has a *prima
facie* pre-settlement character it must necessarily be anachronistic.[3]
Promise is an original constituent of 'the god of the fathers' cult,
the promise of posterity at the pre-sedentary stage and the promise
of land subsequent to the anchoring of these cults in Canaan.[4]

[1] Above, p. 114.
[2] *op. cit.*, pp. 58-62.
[3] A. Alt, 'The God of the Fathers', pp. 9, n. 19, 29, 48 f.
[4] *ibid.*, p. 65; cf. J. Hoftijzer, *Die Verheissungen an die drei Erzväter* (1956),

Hence (and this is Noth's position) the patriarchs find their way into the Pentateuch not as personalities but as founders of cults, and, at the point where the patriarchal theme is linked to the other main themes of the creed, it is the nature of the patriarchal cults and not the patriarchs as personalities which promote this union. The gods of the patriarchs (Abraham, Isaac and Jacob) were family or clan deities and the cult corresponds to a nomadic or semi-nomadic state of existence in which a hunger for land and a desire for a settled life are major concerns. The god promises to the founder of the cult, and to the group which subsequently adheres to the cult which he has founded, posterity and land.[1] The gods of the patriarchs are thus originally clan deities,[2] but this type of cult has an interesting affinity with Yahwism in so far as it is concerned, in its semi-nomadic context, with the relationship between god and community rather than the attachment of a god to a sacred place.

Noth supposes that the Israelite tribes who settled in Palestine brought with them cults of this type, all bearing the names of the gods of their founders and that consequently the 'god of the fathers' type of cult was widespread among these tribes. In the process of transition from a semi-nomadic to a sedentary state of existence these cults were attached to Canaanite sanctuaries up and down the land. The main theological element of the cult is Promise, and, since this was a promise of land, it had been fulfilled for the several tribes as they established themselves in Canaan. This achievement of settled status would appear to the tribes concerned as a fulfilment of the promise made to the founder of the cult and his posterity. If we then look at the place of the patriarchal element in the total creed, we have to say that it contains a promise which was fulfilled when Canaan was occupied by the Israelite tribes. Hence the fulfilment of the Promise which originally attaches to the 'god of the fathers' cult is gathered up into the credal theme 'possession of the land' or 'occupation of the land'.[3]

---

p. 4. Hoftijzer remarks that von Rad and Noth do not observe the distinction drawn by Alt between promise of posterity at the pre-sedentary stage, and promise of land subsequent to the anchoring of the cult at Canaanite sanctuaries.

[1] See above, p. 116, n. 4, where I have noted Hoftijzer's criticism of Noth's alteration of Alt's statement.

[2] 'God of Abraham', '*paḥad* of Isaac', '*ābīr* of Jacob'. For a detailed treatment see chapter iv.

[3] Cf. G. von Rad, 'The Form-Critical Problem of the Hexateuch', pp. 54-63.

What emerges from this is that the patriarchal element of the creed, which is originally non-Israelite in the sense indicated above, has special connexions in the creed with the theme 'possession of Canaan'. The ultimate significance of the incorporation of the patriarchal element in the creed is, however, more comprehensive than this: in the final shaping of the Pentateuch the theological framework is supplied by a Promise and Fulfilment scaffolding whose origins are to be sought in the incorporation of the 'god of the fathers' cult in the Israelite creed.[1]

If the Aramaean of Deut. 26.5 is to be equated with Jacob, it may be asked why Jacob among the other patriarchs first acquired credal status.[2] This again is to be explained in terms of the dominant position of the central Palestinian group of Israelite tribes. We have to suppose that at a Canaanite sanctuary in this area, and probably at Shechem, there were Israelite tribes who maintained the cult of $'^abir\ ya'^aqob$ (Gen. 49.24), and that the elevation of Jacob to all-Israelite rank reflects the influential role of these tribes in the Israelite confederacy. The cult of the 'god of the fathers' was a family cult concerned with the founder and his posterity, and, on the analogy of this, Jacob acquired the status of 'father' of all the tribes who worshipped Yahweh at Shechem.[3]

At a later traditio-historical stage, and up to the point where the traditions were given a fixed literary shape, the main centre of influence was not in central Palestine but in the south. Noth discusses whether this was a further development confined to the south, and reflecting the dominance acquired by the south and by Jerusalem in particular, or whether other tribes also had their special patriarchal traditions, and that, for the most part, it is only the southern expression of this activity which has survived. He is non-commital on this point, but he observes that the character of the E source of the Pentateuch does lend some credence to the view that there were special northern traditions. The Abraham and Isaac stories are connected with the Jacob story by the simple expedient of extending the genealogical principle which had already been used in order to relate all the Israelite tribes to Jacob. The reference to Jacob in the creed marks the appropriation of a patriarchal cult by all the Israelite tribes who then become 'sons'

[1] Below, p. 239.
[2] M. Noth, *op. cit.*, pp. 86-95.
[3] Cf. above, pp. 99 f.

of Jacob. At a later stage of the tradition founders of patriarchal cults known to the southern tribes were also introduced into the Pentateuch and were connected with the earlier patriarchal constituent by the representation that Isaac was the father of Jacob and Abraham the father of Isaac. Thus the family or clan aspect, which is original to the 'god of the fathers' type of cult, is used in order to unite distinct founders of separate family cults.

There is a traditio-historical connexion between the narrative expression of the 'guidance through the desert' theme and the stories about Abraham and Isaac.[1] This is seen principally in the narratives which are attached to a small number of wells in the desert. These are regarded as the outposts of Palestinian culture, and those who live in the Judaean mountains, especially the semi-nomadic elements of the Negeb, have a close relationship with them. One may suppose that the stories about Abraham and Isaac were also attached originally to sanctuaries in the Negeb, and, if so, the narrative expansion of the themes 'promise to the fathers' and 'guidance through the desert' took place in more or less the same circles. Familiarity with a particular well in the Negeb would evoke thoughts about the Israelites who had come out of Egypt and so encourage the elaboration of the theme 'guidance through the desert'.

Noth discusses the respective claims of Shechem and Bethel to be regarded as the first central sanctuary of the Israelite tribes. He notes that according to Gen. 33.18b (J) Jacob sets up his camp east of Shechem and that he bought a piece of land there in order to erect a *maṣṣēbā* on it (33.19 f., E). In Bethel the holiness of the place was unexpectedly revealed to him through a theophany (Gen. 28.11-22, JE; 35.9-13, 15, P) and he erected there a *maṣṣēbā* and a *mizbēaḥ* (28.18; 35.7). The discussion is tied to the relationship established between Shechem and Bethel in Gen. 35.1-5 (Pilgrimage from Shechem to Bethel) which Noth regards as the cultic foundation of the narrative theme 'journeyings of the patriarchs'. Noth suggests that the event underlying the institution of this pilgrimage from Shechem to Bethel may be the transference of the central sanctuary of the Israelite tribes from Shechem to Bethel and so the transference to Bethel of 'the god who appeared to Jacob'.[2] The connexion of Jacob with Bethel derives from the,

[1] M. Noth, *op. cit.*, p. 63.
[2] M. Noth, *ibid.*, p. 87, n. 231; cf. A. Alt, above, pp. 112 f.

perhaps, brief period when Bethel had the rank of a central sanctuary and before this status passed to Shiloh. At this point the pilgrimage to Bethel would be discontinued.[1]

The conservatism which is to be expected in cultic matters had the effect of preserving a link between the Israelite tribes and Shechem even after the removal of the sanctuary to Bethel, and this took the form of a gathering together of the tribes at Shechem and a pilgrimage from there to the central sanctuary. There is the possibility that this pilgrimage may have been a pre-Israelite, Canaanite religious observance in which case one should conclude that the original connexion of the Jacob traditions was with Bethel rather than Shechem. Noth, however, inclines to the view that the Jacob traditions are originally anchored at Shechem and he observes that the suppression of an earlier stage by a later one is a common traditio-historical phenomenon. His considered conclusion is that the promise of land and posterity, which is the kernel of the 'god of the fathers' type of cult, has, in the case of Jacob, been transferred from Shechem to Bethel (cf. Gen. 28.13b, 14, J). Further connexions with Bethel are established through Rachel (Gen. 35.16-20; Jer. 31.15) whose grave is located in Ephraimite-Benjamite territory (south of Bethel between Ephraimite Bethel and Benjamite Ramah) and through Rachel's nurse, Deborah, whose grave is located at Bethel (Gen. 35.8).[2]

If we assume that the Jacob theme acquired all-Israelite status at Shechem, we are touching the tradition at a point when it knows nothing of Jacob in Egypt. The historical situation reflected by the entrance of Jacob into the Israelite creed is the establishment of Israelite tribes in central Palestine and the status of Shechem as a central sanctuary. The notices about Jacob's acquisition of a piece of land at Shechem (Gen. 33.19, E) and his establishing of a camp east of Shechem (33.18b, J) are connected by Noth with the circumstance that within the territory of the Canaanite city-state, Shechem, a well-demarcated piece of land which formed a kind of enclave east of the city belonged to the confederation of Israelite tribes. This acquisition of land is indicative of friendly relations with the city-state of Shechem, and, probably, was the result of the location of the Israelite central sanctuary at the ancient and celebrated sanctuary of the city-state. The ritual preparations

[1] M. Noth, *ibid.*, p. 91, n. 243.
[2] M. Noth, *ibid.*, p. 88.

could then be made by the Israelites on their own soil and the cultic transactions would be consummated at the sanctuary within the boundaries of the city-state. The Israelite piece of land would be in the immediate proximity of the sanctuary (cf. Gen. 33.20, 'there' is not to be taken too stringently). The '*ēlōn* of Judg. 9.6 (cf. Deut. 11.30 and Gen. 12.6) refers to the tree sanctuary east of Shechem which is not to be identified with the 'terebinth tree' (*'ēlāh*) of Gen. 35.4 and Josh. 24.26. This *'ēlāh*, according to Noth, is the place where the Israelites carried out their preparatory rite and was located on their own piece of land. Tree and stone (Josh. 24.27) were witnesses of statutory readings of the Law and this may, perhaps, be related to the putting away of strange gods (Josh. 24.23), all of which constituted a preparation for the cultic celebration which subsequently took place at the ancient sanctuary of the city-state.[1]

Similarly nothing is known about the Egyptian connexions of Joseph at this stage of the tradition. The notice concerning Joseph's grave (Josh. 24.32) coheres with the view that the land beside Shechem had become the property of Joseph and his sons. According to Gen. 48.22 (the conclusion of the Jacob history as transmitted by E) Jacob handed over possession of his territory at Shechem to his son Joseph. Although the conveying of Jacob's property to Joseph and the blessing of all of Jacob's sons (Gen. 49.1-27) is set in Egypt in the extant narrative, the original setting must have been Shechem. In the earlier form of the narrative Joseph and his sons, Ephraim and Manasseh, must have been located in Palestine, and the story may have told how Jacob's descendants, perhaps his sons, journeyed to Egypt after his death. The development of the special Joseph traditions (i.e., the account of the blessing of Ephraim and Manasseh in Gen. 48) may have taken place after the removal of the central sanctuary to Bethel. The diminishing importance of Shechem as the focus of all-Israelite traditions allowed room for these special Joseph traditions which deal with internal tribal circumstances and rivalries and whose location is certainly Palestine and not Egypt.[2]

Further the connexion of Jacob with the Levi and Simeon episode in Gen. 34 is secondary and the story was not originally told with censorious intent. Rather it celebrated the heroic exploits of

---

[1] M. Noth, *op. cit.*, pp. 89 f.
[2] M. Noth, *ibid.*, pp. 90-92.

the two tribes and delighted in the stratagem by which they incapacitated the men of Shechem and so laid the foundations for their victory. It is connected with the process by which the tribes adjusted themselves to a sedentary life, or, perhaps, with their claim to summer pastures in the area of central Palestine west of the Jordan, but it is unlikely that it preserves the recollection of a particular historical occurrence. Hence it is, according to Noth, an 'ethnological aetiology' (using Gunkel's terminology). Joseph and Benjamin tribes were settled in central Palestine before Jacob had attained the status of 'father' of the twelve tribes, and Shechem may have served as a connecting link between the Simeon and Levi episode and Jacob. This secondary entrance of Jacob into the story is connected with the search for a reason for the decline and disappearance of the tribes of Simeon and Levi, and, in association with this secondary aetiological application of what was originally a heroic tale, their conduct is held up for censure and condemnation. Jacob is assigned the role of investigator (vv. 5 ff.) and denouncer (v. 30), although his sons are left with the last word (v. 31). Also in Gen. 49.5-7 the curse and threat of dispersion uttered by Jacob are related to the entirely pejorative construction which is put on the Shechem incident.[1]

The attachment of the Jacob-Esau and the Jacob-Laban stories to the area east of the Jordan is shown by the fact that the older sources of the Pentateuch still contain notices which must originally have stated that Jacob was buried east of the Jordan (Gen. 50.10a, J; 50.11, E). We do not know the location of the threshing-floor of Atad, and Abel-mizraim is aetiological. It has been attached to an account of the mourning rites, because Abel in Abel-mizraim has been associated with '*ēbel* 'mourning' in vv. 10 and 11, and the words 'How bitterly the Egyptians are mourning'! (v. 11) then serve as an aetiology of Abel-mizraim. Another factor is P's representation that Jacob died in Egypt. In P (Gen. 49.29-32; 50.13) Jacob's grave is located at Hebron (which had become the family grave) and, as a consequence, what was said about Jacob's burial place in the older sources has been changed into a notice about where the mourning rites were carried out. The place where the mourning rites were discharged must have been originally the burial place. The lateness of the representation in P is indicated by the fact that it presupposes the episode of Jacob's stay in

[1] M. Noth, *op. cit.*, pp. 93-95.

Egypt and his death there which itself belongs to a late stage of the history of the tradition. Hence Abel-Mizraim in 50.11 (E), which presupposes that Jacob died in Egypt, is also late.[1]

The east Jordan grave tradition is an indication that the east Jordan Jacob stories have an original attachment to that area: Jacob is buried in the place where he lived and possessed land. The historical circumstances which can be correlated with the east Jordan Jacob narratives are the settlement of west Jordan Ephraimite colonists in Gilead. The land which they settled was uncleared woodland, and this circumstance makes it impossible that the east Jordan Jacob is the original Jacob.[2] That the east Jordan Jacob was originally separate from his west Jordan counterpart is suggested by the differences between the two complexes of tradition and the divergent portrayals of Jacob which they contain. It is unlikely, however, that there could have been an indigenous Jacob tradition in an area which was uncleared woodland until it was settled by the west Jordan Ephraimite colonists, and the difference between the west and east Jordan Jacob traditions is rather to be explained by the new conditions of life with which the colonists had to contend. Hence the historical events which lie behind the two complexes of tradition are first the settlement of west Jordan by the central Palestinian tribes out of which comes the west Jordan Jacob with his attachment to Shechem, and, in the second place, the colonizing of Gilead by west Jordan Ephraimites which gives rise to the east Jordan Jacob. We should therefore conclude that the Ephraimite colonists brought with them to Gilead the traditions of the west Jordan Jacob which were by this time firmly established at Bethel, the most celebrated sanctuary in Ephraimite territory.

The Jacob-Esau-Laban cycle is a relatively late growth in relation to the formation of the Pentateuch, as is evident from its expansive saga style and the composition of originally separate parts which is a feature of it. The elements which are thus composed (the Jacob-Esau and the Jacob-Laban stories) themselves belong to a stage of the Jacob tradition, subsequent to that represented by the west Jordan Jacob. The Jacob-Esau cycle supplies the foundation and framework for the combined Jacob-Esau-Laban cycle,[3] but this is not to say that the Jacob-Esau story has an

---

[1] *ibid.*, pp. 95-97.
[2] For a contrary view, expressed by Gunkel, see above, pp. 105 ff.
[3] Cf. Gunkel, above, p. 105.

absolute temporal priority. Rather both cycles are originally independent and have developed separately and concurrently. Both in their individual characteristics and in the form in which they have been combined they are representatives of a later, more discursive, saga style than that exemplified by the stories about the west Jordan Jacob. The literary inventiveness which has developed the east Jordan Jacob stories in many directions, through the exploitation and complication of the basic themes, has not yet made its appearance in the west Jordan Jacob stories. The differing literary characteristics of the west and east Jordan Jacob stories can be correlated with a functional divergence which is conditioned by their differing contexts. The east Jordan Jacob stories have a looser connexion with the credal kernel than do those in west Jordan. In an area which had been uncleared woodland until it was colonized by the Ephraimites there were no ancient and celebrated sanctuaries, and hence the east Jordan Jacob stories are not attached to sanctuaries. Further the loosening of the east Jordan Jacob stories from the credal theme out of which the west Jordan Jacob stories grew is to be explained by the changed circumstances of the colonists. For them the fulfilment of the Promise once made to Jacob no longer had credal urgency – it was not a claim which they felt compelled to make. They were not semi-nomads contesting possession of the land of Canaan; they had come out of a community already settled in Canaan in order to settle an area which was unoccupied until they came and for whose possession they did not have to fight. Their concerns were consequently different from those reflected in the west Jordan Jacob traditions.[1]

The Jacob-Laban story differs from its Jacob-Esau counterpart in that it has a local attachment. The account of the pact between Jacob and Laban on Mount Gilead (Gen. 31.44-32.1, JE) rests on the historical circumstance that a heap of stones or a stone pillar on Mount Gilead served as a boundary marker for use and wont arrangements between the east Jordan Ephraimite colonists and their Aramaean neighbours in respect of pastures and water holes. It is this which gives rise to the story of the pact between Jacob and Laban which is therefore (in Gunkel's terms) an ethnological aetiology. Jacob represents the Gileadite Israelites and Laban and his brothers their Aramaean neighbours – large tribal groups of Aramaeans. The historical reality behind the representation of a

---

[1] M. Noth, *op. cit.*, pp. 97-99.

pact or treaty between Jacob and Laban is the first encounter between Israelites and Aramaeans. Whether Laban was an historical
figure of that period (an Aramaean tribal chief) or whether he is
an eponym of Aramaean tradition, or even a literary creation (an
Aramaean type created by the Israelites and given a name current
at that time) cannot be determined. Jacob has taken on a tribal
function and the cultic and credal significance which he has in the
west Jordan stories has faded. The concerns and interests of the
colonists are gathered up in his person.[1]

The original significance of this mutual pact is accurately indicated by the formula in Gen. 31.52 (J). It probably also stipulated
that the pursuit of an offender would come to an end when the
boundary marker was reached, so that the delinquent would be
safe from punishment as soon as he had passed it, since no extra-
dition arrangements would obtain. It was perhaps this which
encouraged the one-sided interpretation of the pact which appears in the Jacob-Laban narrative, where it is viewed as an
arrangement which enables Israelites to hold safe possession of
property stolen by cunning and resolute action from the Aramaeans. The Jacob-Laban story consequently unfolds not as an
expansion of the negotiation between Israelites and Aramaeans
concluded for the benefit of both, but rather as a story about how
Jacob outwitted Laban by arriving at the boundary with his loot
and then concluding a pact in order to ensure its safe custody.
Another literary motif – the outwitting of Laban – has taken control, and for this reason it is difficult for the story-teller to find a
convincing role for Laban in the negotiation. It comes as a surprise
when Laban is willing to conclude a treaty (Gen. 31.44, E; 31.46,
51, J), for why he should do it is not at all clear in the context of
the narrative. This is an indication that the theme of the pact was
an earlier stage in the history of the tradition than the theme of
the out-witting of Laban, and the effect of the ascendancy of the
latter in the developed narrative is to destroy the credibility of
Laban's role as the Aramaean representative in an agreement between Aramaeans and Israelites. The fact that this lack of credibility is tolerated is in itself an indication that the narrative had no
alternative but to develop from the earlier tradition of a pact and
to accept the consequent unevenness. Thus as things now stand
we cannot refrain from asking why Jacob's unilateral action should

[1] M. Noth, *op. cit.*, pp. 100 f.

induce Laban to conclude a treaty with him. What has Laban to gain from such a treaty? Despite Jacob's complaints against Laban (Gen. 31.38-40, J; 31.41-42, E) it is Laban and not Jacob who has reason to be angry. The rich literary development of the Jacob-Laban story thus follows from the utilization of the motif 'out-witting of the Aramaean'. Laban, a character of consummate craftiness, who had had the better of many encounters, is at last out-witted by the Israelite Jacob – the Ephraimite colonists are more than a match for their Aramaean neighbours.

The original booty was probably Laban's daughters. Jacob justi-fies his flight by expressing the fear that Laban might try to take back his daughters from him (Gen. 31.31). According to E (31.28; 32.1) it is a special concern of Laban that he has been separated from his daughters. His particular complaint is that Jacob has carried them off like prisoners of war (31.26) and he requires that provisions for their protection should be written into the pact (31.50). The concern of the section in E (31.4-26) is to establish that Laban's daughters had gone with Jacob of their own choice and that he had discussed plans for the escape in a conversation which he had had with them. Their willingness had its ground in the love for him which had grown within them, and their desir-ability consisted in their being child-bearing Aramaean women (Leah 'cow'; Rachel 'ewe').[1] Noth queries whether the prominence given to the Aramaean wives of Jacob may not reflect a practice of intermarriage between the Ephraimite colonists and the neighbour-ing Aramaeans, perhaps the practice of raiding each other's terri-tory in order to carry off women. The account of the devices by which Jacob plunders part of Laban's wealth in flocks and herds is a ramification of the 'out-witting of Laban' motif. This is one of the ways in which the Jacob-Laban narrative is elaborated and complicated by the inventiveness of narrators. Another subsidiary theme of the story is the stealing of Laban's household gods (Gen. 31.19b, 30b, 32-35, 37, E), interpreted by Noth as a mocking of cult objects which were prized by the Aramaeans but for which the Israelites had no regard.[2]

Closely intertwined with the Jacob-Laban story in the Penta-teuchal tradition is the Jacob-Esau story. This circumstance, to-gether with the relatedness of the literary styles of the two narra-

[1] M. Noth, op. cit., p. 103, n. 273.
[2] M. Noth, ibid., pp. 100-103.

tives, is an indication that the Jacob-Esau story is to be located among the east Jordan Ephraimites, although it is not attached to any particular locality. It is concerned with two brothers and their different occupations, their conflict over the right of the first-born (Gen. 25.29-34, J) and over their father's blessing (Gen. 27, J). The latter in the masterly, extended narrative of chapter 27 is the version which has been pushed into the foreground. The story of the catching of Esau's heel by Jacob at birth (25.26a, J) originates merely as an aetiology of the name Jacob. The story about the oracle delivered to Rebecca before the birth of the twins (25.22 f., J) is relatively late, since it already views Esau and Jacob as founders of nations and so presupposes the secondary equation of Esau with Edom. Noth[1] supposes that this story existed in an earlier form in which Esau and Jacob were differently designated, not as two nations, nor as older and younger, but as hairy and smooth (cf. Gen. 27.11).

These are all narrative themes which by their nature do not demand a local connexion. Hence the kernel of the Jacob-Esau story contains no notice of locality. The account of the meeting of the two brothers at Mahanaim belongs to a form of the narrative whose extant literary connexions presuppose the union of the Jacob-Esau and the Jacob-Laban narratives. Moreover the mention of Manahaim is aetiologically conditioned ('two camps', i.e., one of Esau and one of Jacob), so that the place Mahanaim is drawn secondarily into the Jacob-Esau narrative in order that an aetiology of it may be supplied from that narrative. The aetiology of Mahanaim given in Gen. 32.2 f. is therefore not the original one; it has been introduced by E and has had the effect of effacing the aetiological orientation which was once extant in 32.14b-22 (E). When J was combined with E, the aetiological conclusion of 32.4-14a (J) was left out.

Again the story localized at Penuel (Gen. 32.23-33) is an independent cultic legend with subsidiary aetiological functions and had no original connexion with the Jacob-Esau story. In its present position it interrupts the account of Jacob's meeting with Esau. It is therefore only loosely attached to the Jacob-Esau story, and its attachment is subsequent to that of Mahanaim. The mention of these localities does, however, show that the work of combining the Jacob-Esau and the Jacob-Laban stories was done in the area

[1] M. Noth, *op. cit.*, p. 107.

of east Jordan which had been settled by the Ephraimite colonists, since both Mahanaim and Penuel lie within this area of settlement. The conclusion that the Jacob-Esau narrative originated and was transmitted in this area is then probable, and, if so, the Jacob of the Jacob-Esau story is none other than the Jacob of the Jacob-Laban story.[1]

Esau is not a type of the foreigner but is rather a figure whom the Ephraimite colonists brought with them from their west Jordan home. Esau belongs to the west Jordan hill country and preserves the memory of the cultural past of the community. From Gen. 25.27 (J) it can be gathered that Esau is a stereotype of the hunter and as such is opposed to Jacob who represents the shepherd. The hunter appears to have priority or, at least, thinks that he has, but through his indifference or stupidity he loses it to the cunning shepherd. In many variants which are not simply literary (i.e., variant versions of the same story from the different documentary sources), but whose arrangement goes back to oral tradition, this subject was explored within the framework of a story about two rival brothers – a familiar folk-tale motif. The two characterizations reflect the stages of cultural transition through which the Ephraimites had passed, from a hunting culture to a pastoral culture, and the stage through which they were passing, from a pastoral culture to agriculture. The narrative is identified in its sympathies with the shepherd rather than the hunter, with the intellectually agile and scheming Jacob rather than the slow-witted, yet thoughtless and impulsive Esau. The transition from a pastoral culture to agriculture is best reflected in the terms of Isaac's blessing (Gen. 27.27-29) whose components are individual and originally independent proverbial sayings about the smell of the field which Yahweh has blessed, the fatness of the earth, the corn and the wine. Despite the impression created by the present context of these sayings, they originally referred to the smell of arable land and it was from these proverbs that the narrative motif of 'smell' entered Gen. 27 as a subsidiary theme (cf. v. 27 in which the smell of the clothes is associated with the smell of the fields).

If Esau is a stereotype of the kind described, the connexion of Esau with Edom must be regarded as secondary (Gen. 25.30, J). Moreover the circumstances of Esau's meeting with Jacob within the area of the Ephraimite settlement of east Jordan are only ex-

[1] M. Noth, *op. cit.*, pp. 103 f.

plicable on the assumption that Gilead and not Edom is Esau's home. Otherwise we have to assume that Esau comes from Edom with the sole purpose of meeting Jacob – not even with a view to hostile action against him which would be more credible – and then having met him immediately begins the return journey to Edom. The name of Esau is an unsolved problem, but it may be a sobriquet for Blockhead, since there can be no doubt that the intention of the narrative is to represent Esau as something of a blockhead.[1]

The Jacob-Esau and the Jacob-Laban stories are combined by the skilful use of the motif of 'flight'. What was originally conceived as a short absence from home in order to allow Esau's anger to cool (Gen. 27.45, J) becomes a long contract with Laban after a probationary period of one month (29.14, J), in the course of which Jacob acquires two Aramaean wives and wealth in livestock. In this further elaboration of the 'flight' motif the original thought that Jacob should stay away from home only until Esau's anger cools is dropped, and, according to Gen. 31.1 f. (JE), the decision of Jacob to return home follows on the awakening of Laban's dislike for him consequent on the great growth of Jacob's wealth. Then there arises as a further complication of the already combined narratives the representation that Jacob had served Laban for years in return for his two wives and his wealth in livestock, and that Laban's hesitation in giving up his daughters was overcome by Jacob's craftiness.

Although a literary separation of the closely intertwined west and east Jordan Jacob narratives is no longer possible, they can be separated by traditio-historical criteria along the lines already indicated. The two complexes of tradition differ in respect of the degree of their attachment to the patriarchal article of the credal kernel of the Pentateuch ('A wandering Aramaean was my father' or 'An Aramaean at the point of death was my father'), and also in respect of their relationship to sanctuaries and their literary characteristics. The east Jordan Jacob narratives cannot be attached to credal concerns or even to historical and cultural circumstances with the same degree of precision as the west Jordan narratives. In the east Jordan setting the stories are no longer necessarily the vehicle of credal convictions or political claims or inter-tribal rivalries. It is no longer certain that they have this function of reflecting circumstances and concerns other than those which

---

[1] M. Noth, *op. cit.*, pp. 104-108.

appear on the face of the stories themselves. The story tends to become an end in itself rather than a means to an end, and control is then vested in the narrative interest itself and not in something outside it. Development is dictated by the artistic and aesthetic pleasure of devising new motifs and complications, and extra-literary concerns and objectives disappear from view.[1]

The east and west Jordan Jacob stories have been combined into a single narrative and this union was effected in the west Jordan area. On general grounds it is understandable that the traditions about the east Jordan Jacob tribes should find their way back to the territory of west Jordan from which the colonists had come, since they would maintain relations with their own tribe and other Israelite tribes in these parts, especially through the central sanctuary which was the principal institutional expression of the coherence of these tribes. More particularly, it can be said that the east and west Jordan Jacob traditions were combined at a time when Bethel, the most important sanctuary in Ephraimite territory, was the central sanctuary of the Israelite tribes and when the west Jordan Jacob traditions had been transferred there from Shechem.

When the west and east Jordan Jacob traditions are worked together we have a story about the 'journeying' of Jacob in his youth – the motif of the 'journey' deriving ultimately from the Shechem to Bethel pilgrimage.[2] It is in the course of a journey after his flight from Esau that Yahweh appears to him at Bethel and promises him land and posterity. This is the west Jordan Jacob tradition of Jacob as the founder of a 'god of the fathers' cult which has been taken up into the creed of the central Palestinian Israelite tribes. Thus we can say that at a given time and place – when the west Jordan Jacob traditions were attached to Bethel – the union with the east Jordan Jacob traditions took place. The combined story went on to tell what happened to Jacob during the years of his service with Laban, of his return and meeting with Esau and of his last journey back to the west Jordan heartland. There the story ended with the account of Jacob's death.

The Joseph narrative, according to which Joseph went to Egypt and died there, was not in existence at this stage of the history of the tradition. The blessing of Ephraim and Manasseh (Gen.

---

[1] Above, pp. 60 f.
[2] Above, pp. 119 f.; cf. Gunkel, above, p. 105.

48.8 ff.), which is set in Egypt just before Jacob's death, belongs originally to the territory of the Joseph tribes in west Jordan and has been secondarily transferred to Egypt. The story of the birth of Jacob's sons (Gen. 29.29-30.24), to which originally belonged the story of Benjamin's birth (Gen. 35.16 ff.), came into existence after the combination of the east and west Jordan Jacob stories. The allocation of Israelite tribes to wives and slave girls[1] is an elaborate drawing out of the implications of the status first attained by Jacob at Shechem as 'father' of the Israelite tribes who had entered into the Promise which he had received as the founder of a 'god of the fathers' type of cult.[2] The transference of the birth of Benjamin to the traditional site of Rachel's death was probably an innovation of E and was taken up into the combined Pentateuchal narrative as special E material.[3]

III

Abraham and Isaac like Jacob were founders of 'god of the fathers' cults and the promise of land and posterity made to them had been fulfilled for their descendants in south Palestine, so that the worship of the 'god of Abraham' and the 'god of Isaac' was established at sanctuaries in that area. In virtue of their connexion with the theme of Promise, the Abraham and Isaac traditions are similar in kind to the west Jordan Jacob traditions, and were probably already in existence before the east Jordan Jacob traditions became part of the portrayal of Jacob. The development of the Abraham and Isaac traditions and the status which they acquired as Fathers of Israel belongs to the south Palestinian stage of the growth of the Pentateuchal tradition. All the notices and narratives which had accrued to Jacob west and east of the Jordan were at some point received in south Palestine which then became the centre for all subsequent growth of the Pentateuchal tradition up to the point of literary fixation.

The achievement of all-Israelite status by Abraham and Isaac follows the lines already indicated for Jacob. This is not simply a process of genealogical extension in terms of which Isaac is made the father of Jacob and Abraham the father of Isaac. This could

---

[1] Leah: Reuben, Simeon, Levi, Judah, Issachar, Zebulon; Rachel: Joseph, Benjamin; Bilhah: Dan, Naphtali; Zilpah: Gad, Asher.

[2] Cf. M. Noth, *op. cit.*, p. 110, n. 293.

[3] *ibid.*, pp. 109-111.

have been carried out and yet Jacob could have remained the first Father of Israel. What is also involved therefore is the transference to Isaac and then to Abraham of the status of Father of the Israelite tribes which had been attained first by Jacob. The process was made easier by the circumstance that all three were founders of 'god of the fathers' type of cults, so that the taking up of the theme of Promise into the Israelite creed, which had enhanced the status of Jacob, would work similarly for Isaac and Abraham.[1]

If this is the way in which Isaac and Abraham became Fathers of Israel, it is clear that Isaac must have acquired this status before Abraham, since he is the link between Abraham and Jacob and the genealogy could only have been carried back to Abraham through him. The prominent position now occupied by Abraham in the Pentateuch is to be explained on the ground that he has been pushed into the forefront at the expense of Isaac; consequently, traditions and localities which are now associated with both were original to Isaac. Moreover, the fact that development was concentrated on the figure of Abraham had the effect of stunting the growth of the Isaac traditions which are consequently exiguous in the extant text.

The relative lateness of the Abraham tradition is shown by the circumstance that even at the stage of literary fixation it is possible to read off its continued growth in the progress from G^2 to J and E. Whatever is retained as an Isaac tradition was probably told originally about Isaac. This material is small in quantity and does not include the Jacob-Esau story which was originally about two rival brothers whose anonymous father was later identified with Isaac. As the promised and, finally, late-born son of Abraham, Isaac has a place in the Abraham story only after the genealogical series Jacob-Isaac-Abraham has been established. Hence all the references to Abraham in Gen. 26, in which J has strung together the bits and pieces of tradition which he knew about Isaac, are secondary. They are subsequent to the extension of the genealogical line to Abraham who has nothing to do originally with traditions which had Isaac as their proper subject. Since Gen. 24 (the acquisition of a bride for Isaac, J) is a late connecting piece,[3] all that remains

---

[1] M. Noth, *op. cit.*, pp. 112 f.

[2] G = *Grundlage*, a source which, according to Noth, underlies J and E (*ibid.*, pp. 40-44).

[3] Below, p. 143.

of Isaac traditions outside Gen. 26 is the short notice in 25.11b (connecting Isaac with Beer Lahai Roi, J).[1]

The material in Gen. 26 has not reached its present shape by traditio-historical processes of growth and one cannot therefore hope to recover from it information about the history of the Isaac traditions. J has strung together laconic and fragmentary notices which were all that he knew about Isaac, and the narrative thread on which he has strung them is 'Isaac and the inhabitants of Gerar'. Hence Gen. 26 is a literary compilation and the order of its parts has no significance for the task of recovering the history of the Isaac tradition. Yet the account of a theophany, with blessing and the promise of descendants and land, comes not inappropriately after the general introduction in v. 1, since Promise was the essential theme of the patriarchal traditions.

Isaac experiences the fulfilment of the divine promise not through his occupation of the land but as a *gēr* – a semi-nomadic shepherd who finds summer pasture for his flocks and herds on the edges of the settled land (26.6) and who enjoys a bumper corn harvest and great prosperity in livestock. This is expressed in a general and exaggerated literary formulation in vv. 12-14 which has no original connexion with vv. 7-11. The Isaac stories thus belong to an earlier cultural stage than the west Jordan Jacob stories. They reflect a period when the Israelite tribes in the south were in contact with the inhabitants of the settled land in the areas which they used for summer pastures, but had not themselves adopted the style of sedentary life.

There are a number of notices in Gen. 26 which deal with the relations between Isaac and the settled population on the subject of the right to make use of wells. The theme mirrors the conditions of life in the cultural setting to which these stories belong, and the intention is to furnish aetiologies for a group of wells (vv. 17, 19-23, 25b-33).

In vv. 7-11 we have the story of how Isaac was afraid that the lusty Canaanites might be attracted by the charms of his wife and his fear that this might have evil consequences for himself. The original form of the story is better preserved here than in the other two variants of it (Gen. 12.10-20, J; 20.1b-18, E). In 26.7-11 the story has a secular character which is superseded in the other two places by elements of miracle and piety. Abimelech learns the

[1] M. Noth., *op. cit.*, pp. 112-114.

truth because he sees Isaac making love to Rebecca. In Gen. 12 Pharaoh suffers from plagues because of Sarah and in chapter 20 Abimelech is undeceived as a result of a divine communication given in a dream. We can conclude that this narrative theme is a contribution to the subject of relations between the semi-nomadic Israelites and the sedentary Canaanites – in Gunkel's terms it is an ethnological aetiology. The Canaanites are characterized as susceptible to feminine charm and so lacking in self-control that they would murder a husband in order to acquire a beautiful wife. In so far as they are driven to murder they exhibit scruples about avoiding the guilt of adultery. The story has its own particular Israelite orientation, for the narrator chuckles over the success of Isaac who is ultimately an object of special awe and deference for the Canaanites. In passing off his wife as his sister he had exposed them to the danger of adultery and they would leave him alone in the future.[1] The description of the area of Gerar as 'the country of the Philistines' (21.32) is probably an innovation of J, explained by the fact that this was the area which the Philistines subsequently occupied. It is not the view of Gen. 20 and 21 (E) that Abimelech was a Philistine.[2] He is the ruler of a city-state with whom the Isaac group have contacts of a friendly kind, regulated by agreements, in connexion with their search for summer pastures. This means that in the case of Abimelech and his officials we may have to reckon with historical characters who presided over the destiny of the city-state of Gerar at a time when the Isaac group appeared in this area. Another possibility is that these figures originate as a later literary elaboration of a folk tale. They are then typical figures of a Canaanite city-state bearing names which were familiar in this milieu in the Late Bronze Age. It is impossible to decide between one or other of these alternatives.[3]

Isaac is the one who receives the divine promise and who already tastes the blessings of the arable land. He knows how to acquire rights in this and that well and how to establish a *modus vivendi* with the settled population of Canaan. Not only is he a recipient of the Promise but he has taken the first steps towards its realization, and as such his cult is practised by semi-nomadic Israelite

---

[1] Cf. above, pp. 7-9.

[2] Cf. M. Noth, *op. cit.*, p. 171. The reference to the land of the Philistines occurs only in 21.32, 34 and these are secondary verses which give expression to an idea of J.

[3] *ibid.*, pp. 114-116, 171.

clans in the south. These stories do not furnish us with biographical details about an historical individual, but they do inform us
about Isaac as the founder of a cult whose god (*paḥad yiṣḥāq*)
issued a promise which has been partly fulfilled for his descendants.

There is no notice in Gen. 26 about the place where the god
appeared to Isaac, and the locality of the Isaac tradition cannot be
ascertained from the passage. Such a notice may have been a
victim of the literary compilation of the chapter which does not
show any particular interest in cultic sites.

According to Gen. 26 the district of Gerar (about twenty kilometres north-west of Beersheba) was frequented by Isaac in a time
of famine and this is interpreted by Noth as an ethnological aetiology – the worshippers of the 'god of Isaac' had their summer
pastures in the vicinity of Gerar. They made use of the wells of
Rehoboth in the valley of Gerar (v. 19), while other wells near by,
whose names are supplied but whose sites cannot be exactly fixed,
were claimed by the settled Canaanite population. The Israelites
also had a share in the well of Beersheba (vv. 23, 25b-33). If Gerar
is to be equated with Tell-esh-Sheri'a, Beersheba cannot have belonged to its territory, and the drawing of Abimelech and his
officials into the Beersheba story, which is concerned to supply an
aetiology for the name Beersheba, is the consequence of a tendency
to attach all the Isaac stories to Gerar and its king.

One would have expected in chapter 26, in connexion with the
promise made to Isaac, an indication of the place where the god
appeared to him and also a notice about the erection of a pillar and
an altar at a place which would be hallowed for ever after. This,
as already suggested, may have fallen out in the process of the
literary compilation of the pieces of the Isaac tradition. From
26.7-11 it would appear that Isaac was resident in the town of
Gerar, but this impression has been created by the literary compilation itself and is connected with the attraction of all the Isaac
traditions to that place. It can hardly have been the intention of
the original tradition to represent that Isaac lived in the city, but
rather that he had connexions with localities which were within
the territorial limits of the city-state. So far as we know Gerar
had no sanctuary at which Israelites worshipped and to which
stories about the god of Isaac could have been attached.

According to Gen. 24.62a and 25.11b (J) Isaac dwelt in Beer
Lahai Roi before a famine forced him to go to Gerar. These notices

do not belong to the nucleus of the old narratives and are clearly
of literary origin. They show, however, that an original connexion
between Isaac and Beer Lahai Roi was still posited at the time of
literary compilation and fixation. The J account of the Ishmael
story in Gen. 16* establishes a connexion between the birth of
Ishmael and the well of Lahai Roi. In respect of its content (i.e.,
as a birth story) and its association with Beer Lahai Roi it preserves
the Ishmael story in a more original form than the E version
(21.8-21). In the history of the tradition Ishmael was first the
brother of Isaac and only secondarily the son of Abraham. In
Gen. 21.8 ff. what is retained is original in so far as Ishmael and
Isaac are juxtaposed, while in Gen. 16 the Hagar and Ishmael story
has, for reasons unknown to us, been transported into the period
before the birth of Isaac. Isaac and Ishmael are 'brothers' in that
they are founders of cults both of which are localized at Beer Lahai
Roi. There the worshippers of the god of Isaac and the god of
Ishmael had rights in the well and each group identified the god
of the founder with the local deity El Roi (Gen. 16.13, J).

The figure of Ishmael gained admission to the patriarchal traditions only because of this link with Isaac. We have to suppose an
original Ishmaelite tradition according to which the nomadic cult
founder Ishmael was born in the desert at a sanctuary where a
deity revealed a well to his mother (in Gen. 21.19 this original
element of the tradition is maintained). In virtue of this theophany
the holiness of the place was confirmed for all time. To the Ishmaelite foundation of the narrative belongs also, presumably, the
theme of Promise to the mother concerning the future descendants
of the child. Thus the Ishmael story features a well and mentions
the place Beer Lahai Roi. Isaac is also associated with wells in the
areas of Gerar and Beersheba and this is a reflection of the stage
of culture which had been reached by the worshippers of the
god of Isaac. The locality of Beer Lahai Roi is associated with both
Isaac and Ishmael and we know from the name itself and from the
Ishmael story that a well was sited there. It is likely then that the
'brotherhood' of Isaac and Ishmael is best explained by the assumption that the two groups had come into contact at the well
and sanctuary of Beer Lahai Roi. The worshippers of *paḥad yiṣḥāq*
had attached their cult to this sanctuary on the ground that Isaac's
god (presumably now identified with the local El Roi) had appeared to him there with the promise of land and descendants.

The Ishmaelite tribes or clans were attached to the sanctuary, because they narrated that there El Roi had revealed the well to Hagar and had made the promise that her son would be the progenitor of a great people.

The site of Beer Lahai Roi cannot be exactly determined. According to Gen. 16.14 (J) it lies between 'Kadesh and Bered', but this can tell us no more than that it was a well on the caravan route between these two places. Hence all we can say is that Beer Lahai Roi was located in the Negeb, the area of desert and pasture south of the arable land of west Jordan. The Isaac stories were taken up into the Pentateuch to enrich the theme of 'Promise to the Fathers' which had already been treated in the Jacob stories. Since the Isaac stories deal with the occupation of areas on the borders of the settled land which were sought as summer pastures, they represent a more primitive treatment of the theme of Promise than that which appears in the west Jordan Jacob traditions where the promise operates within areas of sedentary life.[1]

If much that belonged to Isaac has been transferred to Abraham, the original compass of the Abraham traditions has to be considered. The narratives which are attached to Mamre-Hebron do not belong originally to the Abraham tradition. They arise in connexion with the secondary transfer of the figure of Abraham to the central sanctuary of the southern tribes. This is still unknown to G and is first introduced by J as special material into the Pentateuch as part of the Abraham-Lot saga. This saga is not a purely literary creation, but is based on a narrative which has developed through processes of oral tradition and which has a popular foundation. Nevertheless, it belongs to a relatively late stage of the history of the tradition of the patriarchal narratives as is confirmed by its expansive literary style.

Since grave traditions often disclose the original home of the nucleus of a complex of tradition, we might suppose that the grave tradition of Gen. 23 (P) concerning the cave of Machpelah ('double cave') is old and original. But for the patriarchs, as recipients of the Promise, the nucleus of the tradition is the holy place of theophany and not the grave. Thus there is no grave tradition for Isaac nor is there one for the west Jordan Jacob. The grave tradition attaching to the east Jordan Jacob could not subsequently have arisen if one had existed for the earlier west Jordan Jacob. The

---

[1] M. Noth, *op. cit.*, pp. 117-120.

Abraham grave tradition arises as a consequence of the attraction of a local story to the figure of Abraham and this could only have taken place after the transfer of the figure of Abraham to Hebron. In Gen. 23 P worked over a tradition which had come down to him concerning the grave of Abraham. In its earlier form it was probably a story of a double grave for Abraham and Sarah, and out of this P made the story of the grave which Abraham sought out for Sarah and in which subsequently Abraham himself and the other patriarchs and their wives were buried (cf. Gen, 49.31, P).

If the stories about Abraham connected with Hebron are left out, there remains the material which is common to J and E (i.e., the G material, according to Noth), but original Abraham traditions are hard to find in this. The story of a wife passed off as a sister belongs originally to Isaac, and similarly the story of a conflict with the king of Gerar over a well at Beersheba, together with the aetiologies of that name (21.25 ff.). The Ishmael story belongs from the outset to Isaac and its present connexion with Abraham assumes the genealogical scheme Jacob-Isaac-Abraham. It cannot therefore be an original constituent of the Abraham story prior to the stage where Abraham and Isaac were related. The same is true of the narrative about the birth of Isaac (21.1 ff.) and of the expanded narrative concerning the acquisition of a bride for Isaac (Gen. 24).

There remains Gen. 15 whose literary-critical analysis is difficult and the discovery of whose place in the tradition is a complicated task. It appears to constitute the introduction to the patriarchal narratives in G and so the introduction to the entire Pentateuchal narrative in that source. This introduction contains as a kernel of tradition the account of a theophany to Abraham with the promise of descendants and land. This is the fundamental theme of 'Promise to the Fathers' and the fact that Abraham and Isaac (like Jacob) are founders of 'god of the fathers' cults is the common factor which explains why Abraham becomes the magnet for stories which were originally told about Isaac.

The appearance of this god to Abraham must have been attached to a place, but we do not know its location. The notice about Beersheba in Gen. 22.19 (E) should be discounted, because it arises in connexion with the special E material in 22.1 ff. and goes back no further than the literary work of E in 21.22 ff. The notice about the place of Abraham's theophany has perhaps been lost conse-

quent on the use of Gen. 15 as a general introduction to the patriarchal history and so to the entire Pentateuch. All that we can
conclude from J (12.9; 13.1; 20.1a) is that Abraham belongs to the
Negeb. The fusion of the Abraham and Isaac stories is to be explained partly by the circumstance that they belonged to neighbouring areas. The worshippers of the god of Abraham had come
into contact with the worshippers of the god of Isaac in the vicinity
of Gerar and at the wells beside Beersheba and had appropriated
the Isaac traditions.[1] Isaac was not entirely suppressed because he
had become a figure of Pentateuchal (i.e., of all-Israelite) stature
before this attraction of Isaac traditions to Abraham took place.
Abraham having himself acquired a like status by becoming the
father of Isaac, then assumed the role of supreme Father and so
much Isaac material was then attached to him that Isaac stories
now appear as if they were doublets of Abraham stories, although
in reality they represent an earlier stage of the history of the
tradition.

When Abraham became the supreme Father, he was the principal subject of stories told at the central sanctuary of the six-tribe
amphictyony at Mamre-Hebron,[2] including not only original Isaac
stories, but also local stories which were already old when Hebron
became the central sanctuary of the southern tribes. As in the case
of the east Jordan Jacob narratives we have to do here with material
which has no intrinsic connexion with the theme of Promise.
Questions which were suggested by the view from the heights of
the west Jordan mountains eastwards towards the Dead Sea with
its surrounding wilderness, and further east towards the mountains
of trans-Jordan, were answered in aetiological narratives about a
terrible divine judgement executed on a once flourishing city in a
region of paradisial fertility of which the magnificent oasis of the
lower Jordan valley appeared as an isolated, truncated residue.

There were stories about the origin of the occupation of the east
Jordan mountains by those who happily escaped from the great
divine judgement; about the intimation of this judgement to a man
who lived in the west Jordan mountains at Mamre, who unlike the
rich and corrupt inhabitants of Sodom was pious and who – this is
a well-known and widely distributed narrative motif – observing

---

[1] Cf. Alt, above, pp. 111 f.
[2] Judah, Simeon, Caleb, Othniel, Jerachmeel and Cain, see M. Noth, *Das
System der zwölf Stämme Israels*, pp. 107 f.

the duty of hospitality had treated divine beings with kindness, although he did not know who they were. Stories arose about the relationship of this pious man to those few who because of their righteousness escaped from the doomed city at the last moment and who then became the progenitors of the inhabitants of the east Jordan mountains. The kernel of the great narrative composition of Gen. 18-19 was the account of the destruction of the city below in the valley, but it is no longer possible to trace its growth step by step. It is not clear how much was already there when the figure of Abraham came into its ambit and how much further development there was subsequent to Abraham's attraction to it.

It is at least clear that we are here far removed from the central motif of the patriarchal history (Promise to the Fathers) and we have to reckon with a kind of narrative material which has originated and developed independently of this motif. Its home is in the heights of the Judaean mountains, west of the Jordan, at Mamre, and there is no reason to suppose that it originated within the circle of the Israelite tribes. After the old tree sanctuary at Mamre became the sanctuary of the southern Israelite tribes, this material made its way into the Israelite tradition and the figure of Abraham was established at its centre. This certainly happened at a relatively late stage of the history of the tradition of the patriarchal narratives. We may suppose that the absence of Abraham from this material in G and his presence in J is susceptible of a simple chronological explanation, namely, that at the time of G the material was still unrelated to Abraham. We are not, however, to conclude that the connexion of Abraham with these stories was achieved by J, as an aspect of the final literary fixation of the Pentateuchal tradition, since there are clear traces of organic growth in the final shaping of the tradition. The literary work of J in Gen. 18-19 is distinguishable as an addition to the body of the popular narrative already related to Abraham which J had taken over.

Still later – if we can again employ the first literary appearance as a criterion – there follows in P (Gen. 23) the popular story of Abraham's and Sarah's grave which has arisen out of the local phenomenon of a double grave (Machpelah) in the field of Ephron beside Hebron. Once Abraham had been transferred to Hebron the conditions were created for the attachment of a story about him and his wife to this local phenomenon. The double cave had from the outset, and independent of Abraham and Sarah, encouraged the thought of a double grave. A local story about a double grave is so developed that Abraham is represented as having acquired the cave for the burial of Sarah, who has just died, a place being left for him to lie alongside her. The scene in which he acquires it is so elaborated that the grave now appears as Sarah's in the first place, although neither in the Hebron story nor elsewhere had Sarah an independent role to play, so that a special grave tradition for her is not to be expected. This can only have come about because the appearance of the cave required the thought of a double grave. At the same time it is clear that there lies behind Gen. 23 a process of oral tradition in the course of which the narrative has gradually developed and that P has simply given a final literary form to the material which he has taken over. The Rachel grave tradition is a different case, since, as the tribal mother of the Rachel tribes, she acquired an importance of her own and there was a particular motive to site her grave on the border between the areas occupied by the tribes of Joseph (Ephraim and Manasseh) and Benjamin.

The special E material which comprises the story in Gen. 22.1-19 stands apart from the history of the Pentateuchal traditions. There is no reason to doubt that it too was a narrative which was transmitted by popular and oral processes. For the rest, so much of it is enigmatic that its place in the history of the Pentateuchal tradition can no longer be ascertained. Its local attachment is unknown; according to E it is to be located at the place Yahweh-yireh[1] in the land of Moriah (v. 14), three days journey from Beersheba. There is probably at the base of the story a custom at the holy place in question, which is known elsewhere, of the substitution of an animal sacrifice (a ram) for the sacrifice of a first-born son (cf. Ex. 34.20b – the first-born of an ass is to be redeemed by a sheep). It appeared as if the child were to be sacrificed, but, at the last minute, as he lay bound on the altar, a ram was substituted for him. Part of the aetiology of this substitution is a theophany. It is not clear whether the figure of Abraham was connected with this aetiological tale from the outset and the question where and why Abraham became the centre of the story must remain unanswered. It may be that the name of the son was not originally given and that Abraham's association with the story precedes the point at

---

[1] Perhaps, according to Noth, a corruption of the original name dictated by the exigencies of the aetiology.

which he became the father of Isaac. The fact that the narrative is found only in E suggests that it is not an old component of the Abraham traditions, and this conclusion is supported by the other circumstance that it is far removed from the theme of Promise. As with the Hebron stories (J) Abraham had already achieved the rank of founding father of Israel when this material was connected with his person.[1]

IV

Those named in Gen. 38 as sons of Judah are doubtless eponyms of the clans which made up the tribal confederacy of Judah. Er and Onan represent older clans which no longer retain their independence, while Shelah, Perez and Zerah are the chief Judaean clans at the time of the origin of the narrative.[2] This chapter is not an account of earlier tribal history clothed in the garment of family history. It does not inform us about the past of these clans but about their inter-relationships at the time when the account was written. The aspect of personification is therefore related to an aetiological concern and is not a convention whereby past tribal history is metamorphosed into family history. Hence, although the aetiology has the form of an historical narrative, it has no authentic historical dimension and it operates on a flat, contemporary surface. Thus the point is not that the other clans as 'sons' of Judah come on the scene later than Judah; rather as 'sons' of Judah they are at the time of writing members of a tribal confederacy which bears the name Judah. The aetiology therefore tells us nothing about the past of Judah or of any of the other tribes and clans mentioned, but only about their present organization into a tribal confederacy which it explains by means of a family analogy – Judah (the name of the confederacy) is the 'father' and the component tribes or clans are his 'sons'.

The same kind of explanation probably holds for Hirah of Adullam (38.12) and the Canaanite Bathshua ('daughter of Shua') whom Judah is said to have married (38.2). This notice of Judah's marriage may reflect a connubium between the Judahite residents of Kezib (v. 5) and the neighbouring Canaanites of whom Shua was an eponym. The friendship of Judah with Hirah of Adullam may have its foundation in a similar relationship – perhaps a cove-

---

[1] M. Noth, *Überlieferungsgeschichte des Pentateuch*, pp. 120-127.
[2] Cf. above, pp. 67, 73.

nant between the Judahites and an Adullamite clan of whom Hirah was an eponym.[1]

Further Rachel and Leah do not function within the system of the twelve tribes as the personifications of tribal groups. They do not as 'mothers' of Israelite tribes reflect a historical period earlier than that in which the tribes themselves came into existence. The history of these tribes begins in central Palestine, west of the Jordan, and the west Jordan Jacob acquires the status of 'father' of these tribes at Shechem, where they confess that they have entered into the promise of land and descendants once made to Jacob by his god. But Rachel and Leah only emerge with the development of the Jacob traditions east of the Jordan in connexion with the narrative elaboration of the Jacob-Laban story. Hence they only achieve their rank as 'mothers' of Israelite tribes once the east Jordan Jacob traditions were combined with their west Jordan counterparts. It was the key position occupied by the west Jordan Jacob traditions in the Pentateuch which brought the two Aramaean wives of the east Jordan Jacob more into the forefront than other women who appear in the narratives. As presumably pure, artistic creations they appear along with their two slave girls, Bilhah and Zilpah. In so far as Rachel and Leah reflect historical conditions these are the conditions of the Ephraimites in east Jordan and their dealings with Aramaean neighbours. Even then, Rachel and Leah belong to an advanced stage of the development of the east Jordan Jacob tradition and are products of literary invention and elaboration rather than a mirror of the conditions of life of the Ephraimite colonists in east Jordan.[2] Rebecca (perhaps a dialectal form of bikrā 'young she-camel') belongs like Jacob's wives to an Aramaean family and in the story of her acquisition as Isaac's bride the same motive of relatedness to the Aramaeans as played a part in the Jacob story again operates. The Israelites have a kin relation with the Aramaeans and this is a way of emphasizing their non-relatedness to the Canaanites. It cannot be doubted that this aspect of Gen. 24 is a secondary parallel to the Jacob story in which the Aramaean connexions are original, and this process is a consequence of the general, reciprocal equalizing of the figures of the Fathers. Rebecca is an ad hoc figure–a product of literary inventiveness.[3]

[1] M. Noth., *op. cit.*, pp. 162 f.; cf. Eissfeldt, above, p. 73.
[2] Cf. above, pp. 86 f., 99 f.
[3] M. Noth, *op. cit.*, pp. 165-167.

The Lot narratives have had a complicated prehistory as can be gathered at once from the uncle-nephew relationship which can hardly have been an original feature of a folk tale. Haran, who in the final form of the story is Abraham's brother and Lot's father, must originally have had a more significant and essential role which has been taken over later by his son, Lot. In the stories which were transmitted about Lot disparate elements have been joined together. The location is Hebron, but the stories are about the fate of the Dead Sea area and so are derived from east Jordan traditions.

The name Haran cannot be dissociated from Beth Haran on the eastern edge of the Jordan valley at the outlet of the Wadi *Hesbān* into the Jordan valley, a few kilometres from the north end of the Dead Sea. Haran was one of the settled oases which encouraged the idea that the area had once been fertile and that there were only a few remains of this fertility. On this view the Dead Sea had come into existence as a consequence of a catastrophic divine judgement executed against the inhabitants of these parts which brought about the destruction of Sodom and Gomorrah. Haran was originally the name of a local deity worshipped at Haran. Later, and perhaps outside the limits of Haran, Beth Haran was taken to mean 'residence of Haran' rather than 'temple of Haran', and Haran was portrayed as a pious man who had escaped from the disaster which had overtaken the region and had found asylum in Beth Haran. We can no longer ascertain how a relationship between Beth Haran and Hebron originated which could lead to the story that in Hebron-Mamre there lived another pious man who was Haran's brother. We must, at any rate, assume that a secondary understanding of the name Beth Haran was taken up in Hebron, since the story which we have in Genesis originated and was developed there.

This secondary understanding of the name Beth Haran in Hebron probably rests on the fact that among the settled oases of the lower Jordan valley which were known there only Beth Haran would suggest a connexion with a personal name. Hence it would be posited that the brother of the pious man of Hebron-Mamre, who had settled in the once paradisial region down in the valley, and who had escaped from the catastrophe which overtook it, became the progenitor of those who now lived in the region of the Dead Sea. The fact that there were still scattered settlements in this area must have given rise to the thought that one person at least had escaped from the general destruction. Certainly he had escaped with his life and nothing else, while his brother – so they would take pleasure in telling at Hebron – had chosen a home which was not so fertile but which proved to be safer and more enduring.

It is at this point that the figure of Lot emerges. Originally he was the centre of an independent local tradition which was attached to a cave beside Zoar (modern *Ghōr-eṣ-ṣāfi*) at the southern end of the Dead Sea. This local tradition would become known in Hebron because of the caravan traffic which moved between Hebron and the south-east area of the Dead Sea. It is no longer possible to ascertain the original content of the kernel of this tradition and the meaning of the name Lot is obscure. At any rate the nucleus of the narrative in Gen. 19.30-38 will have been attached originally to Lot who lived in a cave along with his daughters and who, for reasons unknown to us, became the eponym of those who occupied the mountainous country above Zoar. The narrative perhaps comes from a period when the area of south-east Jordan had not yet been occupied by Edomites, Moabites and Ammonites. The derivation of the Moabites and the Ammonites from Lot's daughter with the aetiologies of their names in Gen. 19.37 f. rests on a later elaboration of the narratives, since the Ammonites, at least, dwelt too far away from the cave to have had an original place in the story. Only subsequently, and from the point of view of Hebron-Mamre, there arose the thought of the Moabites and Ammonites who in the interval had settled on the opposite side of the Dead Sea.

After the local story of the cave beside Zoar had become known at Hebron-Mamre as an aetiology of the origin of those who lived east of the Jordan, it was a small step to connect it with the story of Haran who had been portrayed independently as the progenitor of those who lived in the environs of the Dead Sea. Since the Haran story was probably the earlier of the two, it was quite appropriate that Lot should be represented as the son of Haran and so the nephew of the pious man of Hebron-Mamre in whose place Abraham later appeared. The story of Lot contained more concrete details than that of Haran and so Lot became the more popular character of the two in Hebron-Mamre and soon attracted to himself the entire content of the Haran story, namely, the settlement in the paradisial region which later became the Dead Sea and the escape from the catastrophe in which this area was engulfed. This was facilitated by the circumstance that both Haran and Lot, as progenitors of those who had settled around the Dead Sea, had been allotted identical roles in their respective and originally independent traditions.[1]

V

Noth's treatment of the Joseph story[2] may be conveniently considered at this point. The patriarchal history flows out towards the Joseph story which deals extensively with the emigration of the patriarchal family to Egypt and which is loosely connected with the 'Deliverance from Egypt' theme by the remark that there arose finally in Egypt a king who did not recognize Joseph's worth (Ex. 1.8, J) and that the family of Jacob had, in the interval, grown into a strong and numerous people (Ex. 1.7, P; 1.9, J). The Joseph story, which is a masterpiece of narrative art, is a late arrival in the history of the Pentateuchal tradition as is shown by its function as a connecting link between the two themes 'Promise to the Fathers' and 'Deliverance from Egypt'. The extant form of the 'Little Creed' (Deut. 26.5-9) contains no reference to it: all we are told is that Jacob went down to Egypt or that Jacob and his sons went down to Egypt (Josh. 24.4) – perhaps impelled by famine. To this corresponds the circumstance that the Joseph story is the most finished and best articulated of all the Pentateuchal narratives. The elements which constitute it are so combined that it is no longer possible to separate them into independent units, and hence the story gives the impression of having been created *ab initio* as a complicated work of art rather than of having reached its present complexity by a process of fusing originally independent elements.

The story as we have it is not the consequence of elaboration in oral tradition, since no kernel from which such a growth could have taken place is discoverable. The story, therefore, was conceived as an artistic whole and this whole is a relatively independent complex of material which could have been told for its own sake. It presupposes, however, as something which is assumed to be generally known, although it is not explicitly mentioned, the tradition about the emigration of Jacob and his family to Egypt, and

[1] M. Noth, *op. cit.*, pp. 167-170.
[2] M. Noth, *ibid.*, pp. 226-232.

so the ordering into a series of two of the great Pentateuchal
themes – 'Promise to the Fathers' and 'Deliverance from Egypt'.
In this way the positioning of the Joseph story within the process
of growth of the Pentateuchal narrative is fairly clearly determined.
It does not belong properly to any of the major themes; neither in
its original nor in its secondarily developed content does it belong
to the patriarchal theme, apart from sharing the circle of personalities on whom the dramatic working-out of this theme depends.
Again it is only loosely connected with the theme 'Deliverance
from Egypt'. It is best described as the result of an ample artistic
development of what functions as a connecting piece between these
two themes.

The use of universal narrative motifs to which Gunkel and
Gressmann[1] have called attention is conditioned in a particular
way. We are not dealing here with the attachment of those universal motifs (the badly used younger brother who eventually gets
the better of his older brothers; the slave who becomes the highest
minister of the land) to a particular historical person in the course
of a process of story-telling, with a view to achieving the most
concrete representation possible and enriching the tradition concerning this person. Rather the impetus for the construction of
the Joseph story is supplied by presuppositions given by the
Pentateuchal themes and their inter-connectedness. Jacob and his
sons had once been in Egypt (Josh. 24.4). How did this come
about? Such a question could well arouse the power of imagination
of a gifted story-teller. So there was developed by means of universal narrative motifs the wide-ranging and artistically constructed
Joseph story.

How did it come about that among all the sons of Jacob it was
Joseph who became the centre of interest? Joseph was not the
youngest brother and so the narrative motif concerning the youngest brother, who is his father's favourite and who awakens the
hostility of his older brothers, does not explain this choice. The
system of the twelve tribes is older than the connexion of their
eponyms with Jacob, and so from the outset the entire series of
twelve tribes must have been associated with Jacob. In the Joseph
story, however, Benjamin is represented as being so young that
he does not play an independent role; he is closely connected with
Joseph, but he does not count as an independent person. Through

[1] Cf. above, pp. 101-103.

this setting aside of Benjamin as a brother in his own right, Joseph is portrayed as a quasi-youngest son. Hence the motif of the youngest son does not properly apply to Joseph and the ingenuity and artistry of the author is exercised in order to present Joseph as effectively the youngest son, and this is done by denying Benjamin sonship in his own right. If this is a correct account of the matter, the original reason for the choice of Joseph cannot have been that he was the youngest son and must therefore have been determined by other considerations. He has been secondarily attracted into the rôle of the youngest son and this has been achieved by the conscious literary device of placing Benjamin in the shade of Joseph.

The setting apart of Benjamin from the other brothers is a secondary feature which has its cause in the treatment of Benjamin in the Joseph story. It can be seen in his omission from Gen. 29.31-30.24 and in his association with the story of the death of his mother which has an original attachment to the site of Rachel's grave. The explanation of the late birth of Benjamin, which is still widespread to-day, is the relic of a long antiquated premise that the details of the patriarchal stories represent the transposition into personal relationships of the history of tribes.[1] The late birth of Benjamin is then elucidated as the circumstance that the tribe of Benjamin was constituted for the first time in Canaan through a division of the 'House of Joseph'. But all the tribes were constituted for the first time on the soil of Canaan and the twelve-tribe system, including Benjamin, is the primary datum of the tradition, while the details about the births of the tribal eponyms are, on the other hand, secondary.[2]

Further, the emergence of Joseph cannot be explained, as was believed at an earlier period, by the fact that the House of Joseph in particular or the entire group of Rachel tribes were the only part of the later confederation of Israelite tribes which had been in Egypt. Such a piece of historical information is not to be expected from the Joseph story which belongs to a late stage of the history of the Pentateuchal tradition. Long before its appearance, and at an earlier stage of the tradition, it was already affirmed that all of Israel had been in Egypt. In other words the theme 'Deliverance from Egypt' had become an all-Israelite theme at a much earlier

[1] Cf. my criticism of Eissfeldt, above, pp. 85 ff.
[2] Cf. above, pp. 99 f.

stage of the history of the tradition than that which is represented by the Joseph story. It is to be noted particularly that the credal kernel of the Joseph story (Josh. 24.4) is not about Joseph by himself but about all the sons of Jacob. It was not just Joseph who emigrated to Egypt but 'Jacob and his sons'. It is inconceivable that there was an earlier form of the story according to which only Joseph arrived in Egypt, since the final appearance of the brothers before Joseph in Egypt and their settlement there under his magnanimous protection belongs so essentially to the necessary constitution of the whole that without this ending it should never have been told.

That the choice among Jacob's sons fell on Joseph has its explanation in the simple circumstance that the Joseph story originated and was developed in the circle of the House of Joseph. The original central Palestinian story of Jacob and his twelve sons was enriched by the Joseph *Novelle* in the milieu of the central tribes, just as the original patriarchal figure of Jacob was resumed by those of Isaac and Abraham who were then given precedence over him. By means of the Joseph story the west Jordan Jacob tradition was connected to the theme 'Deliverance from Egypt'. The Joseph story does not have individual traditions with attachments to particular sites as its foundation. It is rather constructed out of universal narrative motifs. Nevertheless, there is an indication in the mention of Dothan (Gen. 37.17; modern Tell Dōthān, cf. II Kings 6.13) that at the beginning of the Joseph story Jacob and his family were thought of as living in the mountain country of Ephraim and particularly in the region of Shechem, that is, in the territorial area of the House of Joseph. The mention of the valley of Hebron (Gen. 37.14) is secondary; it is to be connected with the combination of separate patriarchal stories which brought Jacob finally to Hebron which had become the site of important Abraham traditions. Alternatively it may be a redactional adjustment related to the mention of Hebron-Mamre (35.27, P) which has had the effect of suppressing the place originally mentioned. According to 37.14 Joseph came to Shechem and he probably began his journey from a place within the territory of the House of Joseph. The arrival at Shechem is the point at which the Joseph story had its origins. The theophany granted to Jacob at Beersheba (46.1-5,* E) comes expressly from the god of his father Isaac and belongs again to a secondary narrative which conflates the patri-

archal figures and which feels the necessity to report the presence
of Jacob at the sanctuaries of Isaac and Abraham. It does not
therefore show that the beginnings of the Joseph story were in
south Judah or that the story was thought to have originated there.

Alone among all the sons of Jacob, Joseph is the one who made
his fortune. From being the son of a Palestinian shepherd who was
badly treated by his brothers he rose to be the all-powerful
minister of the great and rich land of Egypt. From such an eponym
the House of Joseph took its rise and as he was separated from his
brothers (Gen. 49.26; Deut. 33.16), so the House of Joseph, in its
own estimation, and, for a time, in its actual historical significance,
occupied the first place among the Israelite tribes. The dreams in
Gen. 37.5 ff. were told in order to supply motivation for the
jealousy and hatred of the remaining sons of Jacob. They make the
narrative work by furnishing grounds for the subsequent actions
of Joseph's brothers. They would, however, be narrated within the
House of Joseph with the thought that they constituted a predic-
tion not only of Joseph's position within the circle of his brothers,
but also of his successors within the circle of the tribes.

The Joseph story reaches its goal with the rise of Joseph to
power in Egypt and it is told for the greater glory of his descendants who are united in the House of Joseph. Within the context
of the Pentateuchal narratives it is no more than an episode without
considerable consequences. In the last scene Joseph is simply
again one among his brothers. The end is reached in a scene of
final reconciliation with his brothers after his father's death and
this is followed by his own death (50.15-26, E). In his death he is no
longer one of the highest ministers in Egypt but one of Jacob's
sons, albeit the one singled out by God. Thus the Joseph story is
an independent structure which originates in the House of Joseph
in accordance with the presuppositions supplied by the connected
Pentateuchal narrative. It then, however, in terms of the narrative
motif which it has appropriated, develops according to its own
laws without marked deference to the composite Pentateuchal
narrative and grows into a special and comprehensive narrative
complex.

VI

The point at which the connecting pieces are inserted in order to
make an interconnected whole of the patriarchal history is near to

the period of literary fixation.[1] Often it is no longer possible to make out whether a particular connecting piece belongs to a development which is still oral or is to be reckoned as a literary contribution. On the whole, however, the joining together of the elements of tradition should be attributed to the pre-literary stage of development.

The theme 'Promise to the Fathers' is complete in itself and stands apart in a position of relative isolation from the other themes. Within it there is a fusion of the three figures of the patriarchs and narratives about each have been transferred from one to the other. Nearly all that was told about Isaac has been attracted to Abraham and almost nothing that was told originally about the latter has been retained. This process of fusing the three figures of the patriarchs belongs to the pre-Pentateuchal (i.e., pre-literary) stage of the construction of south Judaean traditions. The genealogical connexion between Abraham and Isaac joined to the narrative motif of the barrenness of the mother, which allows the birth of the son to appear as a special gift, has been worked secondarily into the Hebron stories (Gen. 18.9-15, J).

The most important factor in this connexion is the transfer of features which belonged originally to the central Palestinian Jacob to the south Palestinian figures of Isaac and Abraham. Abraham is represented as having associations with Shechem and Bethel (Gen. 12.6, 8), sanctuaries which had an original association with Jacob.[2] The motif of the 'journey' which originated in the pilgrimage from Shechem to Bethel within the Jacob tradition[3] was also transferred to Abraham who was portrayed as journeying from north to south, a representation which may have given an impetus to the preference for the Hebron stories, which belong to a late stage of the Abraham tradition, over the older Abraham stories.

Another important departure was the carrying over of the Aramaean connexions of Jacob into the traditions about Isaac and Abraham. As south Judaeans these two had originally nothing to do with Aramaeans. The thought arose in connexion with the story of Jacob's marriage to two Aramaean women and their status as 'mothers' of the Israelite tribes that the Israelites were related to the Aramaeans who lived on the eastern edges of the arable land

---

[1] M. Noth, *op. cit.*, pp. 216-219.
[2] Cf. Eissfeldt, above, pp. 109 f.
[3] Above, p. 120.

of Palestine. The thought was historically not inappropriate, that is to say, there are general ethnic connexions between the Israelites and the Aramaeans and the Israelites may be reckoned as part of an Aramaean immigration.[1] In Noth's view, however, it is not an historical interest which leads to the establishment of this relationship between the Aramaeans and the patriarchs. It is rather the inner history of the tradition, whose laws are not those of historiography, which explains why all of the patriarchs are represented as having Aramaean connexions. What was originally told of Jacob influences what was told of Isaac and Abraham. Thus Isaac too has an Aramaean wife, and the masterly story of Gen. 24, whose discursiveness shows that it belongs to a late stage of the tradition and whose beginning originally presupposed that Abraham was at the point of death, appears within the circle of the patriarchal stories.[2]

With this extension on the patriarchal side of the originally local and bounded relations between Jacob and Laban there goes a corresponding widening of the horizons on the Aramaean side. After the town of Harran had become known as an Aramaean centre through contacts with merchants travelling in caravans, Laban, who was at first the neighbour of the east Jordan Jacob, was transferred to Harran (Gen. 27.43; 28.10; 29.4). Thus neighbourly relations were transformed into a kin relationship and this had the consequence that the patriarchs themselves, who were not settled in the land of Canaan but had the promise of it for their descendants, were represented as originating from the circle of those Aramaeans to whom they were said to be related and so as having come from their territory. Hence, according to P, Abraham came out of Harran and journeyed to Palestine (Gen. 11.31 f.; 12.4b, 5). In this way something which is historically appropriate is adumbrated (i.e., the Aramaean origins of Israel), but the basis is not historiographical enquiry. The final view of the relations of the patriarchs to the Aramaeans has been reached by traditio-historical processes which derive from the Jacob-Laban story. The ultimate historical basis is the territorial contiguity of Ephraimite colonists and Aramaeans in east Jordan.

The reverse process whereby elements of Isaac and Abraham traditions find their way into the Jacob story occurs only rarely.

[1] Cf. above, p, 4, n. 2.
[2] Cf. above, p. 143.

All that need be noted in this connexion is the association established between Jacob and *paḥad yiṣḥāq* whose attachment is with southern Judah, especially Beer Lahai Roi (Gen. 31.42, 53).

A fusion between the other Pentateuchal themes and the patriarchal narratives is to be found only in Gen. 15 which belongs to a late stage of the history of the tradition. The procedure of concluding a covenant, the manifestations of smoke and fire which are indicative of the presence of God, and especially the representation of a covenant between God and man, are derived from the Sinai theophany. Gen. 15 does not belong to the old content of the Abraham tradition; it is a later preface to the Abraham stories or probably to the entire story of the patriarchs, preceding, however, the attachment of Abraham to the Hebron stories. It introduces in a special, ceremonial way the fundamental motif of the patriarchal history – the promise of descendants and of land for those descendants. The theme 'Revelation at Sinai' has supplied significant features of the portrayal and the already complete plan of a unified Pentateuch is adumbrated, that is, the fulfilment of the Promise made to the patriarchs will follow in the other major themes ('Deliverance from Egypt', 'Guidance through the Desert' and 'Possession of Canaan') into which the Sinai tradition has been incorporated.

VII

The brilliance of Noth's analysis and the relentless manner in which he pursues his hypothesis compel admiration. It has been noted[1] that the premise which he takes from von Rad, namely that the scaffolding for the structure of the Pentateuch is supplied by a 'Little Creed', influences profoundly the shape of his history of the tradition of the Pentateuch. This feature of von Rad's form-critical analysis of the Hexateuch and Noth's history of the tradition of the Pentateuch has been subjected to searching scrutiny and doubt has been cast on the validity of such a point of departure.[2] The aspect of these expressions of doubt which applies particularly to Noth's criticism of the patriarchal narratives is the use which he makes of the patriarchal article of the postulated 'Little Creed'. There is no doubt that his account of the history of

---

[1] Above, pp. 112 f.

[2] A. Weiser, *Introduction to the Old Testament* (1961), pp. 83-89 (a translation by D. M. Barton of *Einleitung in das alte Testament (4)*, 1957); A. van der Woude,

the tradition of the patriarchal narratives begins with the clause in Deut. 26.5, 'A wandering Aramaean was my father'. This does not, however, entail that the clause is an indispensable prop and that his account would collapse if it were taken away. Nor does it seem to me to be reasonable to assert that the history of the tradition of the patriarchal narratives which he offers would never have occurred to him if he had not found a clue in Deut. 26.5. A more fundamental assumption, and one which exercises a greater control on his enterprise, is that the history of the tradition of the patriarchal stories begins at Shechem within a twelve-tribe Yahwistic framework into which Jacob, as the founder of the cult of *'ᵃbîr yaʻᵃqōb*, has been integrated. Hence what principally determines the direction of Noth's work on the patriarchal narratives is the relation which he establishes between the Jacob traditions and his hypothesis, developed in an earlier work,[1] that Shechem was the first central sanctuary of a twelve-tribe Yahwistic amphictyony. His view is that the beginning of the history of the tradition of the patriarchal narratives is post-amphictyonic. Since the beginning of the history of the Jacob tradition is the absolute beginning of the history of the tradition of the patriarchal narratives, the historical circumstances reflected in the unfolding history of that tradition are everywhere 'Israelite', that is, post-settlement and post-amphictyonic.[2]

The special place occupied by the Jacob stories in Noth's history of the tradition of the patriarchal narratives can be illustrated by a comparison of Gunkel and Noth. Gunkel supposes that the east Jordan Jacob is prior to the west Jordan Jacob and that the vocational stories about Jacob and Esau (Jacob, the shepherd, and Esau, the hunter) constitute the beginning of the history of the

---

Uittocht en Sinai (1960); Th. C. Vriezen, 'The Credo in the Old Testament', Volume of the Sixth Annual Congress of the Society for Old Testament Study in South Africa (1962), pp. 5-17; C. H. W. Brekelmans, 'Het "historische Credo" van Israël', *Tydschrift voor Theologie* iii (1963), pp. 1-11; L. Rost, *Das kleine Credo und andere Studien zum alten Testament* (1965), pp. 11-25; W. Richter, 'Beobachtungen zur theologischen Systembildung in der alttestamentlichen Literatur anhand des "kleinen geschichtlichen Credo" ', *Wahrheit und Verkündigung* (1967), pp. 175-212; J. P. Hyatt, 'Were There an Ancient Historical Credo in Israel and an Independent Sinai Tradition?', *Translating and Understanding the Old Testament*. Essays in Honor of Herbert Gordon May (1970), pp. 152-170.

[1] *Das System der zwölf Stämme Israels* (1930).
[2] See further below, pp. 189 ff.

tradition of the Jacob stories. What we have basically is a contest motif concerned with trades or occupations, and the shepherd stories about Jacob and Laban, where the contest is between two men who follow the same occupation, are attached to the Jacob-Esau narratives. According to Gunkel the west Jordan Jacob, who is associated with sanctuaries and theophanies, belongs to a later stage of the history of the tradition.[1] Against Gunkel, Noth maintains that a tradition has a structure and that the 'kernel' of the tradition already contains within itself the potentialities which are realized in the processes of future growth and development. The subsequent growth of the credal kernel of the Jacob tradition is controlled by elements of structure which are contained in the kernel from the outset.[2]

Noth maintains that Gunkel argues in a circle. He makes an assumption that the essence of the Jacob tradition is a type of contest story, involving two men who follow different occupations, and then he argues that whatever is not of this character must belong to a later stage of the tradition. He does not weigh the possibility that the extensive narrative elements which are now so much in the forefront may be later and not earlier than those elements which are fragmentary narratives or simply notices. Further, Noth holds that the area east of the Jordan was uncleared woodland until it was settled by Ephraimite colonists from west Jordan, that the east Jordan Jacob stories could have taken their rise only among these colonists and that therefore they are a development of the west Jordan Jacob traditions.[3]

One difficulty which Noth does not deal with very convincingly is constituted by the phrase 'a wandering Aramaean' or 'An Aramaean about to die' (Deut. 26.5). This, according to Noth, is the credal kernel of the Jacob traditions and of all the patriarchal traditions, and it is an article of an all-Israelite creed which was attached to the sanctuary of Shechem in west Jordan. Whatever translation of the phrase is adopted the reference to Jacob as an Aramaean in this context calls for some explanation.[4] Why is Jacob, who has achieved all-Israelite status in a sedentary, west

---

[1] Above, pp. 105 ff.

[2] Cf. Noth, *op. cit.*, p. 111, n. 299, 'eine bestimmte Überlieferungsgestalt das Primäre sein kann an die sich nachträglich allerlei Erzählungsstoffe ankristallisierten'.

[3] M. Noth, *ibid.*, p. 111, n. 299.

[4] Cf. M. Weippert, *op. cit.*, p. 103, n. 5.

Jordan milieu, described as a 'wandering Aramaean' or 'an Aramaean about to die'? On Noth's own premises this can hardly have been an original feature of the credal article referring to Jacob. One would have to suppose rather that this way of characterizing Jacob assumes the union of the west and east Jordan Jacob traditions. There is then the further problem of determining what experiences of the east Jordan Jacob are indicated by the phrase '*ᵃrammī 'ōbēd*. Is it a general reference to Jacob's long stay with the Aramaean Laban? Or is it a more particular reference to a practice of intermarriage between east Jordan Ephraimite colonists and the neighbouring Aramaeans?[1] In any case there does seem to be a problem here which is not resolved.[2] If, as Noth holds, the east Jordan Jacob stories are characterized by their dissociation from sanctuaries, by the disappearance of the element of theophany and by a tendency towards a more independent literary motivation as compared with the credal functions of the west Jordan Jacob stories or notices, it is perplexing to find the mention of precisely this east Jordan Jacob in the credal article which is said to be the germ of all the Jacob traditions. A plain answer, which Noth, however, is precluded by his premises from giving,[3] is that the phrase contains an authentic historical recollection and indicates that the patriarchs came to Palestine from the Mesopotamian area as part of an Aramaean or proto-Aramaean immigration.

Hoftijzer[4] has noticed that Noth's account of the content of the Promise associated with the 'god of the fathers' cult differs from that of Alt. Hoftijzer's own approach to the patriarchal narratives is an attempt to combine a literary-critical with a traditio-historical method, but in a manner different from that of Noth.

Whoever undertakes to enquire into the promises made to the patriarchs must ask the question which method he is to follow. Whether the method of Staerk who seeks to establish the significance of the promises, their function in and their relation to the extant text, or the method of von Rad and Noth who enquire into the previous stages (of the tradition) and into the role of the promises in the *Überlieferungsgeschichte*, but who take practically no account of the forms of the tradition as they have been transmitted to us. . . . Only after an attempt has been made to grapple with this problem should the question be discussed whether there are

[1] M. Noth, *op. cit.*, p. 102, n. 272.
[2] For the treatment of this by Seebass, see below, p. 173.
[3] Above, pp. 151 ff.
[4] Above, p. 116, n. 4.

grounds for assuming previous stages and what the possible form and role of these previous stages may have been. Otherwise the danger lies very near that decisions will be made about the origins of forms of the tradition, the period of their emergence and their relation to other traditions, and that the traditions of Promise in our extant text will be elucidated on this basis without the question being put whether this text agrees well with the solution which is offered, since it is simply assumed that this is so.[1]

What Hoftijzer appears to object to as a methodological flaw is an essential feature of Noth's traditio-historical method. It is not, from Noth's point of view, a flaw of which he is unaware and which has to be brought to his notice; it is a goal which he pursues with a full awareness of all its consequences. It is clear that Noth and Hoftijzer diverge in their understanding of 'History of Tradition' and in their insights into the relationship between literary-critical conclusions and the functioning of a traditio-historical method. In Noth it is evident that history of tradition must necessarily go beyond what can be established by literary-critical methods. Moreover – and this is where Hoftijzer will not accept the implications of Noth's method – it produces results which are strange in relation to the *prima facie* evidence of the extant text.

If one could say that Hoftijzer was a literary-critical positivist of the same kind as Eissfeldt, the issue between him and Noth would be easier to state, but, in fact, it is a much more difficult matter to give clear expression to Hoftijzer's views. It is not always easy to decide whether his judgements are based on literary-critical criteria or traditio-historical criteria. From a literary-critical point of view his assessment of Gen. 15 and 17 is not novel. Thus Gunkel[2] held that chapter 15 came from a period when Israel's possession of the land had become problematic and this agrees with Hoftijzer. In so far as chapter 17 has been generally allocated to P by the source critics its lateness has been indicated.

When we come to the passages which Hoftijzer associates with Gen. 15 (the Genesis 15 Group) and those which he associates with Gen. 17 (the El Shaddai Group) the matter is more complicated. The Promise element in the E-S group is not separable from its context in literary-critical terms, but it is, according to Hoftijzer, secondary in a traditio-historical respect. For the Genesis 15 Group Hoftijzer posits a *Redaktionsgeschichte* as a consequence of

[1] J. Hoftijzer, *Die Verheissungen an die drei Erzväter*, pp. 4 f.
[2] *Genesis (3)*, p. 183.

which the Promise elements became part of our extant text. Hence in the Genesis 15 Group the Promise elements are secondary both in a literary-critical and in a traditio-historical sense.[1]

It is a puzzle to know how Hoftijzer arrives at the conclusion that the Promise elements in the Genesis 15 Group are secondary in a traditio-historical sense. It is a premise of *Überlieferungs-geschichte*, in Noth's sense of the term, that the history of the tradition cannot be read off from the final form of the documents. You cannot by a scrutiny of the documents discern the various stages of the history of the tradition which lead to the final, fixed literary form. It is this aspect of Noth's history of tradition which is unacceptable to Eissfeldt who regards the documentary sources as the furthest limit of scientific criticism. So far as the patriarchal stories are concerned, the evidence of the extant text is that they begin with Abraham and end with Jacob (or Joseph). If we are not permitted to infer from the documents a history of tradition which conflicts with the representation of these documents, and which establishes that the tradition begins with Jacob and ends with Abraham, Noth's method is invalid.

This, however, is not precisely Hoftijzer's position, although in the course of his detailed criticism of Alt[2] one might be pardoned for supposing that he is this kind of literary-critical positivist. Thus his argument that supposed references to patriarchal gods cannot be so understood because these gods are equated with Yahweh in the extant documents makes sense only from such a standpoint. The argument of Noth is not related to how these references to 'god of my father' and so on are understood in the documents. On the contrary, his history of tradition is intended to explain how it came about that these gods were eventually equated with Yahweh in the documents.

Hoftijzer tries too hard to remove all traces of patriarchal gods distinct from Yahweh. To do this in Ex. 3.14-15 he has to assume a conflation of two originally disparate traditions rather than allowing an explanation based on the assumption that the passage is unitary.[3] Similarly he seems to be straining too hard in his exegesis of Gen. 31.42 and 53. In the case of 31.53 we are required to accept the unnatural conclusion that it is Laban and not Jacob who

---

[1] J. Hoftijzer, *op. cit.*, pp. 27 ff.
[2] *ibid.*, pp. 84 ff.
[3] *ibid.*, p. 86.

is a worshipper of the 'god of Abraham'.[1] Then again it is not obvious why Hoftijzer reaches different conclusions in respect of *paḥad yiṣḥāq* from those which he otherwise draws about the patriarchal gods. He says that in the extant text *paḥad yiṣḥāq* is to be equated with Yahweh, but that in this particular case it is possible that the expression stems from the pre-Yahwistic period and did not originally refer to Yahweh. If *paḥad yiṣḥāq* is possibly pre-Yahwistic why is it impossible for 'god of my father', 'god of your father', 'god of Abraham', to have a pre-Yahwistic history despite their equation with Yahweh in the extant documents?[2]

Hoftijzer, so far as I can see, is a historian of tradition who does not accept Noth's view that the documents give no indication of the history of the tradition of which they are the final fixation.[3] A further difficulty in coming to terms with him is his somewhat negative attitude to the scholars (Alt, von Rad and Noth) whose work he reviews. When the positive side of his work is examined, it appears that his conclusions have some affinity with those of Gunkel and that his conflict with Noth is much sharper than his conflict with von Rad, although Hoftijzer himself does not fully understand the differences between von Rad and Noth. Hoftijzer holds that the patriarchal narratives had become a connected history before the Promise theme exercised any influence on their structure and this is Gunkel's position and also that of von Rad who follows Gunkel in this respect.[4] One might therefore say of Hoftijzer that he is offering an alternative explanation to that of von Rad concerning the role of Promise in the *Heilsgeschichte* (i.e., the history of salvation whose basic structure is given by the themes of the 'Little Creed'). According to von Rad the patriarchal stories were integrated into the *Heilsgeschichte* by the Yahwist (J) who employed the 'Little Creed' (Deut. 26.5-9) as the scaffolding of his history and was occupied with the hermeneutical possibilities of the theme of Promise. Hence Promise is the thread of his history – the promise to the patriarchs is fulfilled in the possession of Canaan and the military and political achievements of David bring the Promise-Fulfilment scheme to life in the Yahwist's day.[5] According to Hoftijzer, on the other hand, the entry

[1] *ibid.*, pp. 94 f.
[2] *ibid.*, p. 89.
[3] Cf. the quotation, above, pp. 156 f.
[4] Below, pp. 225 ff.
[5] Below, pp. 241 ff.

of Promise into the *Heilsgeschichte* came much later and had a much narrower theological significance. Before Promise exerted any influence the entire *Heilsgeschichte* from the patriarchs to the possession of Canaan was complete. It was the loss of confidence and the problematic character of Israel's existence in the late pre-exilic or exilic age which was responsible for the elements of Promise in the patriarchal narratives and elsewhere in the *Heilsgeschichte*. This emphasis on Yahweh's promises to his people is a kind of whistling to keep up one's courage. It is the insertion of notes of reassurance which in fact indicate a loss of confidence and an awareness of the precariousness of Israel's position in the world.

Hoftijzer agrees with Gunkel and von Rad that Promise is not a theme which is integral to the patriarchal narratives from the outset. He disagrees with von Rad in his assertion that Promise is not originally integral to the *Heilsgeschichte*. He disagrees with Noth on both counts. According to Noth, Promise is the credal kernel of the patriarchal narratives and the promise to the patriarchs reinterpreted as the promise of the land of Canaan to Israel is fulfilled by the Settlement which is one of the main themes of the *Heilsgeschichte*.

VIII

According to Jepsen[1] the history of the Jacob tradition begins in east Jordan with the story about the contest of Jacob with a deity at the Jabbok (Gen. 32.23-33). This is to be regarded as the account of how Jacob received the revelation which constituted him founder of the cult of *'ᵃbīr yaʿᵃqōb*. Its localization at Penuel is an indication that the clan which worshipped *'ᵃbīr yaʿᵃqōb* had subsequently settled down in that area (hence also the association of Jacob with Mahanaim and Succoth). The Jacob-Esau story is a free narrative expansion of the motif 'brothers in conflict' rather than cultic history or tribal history. The Jacob-Laban story, although it is now integrated into this literary complex, has a different character in so far as it is a reflection of relationships between the tribe of Reuben settled in east Jordan and the adjacent Aramaeans. The cult of *'ᵃbīr yaʿᵃqōb* at the earliest point of the history of the Jacob tradition had its home in the tribe of Reuben which was settled

---

[1] A. Jepsen, 'Zur Überlieferungsgeschichte der Vätergestalten', *Wissenschaft-liche Zeitschrift für der Karl Marx Universität, Leipzig* (1953/4), Gesellschafts- und Sprachwissenschaftliche Reihe, Heft 2/3, pp. 265-287.

with Gad in east Jordan. In support of these statements Jepsen brings forward the following considerations:

(a) The arguments by which Noth[1] seeks to demonstrate that Reuben was settled in west Jordan are not valid. The references to the stone of Bohan (Josh. 15.6; 18.17) are not an indication of an original west Jordan settlement of the tribe but refer rather to a part of the tribe which was settled there after the break-up of an original east Jordan tribal settlement.

(b) The *argumentum e silentio* from the Song of Deborah (Judg. 5.17, cf. v. 15, Gilead is expressly said to be east of the Jordan, Reuben is not) is not a conclusive one. Moreover Eissfeldt's interpretation of Judg. 5.16 establishes the pastoral character of Reuben's existence which accords well with an east Jordan area of settlement. According to Eissfeldt[2] *hammišpᵉtayim* are 'sheep pens' (NEB, 'cattle pens') and *šᵉriqōt ᶜᵃdārim* refers to the bleating of the herds consequent on attempts to steal them and on the efforts of the shepherds to get them to the safety of the pens. The attempt to steal sheep and the counter-efforts to frustrate the attempt are referred to in Gen. 49.19 in connexion with Gad which like Reuben was an east Jordan pastoral tribe. Reuben and Gad (Gilead) were too occupied with the protection of their flocks and herds to answer the call of Deborah (Judg. 5.15-17).

(c) The connexion established between Reuben and Migdaleder (Gen. 35.21 f.) is to be explained in the same way as the stone of Bohan passages.

(d) The reference to Reuben in association with Gilead (Num. 32.1) is to be relied on and is not late as Noth has maintained.[3]

Against Noth Jepsen holds that the evidences of a firm connexion between the Jacob tradition and east Jordan are not adequately explained by the assumption that this belongs to a secondary phase which is to be correlated with the colonization of east Jordan by Ephraimites from west Jordan.[4] Jepsen disputes Noth's interpretation of Judg. 12.1-6[5] and observes that even if, at the

---

[1] M. Noth, *Das System der zwölf Stämme Israels*, p. 77. Noth follows C. Steuernagel, *Die Einwanderung der israelitischen Stämme in Kanaan* (1901), pp. 15 ff.

[2] O. Eissfeldt, 'Gabelhürden im Ostjordanland', *Forschungen und Fortschritte* (1949), pp. 9-11; *KS* iii, pp. 61-66.

[3] M. Noth, *Überlieferungsgeschichte des Pentateuch*, p. 107.

[4] Above, p. 123.

[5] M. Noth, *op. cit.*, p. 98.

period which is reflected in that passage, there were Ephraimite colonists in east Jordan, this does not demonstrate that the original settlers there were Ephraimites. Further he raises the matter of the east Jordan grave tradition relating to Jacob (Gen. 50.10-11). The laments which are raised for Jacob on the threshing floor of Atad on the east side of the Jordan indicate that this was his burial place. The account of his burial there has been suppressed by the later concept of a family tomb at Machpelah where all the patriarchs are buried (Gen. 50.12-14). The east Jordan grave tradition would never have arisen, if Jacob had come to that area as an all-Israelite, west Jordan figure. It is only explicable on the assumption that the tradition had its beginning in east Jordan and subsequently extended its influence west of the Jordan. If the Jacob tradition at its earliest traceable point is attached to the area of the Jabbok, it is understandable that an east Jordan grave tradition should have arisen.[1]

The west Jordan Jacob traditions are of small bulk: they comprise the sanctuary legend located at Bethel (28.10 ff.) and a few loosely juxtaposed notices at the end of chapters 33 and 35. Jepsen asks whether it is probable that the Jacob tradition would be so quickly truncated in what, according to Noth, was its heartland and would assume so impressive dimensions in the 'colonial' area of east Jordan.[2] He postulates a process the reverse of that laid down by Noth. The *'ᵃbir yaʿᵃqōb* cult was first attached to the tribe of Reuben in east Jordan and subsequently spread to west Jordan where it was a unifying factor in a coalition of the tribes who were represented as 'sons' of Jacob by his wife Leah (Reuben, Simeon, Levi, Judah, Issachar, Zebulon). Through these tribes Jacob was attached to Shechem and Bethel. The connexion with Shechem was effected by the tribes of Simeon and Levi (Gen. 34) and that with Bethel perhaps through Judah which may have been settled at Bethel and have anchored the cult of *'ᵃbir yaʿᵃqōb* to that ancient sanctuary. The representation of these six tribes as 'sons' of Jacob and Leah is explained by the circumstance that the cement of this inter-tribal union was the cult of *'ᵃbir yaʿᵃqōb*. Bethel may have become the central sanctuary of the twelve-tribe Israelite amphictyony at the point when hegemony passed from the Leah tribes to the Joseph tribes.[3]

---

[1] Cf. Noth, above, pp. 122 f.   [2] Cf. Noth, above, pp. 155 f.
[3] A. Jepsen, *op. cit.*, pp. 269 f., 272-74.

Joseph, according to Jepsen, is first an historical individual (the leader of the tribe which bears his name) and subsequently the name of a tribe. The history of Joseph begins at Beersheba in association with the clan which worshipped *paḥad yiṣḥāq*. This clan, of which Joseph was the leader, made its way into Egypt, perhaps forced out of Beersheba by Ishmaelite pressure, and there Joseph became the leader of the tribe which bore his name and which adopted *paḥad yiṣḥāq* as its tribal god. Through the contribution of Moses the Joseph tribes embraced Yahwism and on their return to Palestine established a twelve-tribe amphictyony based on the unifying power of Yahwism. This was made up of the Leah tribes (Reuben, Simeon, Levi, Judah, Issachar, Zebulon), the Rachel tribes (Joseph and Benjamin) and the slave tribes (Dan, Naphtali, Gad, Asher). In connexion with this amphictyony there arises the representation that all these tribes are 'sons' of Jacob and, as a secondary elaboration, the relative superiority and inferiority of the constituent tribes is expressed by their allocation among wives and slave girls. The original connexion of Rachel would appear to be with Benjamin. She died in giving birth to Benjamin and her grave is located within the tribal territory of Benjamin.[1] Rachel, as Jacob's favourite wife, becomes a device for asserting the claims of the Joseph tribes to a place of pre-eminence in the tribal coalition. Joseph is Rachel's son and his father's favourite. This state of affairs is reflected in the Joseph story which presupposes the existence of the twelve-tribe amphictyony and which probably originates in the tribe of Manasseh. The representation that four of Jacob's 'sons' were born to slave girls presumably indicates their subordinate status in the tribal union and their distance from the centre of power.

Judah, an original member of the six-tribe Leah amphictyony, was incorporated into the twelve-tribe Yahwistic amphictyony and was also a member of an amphictyony based on Hebron under the hegemony of the Calebites. The latter had occupied the Hebron area about the same time as the Joseph tribes arrived in Canaan, and through its association with the Calebites Judah became a worshipper of the 'god of Abraham'. To what extent this 'god of Abraham' was already identified with Yahweh in this Calebite or Kenite context is difficult to say. A later stage of the Joseph story is represented by the substitution of Judah for Reuben as the

[1] Cf. Noth, above, pp. 147 f.

spokesman of the brothers. Reuben is the first-born according to the genealogical scheme by which the tribes are represented as 'sons' of Jacob and his seniority makes him the natural and appropriate spokesman. Judah has no such right of seniority and when he is represented as the spokesman this must have political significance and must reflect the supremacy and dominance achieved by Judah in the reign of David. Jepsen holds that there are two variants of the Joseph story and his analysis follows the lines of the usual allocation between J and E. He maintains, however, that a source analysis is not appropriate: we should envisage instead that a single author (the Yahwist) incorporated variant and parallel traditions into his work. In this way Jepsen makes the hypothesis of a redaction (J-E) redundant. In the later version, where Judah displaced Reuben, the patriarch is called Israel and not Jacob, and Jepson appears to say that Judah-Israel is a significant correlation and that 'Israel' like 'Judah' has links with the greater political entity established by David.[1]

The history of the Isaac traditions begins at Beersheba. According to Jepsen, Gen. 46.1-5, which is located at Beersheba and deals with the disclosure made to Jacob by the 'god of his father Isaac', is to be regarded as a distinctive Isaac tradition. He says that the promise of this god has been incorporated in the larger context of the patriarchal stories and this, apparently, is his attempt to explain why Jacob features in the extant story. Jepsen holds that the concept of Guidance is special to $pa\d{h}ad\ yi\d{s}\d{h}\bar{a}q$, just as Conflict and Blessing are special to the Jacob tradition and Promise to the Abraham tradition. Guidance is again the motif in Gen. 26 which contains a recollection of contacts between the clan of Isaac (i.e., the worshippers of $pa\d{h}ad\ yi\d{s}\d{h}\bar{a}q$) and the inhabitants of Gerar. The transference of this to Abraham (Gen. 20) is secondary as is also the transference of Ishmael. The original relationship is between the clan of Isaac and the Ishmaelites and this is indicated by the common links which they have with Beersheba and Beer Lahai Roi.[2] The Isaac traditions are small in bulk, but they preserve a recollection of quarrels about wells in the Negeb; also of a settlement at Beersheba and brushes with neighbouring tribes, especially the Ishmaelites, in whose place the Philistines later appear.

Jepsen argues that there is evidence of a special attachment of

[1] A. Jepsen, *op. cit.*, pp. 265-269.
[2] Cf. M. Noth, above, pp. 135 ff.

the Isaac tradition to the northern kingdom of Israel. The mountains of Samaria are called 'the high places of Isaac' (Amos 7.9); Beersheba was a place of pilgrimage for northern Israelites according to Amos and Hosea; Elijah wandered as far south as Beersheba. Moreover, despite its southern location, Beersheba does not seem to have been an important sanctuary in Judah.[1] The link between the Isaac traditions and the north is, according to Jepsen, Joseph. First, Joseph, as an historical individual, who is the leader of a clan which worships *paḥad yiṣḥāq* at the place where the tradition originates – Beersheba; then the Joseph tribes who return to Palestine from Egypt as Yahwists, but who retain their allegiance to *paḥad yiṣḥāq* – their tribal god. It is this circumstance which explains how it came about that Isaac was established in an all-Israelite, Yahwistic context as the father of Jacob. The Joseph tribes, who had played an important part in the formation of the twelve tribe amphictyony, accorded to Isaac the same all-Israelite status as had been conferred on Jacob-Israel.[2]

A great deal has been attached secondarily to Abraham: the sale of the tribal mother into a harim (12.10-20; 20); tribal sagas concerning Ishmael (16.1-9, 10-14; 21.8-21); traditions concerning Moab and Ammon (19.30-38); the late midrash in chapter 14; Isaac narratives (21.22-34; 22.1-14, 19); a *Novelle* (24). There remains the Abraham-Lot cycle (13.2, 5. 13; 19.1-28), the vision in chapter 15 and the Mamre narrative (18.1-15). Chapter 15 is to be regarded as a recollection of a revelation made by the 'god of Abraham' to the founder of that cult, but the developed theological character which it now has is an indication that its extant form is later than chapter 18. The fact that the latter is set at Mamre shows that the clan which worshipped the 'god of Abraham' settled in that area.[3]

The occupation of Hebron by the Calebites is represented as the fulfilment of a promise of land, only this promise is related to Moses and is referred to the events of the Mosaic period (Num. 14.24). Originally, however, this promise arose out of the cult of the 'god of Abraham' of whom the Calebites were worshippers. The extant Caleb tradition is usually explained as an aetiological saga – it seeks to explain why Hebron, the principal city of a

[1] Cf. A. Alt, above, pp. 111 f.
[2] A. Jepsen, *op. cit.*, pp. 271, 274 f.
[3] Cf. Noth, above, p. 137.

Judahite coalition, was inhabited by Calebites rather than Judahites. The assumption then is that this account originated in
Judahites circles. Jepsen argues that the tradition, in the 'original'
form which he reconstructs, is Calebite and that the attachment of
Judah to the 'god of Abraham' cult at Hebron is a subsequent
stage. The Calebites grew out of the clan of Abraham and appropriated the promise of land (i.e., of Hebron and its environs) made
by the 'god of Abraham' to the founder of the cult.

Jepsen develops his argument further and offers a reconstruction
which begins not with the clan of Abraham at Mamre-Hebron but
with the historical Abraham, a *gēr* in the area of Hebron who receives the promise of posterity and land in a revelation from the
'god of Abraham'. This cult was maintained in Abraham's clan
which had been forced out of the Hebron area towards the south.
In connexion with a renewed impetus of semi-nomadic peoples
the clan of Abraham under the leadership of the Calebites (who
had appropriated the cult of the 'god of Abraham' and the promise
of Hebron) pressed forward to possess the land which had been
promised. When later Abraham became the father of all Israel, the
Promise was referred to the whole of the Promised Land and so
the account of the promise of Yahweh to Caleb, communicated by
Moses, to give him Hebron originated.[1]

Judah in virtue of its membership of the confederation of tribes
based on Hebron became a worshipper of the 'god of Abraham'
and made the Abraham traditions of the Calebites its own. The
incorporation of Abraham into the all-Israelite genealogical scheme,
Abraham-Isaac-Jacob, can only have been effected by Judah, and
this dominance of Abraham over Isaac (who is a northern figure
according to Jepsen) is only intelligible in the period of Judaean
hegemony, that is, in the reign of David.[2] Subsequently features
of Isaac and Jacob traditions were transferred to Abraham: the
treaty with Abimelech from Isaac to Abraham (21.22-33); the
founding of the sanctuaries of Shechem and Bethel from Jacob to
Abraham (12.6-8). The fact that the Abraham tradition consists
of a series of loosely connected narratives is an indication that a
relatively late collection of diverse materials lies before us.

The Abraham-Lot cycle contains reminiscences of difficulties

---

[1] Similarly, R. E. Clements, *Abraham and David*, pp. 33, 39; 'Abraham',
pp. 55 f.
[2] Cf. R. E. Clements, *Abraham and David*, pp. 47-60.

which had been encountered by the Abraham clan and the motif of rivalry found in the Jacob-Esau, Jacob-Laban and Isaac-Ishmael narratives is present there also. Different portrayals are now combined in Lot: eponym of Moab and Ammon through his daughters (19.30-38); survivor of the destruction of Sodom; nephew of Abraham. The Ishmael narrative in two versions (16; 21.8-20) has originally to do with the close relationships which obtained between the clan of Isaac and the Ishmaelites and it is in virtue of this that Isaac and Ishmael are 'brothers'. Abraham is drawn into the Ishmael story only after he became the 'father' of Isaac in the Abraham-Isaac-Jacob genealogy. The motif of selling a wife into a harim has also been transferred from Isaac to Abraham (26.7-11; 12.10-20) and was subsequently modified to meet the requirements of theological propriety in chapter 20. The story of the sacrifice of Isaac (22.1-19) probably issues from the same circles as chapter 20. It not only presupposes the close connexion of Abraham and Isaac, but is also aware of the significance of Isaac for the fulfilment of the Promise and is written in praise of complete submission to God as a criterion of piety. Chapters 18.16-33 and 24 belong to the latest stage of the Abraham tradition and are shaped by precise theological concepts – Theodicy and Guidance.[1]

The Jacob tradition was reinterpreted through the elucidation of Esau as Edom and this elaboration belongs to the period when Israel had historical relations with Edom, that is, perhaps to the ninth century B.C. It is here that the history of the tradition of the patriarchal narratives ends.[2]

IX

The basis of Jepsen's account of the history of the tradition of the patriarchal narratives is, for the most part, Alt's 'god of the fathers' thesis. Thus an *'aḇīr ya'aqōḇ* cult is the starting point of the history of the Jacob traditions and a *paḥad yiṣḥāq* cult the starting point of the history of the Isaac traditions. There are two important respects in which Jepsen differs from Alt or exceeds the boundary of his method:

1. While there is a sense in which the cult of the 'god of Abraham' is the source from which Jepsen's account of the Abraham traditions issues, he, nevertheless, attempts to go beyond the

[1] A. Jepsen, *op. cit.*, pp. 271, 275-77.
[2] *ibid.*, p. 278.

bounds of cultic history (i.e., the cult of the 'god of Abraham') and to speak directly about Abraham as an historical individual who lived as a *gēr* in the area of Hebron. This attempt must be regarded as unsuccessful. It is not an economical hypothesis; it requires too many assumptions and can only be described as speculative. The argument runs as follows: Abraham once lived as a *gēr* in the vicinity of Hebron. When his clan was driven towards the south, they perpetuated his cult and identified themselves with the promise of land which Abraham had received from his god. It was thus that the cult passed to the Calebites, with whom the clan of Abraham had become associated, and was established in Hebron when the Promise was fulfilled by Calebite occupation of that area. It is hard to resist the conclusion that Jepsen would have done better to accept the limitation of Alt's method for Abraham as he did for Isaac and Jacob and to have made the 'god of Abraham' his starting point.

2. Jepsen does not work with Alt's typology or phenomenology of the cult of the 'god of the fathers'. The content of the cult, according to Alt, is Promise: the promise of posterity made to the founder of the cult and his clan in a nomadic or semi-nomadic context and the promise of land which is attached to the cult when it is anchored to sanctuaries in settled territory. This presupposes an accommodation of the patriarchal cults with the Canaanite *Elim* of these sanctuaries[1] and this aspect of the matter is entirely ignored by Jepsen. Two issues are raised here: (*a*) Jepsen holds that each of the patriarchal cults has its own typology. The *'aḇīr ya'ʿaqōḇ* cult is concerned especially with Conflict and Blessing; the theme of the *paḥad yiṣḥāq* cult is Guidance; only the 'god of Abraham' cult is about posterity and land. That this has important implications for his history of the tradition of the patriarchal narratives will be shown below. (*b*) Jepsen's account of the history of the Jacob tradition suffers from the lack of an ancient Canaanite sanctuary east of the Jordan. It is not enough (at least in terms of Alt's thesis) to postulate a locality where the clan of Jacob became sedentary and the cult of *'aḇīr ya'ʿaqōḇ* was localized. The localization of a 'god of the fathers' cult requires an accommodation with a Canaanite El at an established sanctuary and Jepsen has not shown that there was such a sanctuary east of the Jordan. Hence in so far as Jepsen accepts Alt's premise that the history of the tradition of the Jacob

[1] Below, Chapter iv.

narratives has its source in the localization of a semi-nomadic cult at a Canaanite sanctuary, his account of that history, beginning as it does in east Jordan, is defective.

In so far as Jepsen sets out from Alt's hypothesis, his history of the tradition of the patriarchal narratives is in general accord with that of Noth. Both hold that the patriarchal narratives are basically cultic history and that they can only be used as historical sources indirectly and inferentially. In other words the historical information which they give is other than what they appear to give, and it is discoverable by correlating the narratives *qua* cultic history with what are thought to be the appropriate historical circumstances. Thus the ultimate dominance of Abraham in the stories tells us nothing about the period in which Abraham is purported to have lived. So far as the history of the tradition is concerned, his dominance, according to Jepsen, reflects the circumstances of the reign of David. When historical conclusions can only be drawn inferentially, differences of opinion are inevitable and these appear as between Noth and Jepsen, but such divergences in detailed interpretation are not incompatible with an agreement in principle about the relationship between cultic history and history in the patriarchal narratives.

There are two important differences between Noth and Jepsen: (*a*) Noth accepts, for the most part,[1] Alt's typology of the 'god of the fathers' cult. (*b*) At the base of Noth's account of the history of the tradition of the patriarchal narratives is von Rad's 'Little Creed'[2] which does not exercise any influence on Jepsen's work. In virtue of these fundamental assumptions Noth's account of the history of the tradition is unitary and organic; Jepsen's is discrete and then composite. At the beginning of Noth's history of the tradition of the patriarchal stories stands an article of a Yahwistic creed: the history of the tradition does not begin in a pre-Yahwistic context, but in an amphictyonic, all-Israelite one, and the subsequent growth of the tradition is entirely within the sphere of Yahwism. It is therefore an indispensable part of Noth's argument that all three patriarchal cults have the same typology, since it is because of their common content of Promise that they are integrated into a Yahwistic creed and finally subsumed under the final article of that creed – Possession of the Promised Land. The inte-

[1] Cf. above, p. 116, n. 4.
[2] Above, pp. 112 f.

gration of the patriarchal cults with the settlement tradition can happen in the way which Noth describes only because all three cults have the same typology.

With Jepsen, on the other hand, there is no single history of the tradition of the patriarchal narratives. The traditions of the patriarchal cults are separate and are combined in circumstances which Jepsen tries to reconstruct. '*ᵃbīr ya*'*ᵃqōb* is first of all the tribal god of Reuben, then the god of a six-tribe Leah amphictyony and ultimately is integrated into Yahwism at Bethel in the setting of a twelve tribe amphictyony. *paḥad yiṣḥāq* is a clan god at Beersheba, then the god of the tribe of Joseph in Egypt and the cult achieves all-Israelite status in connexion with the hegemony of the Joseph tribes in the context of a twelve tribe amphictyony at Bethel. The 'god of Abraham' is a clan god, then the god of the Calebites, then the god of a Judahite amphictyony based on Mamre-Hebron. Finally the 'god of Abraham' becomes dominant in an all-Israelite context and overshadows the other patriarchal elements in Yahwism as a consequence of David's rise to power. The patriarchal narratives are still envisaged as cultic history, but Jepsen has gone beyond Noth's starting point and has described the separate pre-Yahwistic histories of the three patriarchal cults.

The relationship assumed by Jepsen between history of tradition and the extant documentary sources is different from that which underlies Noth's work. According to Noth the sources do not supply direct information concerning the history of the tradition, whereas Jepsen tends to rely on the sources (i.e., on the extant shape of the patriarchal stories) in order to establish where the history of the tradition should begin. This would seem to be in conflict with his own theory which should be the same as that of Noth, namely, that the extant shape of the stories will mirror the end of the history of the tradition rather than the beginning. Thus Jepsen argues statistically from the text of the patriarchal narratives: the bulk of the Jacob narratives are set in east Jordan; Jacob is associated predominantly with places in east Jordan and the west Jordan Jacob traditions are meagre. Therefore the Jacob tradition most probably began in east Jordan. Similarly because the patriarchal narratives, as we now have them, establish a close connexion between Abraham and Mamre-Hebron, Jepsen assumes that this is an original connexion. Noth, on the other hand, applies the same kind of amphictyonic interpretation to Abraham at Mamre-Hebron as he does to Jacob at Shechem. The association of Abraham with Hebron is not significant with respect to the original location of the 'god of Abraham' or the original content of the Abraham traditions. The primary datum is that an amphictyony was established at Hebron, and the transference of the figure of Abraham to Hebron and his attraction to Hebron traditions is a post-amphictyonic development.[1]

The weakest of all Jepsen's arguments is his effort to show that Joseph was the bearer of the Isaac traditions and the following observations may be made about this argument:

1. Jepsen's contention that Gen. 46.1-4 can be regarded as a reminiscence of a revelation made by *paḥad yiṣḥāq* to the founder of that cult is insupportable. The episode occurs in the context of the Joseph story with which Isaac has nothing to do, whereas Jacob, as Joseph's father, is closely involved in it. To suggest, as Jepsen appears to do, that Jacob has made his way secondarily into the passage is wrong-headed. The correct observation is rather that the representation of Jacob seeking guidance at Beersheba from the god of his father Isaac is an indication that the genealogical link Isaac-Jacob was established before the episode was written. At any rate the passage has no bearing whatever on whether or not there is a link between Joseph and *paḥad yiṣḥāq*.[2]

2. Jepsen's assumption that Joseph is an historical individual who becomes the leader of a tribe which is then called after him accords ill with his own method. He recognizes that when the Israelite tribes are represented as the twelve 'sons' of Jacob we have tribal history in the guise of family history. If eleven 'sons' of Jacob are tribes (and this seems to be Jepsen's position) it is unreasonable to say that Joseph, who is the twelfth 'son' in this scheme, is not only a tribe but also an historical individual.[3] It may be granted that there is a case to answer in so far as evidence exists of a special attachment of the inhabitants of northern Israel to Isaac and to the sanctuary of Beersheba. Zimmerli's attempt to explain this in terms of Simeonites who moved north and carried Isaac traditions from the south with them is rejected by Jepsen.[4]

---

[1] Above, p. 137.

[2] Cf. Jepsen, *op. cit.*, p. 280. He says that J probably inserted 46.1-4 into the Joseph story and also reshaped 45.25-46.5.

[3] Above, pp. 146 ff.

[4] W. Zimmerli, *Geschichte und Tradition von Beersheba*, p. 23; cf. Alt, above, pp. 111 f.

Whatever explanation is offered of the special attachment of northern Israelites to Isaac traditions Jepsen's one which assumes an
original relationship between Joseph and the 'god of Isaac' is so
elaborate a piece of speculation that it will not carry conviction.
It requires belief in the existence of a Joseph who was the leader
of the clan of Isaac at Beersheba and then of the tribe of Joseph
in Egypt; it requires belief in a tribe of Joseph which became
Yahwist under the influence of Moses in Egypt, but which retained
paḥad yiṣḥāq as its tribal god whom it ultimately integrated into
the structure of amphictyonic Yahwism. The Joseph story cannot
be regarded as evidence that a leader of a tribe named Joseph was
once in Egypt. The Joseph of the Joseph story is not the leader
of a tribe. In so far as there is a tribal history in the guise of a
family history in the Joseph story, that story is a further development of the representation of the twelve tribes of Israel as 'sons'
of Jacob – a development which has to be correlated with the
emergence of two Joseph tribes, Manasseh and Ephraim, and conditions of rivalry and tension between them. It must be said therefore that with respect to the history of the tradition the primary
datum is the tribe Joseph, and that the Joseph story is to be
regarded as a narrative invention written to celebrate the hegemony of the Joseph tribes in the context of the Israelite confederacy
and reflecting their inner rivalries. At any rate the Joseph story
does not supply evidence that there was an historical individual
called Joseph who was the leader of a tribe in Egypt and whose
tribe was subsequently known by his name.

X

In his monograph on the Jacob traditions Seebass[1] holds that the
Israel intended by Josh. 24.1 f. is the historical Israel (i.e., Israel
consisting of a confederation of tribes) and that the *'ᵃrammī 'ōbēd*
of Deut. 26.5 ('an Aramaean at the point of death', according to
Seebass) is likewise Jacob-Israel, the 'father' of the Israelite tribes.
There is, however, an earlier meaning of Israel and of Jacob than
this. The Jacob-Israel who is the 'father' of the twelve tribes cannot be elucidated in the first place as an historical individual. His
significance is traditio-historical rather than historical, but this is
not the last word that can be said about Jacob-Israel. It is possible
by instituting an historical investigation to trace behind this Jacob-

[1] H. Seebass, *Der Erzvater Israel, BZAW* 98 (1966).

Israel an Israel who is a clan leader and whose clan cult ('god of Israel') was fused with the cult of the ancient Canaanite sanctuary of Shechem. Likewise Jacob is also a clan leader whose clan god ('god of Jacob') was fused with the El Bethel of the ancient Canaanite sanctuary of Bethel. Hence the patriarchal narratives give us direct access to the prehistory of historical Israel: Israel and Jacob migrated into Canaan with the clans that bore their names and established their clan cults in association with the cults of Canaanite sanctuaries.

The original tradition of the renaming of Jacob is preserved in Gen. 35.10 (E, according to Seebass, and not P), while the account in 32.23 ff. is secondary. The significance of the renaming of Jacob as Israel at Bethel (35.10) is that it constitutes a legitimation of the 'god of Jacob' cult at Bethel in terms of the 'god of Israel' cult at Shechem. The original renaming of Jacob as Israel was not therefore related to the later all-Israelite status of Jacob. In the original context of the renaming (35.10) as opposed to the secondary context (32.23 ff.) 'Israel' denotes a clan chieftain and not the historical entity Israel.

Features of the older Israel and of the pre-Yahwistic 'god of Israel' cult are to be traced in the Jacob-Israel of the 'Little Creed' (Deut. 26.5). The earlier Israel was 'an Aramaean at the point of death': his distress is alluded to in Gen. 35.3 as is also the journey which he has made. Shechem is a safe destination which he has reached after a difficult and dangerous journey. That the reference to his emigration from Mesopotamia is not preserved is a consequence of the combination of the traditions of Abraham, Isaac and Jacob, in the total context of which Abraham is the one who left his father's house in Mesopotamia. But the Mesopotamian connexions of the Jacob stories are attributable to Israel rather than to Jacob and the motif of leaving the father's house in order to journey into a strange land has been transferred from Jacob (Israel) to his wives (Gen. 31.13b, 14). Hence the original Israel, the clan leader who established himself with his people at Shechem after having emigrated from Mesopotamia, was an'*ᵃrammī 'ōbēd*.

The Jacob stories proper are connected with east Jordan not Mesopotamia. The east Jordan sagas (32.2-33.16) perhaps stem from a relatively old tradition which preserved the account of the immigration of the Jacob clans. Noth's view[1] that the east Jordan

---

[1] Cf. Noth, above, pp. 122 f.

Jacob stories reflect the circumstances of Ephraimite colonists in Gilead, and so a later stage in the history of the Jacob tradition, than the west Jordan stories is rejected by Seebass. A direct historical link rather than a traditio-historical one between the west and east Jordan Jacob stories is postulated by him. What is indicated is the connexions of a semi-nomadic clan of shepherds with sanctuaries of the settled land (Shechem and Bethel), their attraction to these sanctuaries, their annual participation in the cults and their eventual settling down at them. A large part of this Jacob group remained nomadic after the settlement of these elements in west Jordan and this part eventually settled down in Gilead, where the extent of their territory over against the adjacent Aramaeans was marked by a boundary stone on Mount Gilead. Gen. 27 was originally a hunter-shepherd contest story which now serves to outline the conflict on account of which Jacob had to leave his father's house. The way in which the story is now told partially cloaks the original milieu of the Jacob stories. Jacob is in fact one of the $b^e n \bar{e}$ $qedem$ – not a sojourner with them – and it is from this east Jordan milieu that he leads his clan to Bethel. The fact that Jacob is said to have been buried in east Jordan tells against the view that the east Jordan stories are a secondary phase of the Jacob traditions. Seebass argues that such a grave tradition in east Jordan would not have arisen subsequent to the achieving of all-Israelite status by a west Jordan Jacob.[1]

Seebass offers a different explanation from Alt of 'god of Abraham', 'god of Isaac' and 'god of Jacob'. Thus 'god of Abraham' does not mean 'the deity who is so named because Abraham was the founder of the cult in question', but 'the nameless clan god of Abraham's clan', and similarly with $pahad$ $yiṣḥāq$, $^a b\bar{\imath}r$ $ya^{\prime a}q\bar{o}b$ and $^e l\bar{o}h\bar{e}$ $yiśrā'\bar{e}l$ (33.20). $^a b\bar{\imath}r$ $ya^{\prime a}q\bar{o}b$ (49.24) is to be taken as a reference to an epithet of Jacob's god and not to the name of that deity. 'God of Jacob' occurs only in Ex. 3.6, 15 in the context 'God of Abraham, God of Isaac and God of Jacob', and the existence of an independent expression 'god of Jacob' is problematical. Likewise 'and the god of Isaac' is perhaps a secondary addition to 'I am the god of Abraham, your father' (28.13); $pahad$ $yiṣḥāq$ (31.42) is, according to Seebass, a secondary contraction of $pahad$ $'\bar{a}b\bar{\imath}w$ $yiṣḥāq$ (31.53b) and hence is not the name of a god. It may mean 'the god whom his father Isaac revered' and is then a variant of

[1] H. Seebass, $op.$ $cit.$, pp. 1-48.

'the god of his father Isaac' (46.1) and 'the god of my father Isaac' (32.10). Seebass supposes that the clan god was originally designated by his worshippers as *ᵉlōhē ᵓābī* (Gen. 31.5; Ex. 15.2; 18.4). Hence *ᵉlōhē ᵓābī* or *ᵉlōhē ᵓābīkā* (Gen. 50.17) or *ᵓēl ᵓābīkā* (Gen. 49.25) or *ᵉlōhē ᵓᵃbīkem* (Gen. 31.29; 43.23) did not originally presuppose, as they do now in all the passages which Seebass cites, a religious unification of clan cults associated with the genealogical scheme Abraham-Isaac-Jacob.[1]

Seebass's account of the inauguration of Yahweh worship in an all-Israelite context in Canaan is connected with his view that Yahwism was brought to Canaan by a Moses group. The tradition of the flight of Moses to the Midianites is not understood biographically but as tribal history, and is said to contain a recollection that the Moses group already had relations with the Midianites before their Exodus from Egypt. Yahweh had been the clan god of the Midianites with his seat at Mount Sinai. This Yahweh was appropriated by the Moses group in a decisive way and identified with their own clan god (*Vatergott*) as a consequence of the prophetic contribution of Miriam who perceived Yahweh's presence in the destruction of the Egyptians at the Red Sea (Ex. 15.20 f.). Sinai, as Yahweh's sanctuary and no longer merely the sanctuary of the Midianites, became the cultic centre of the Moses group.

Yahweh like the other clan deities was a *Vatergott* and this facilitated the union of Yahwism with the cult of the nameless clan god ('god of Israel') at Shechem. The union at Shechem was also prepared for by the circumstance that the putting away of alien gods was a ritual which had ancient roots in Shechem in connexion with the cult *ᵓēl ᵉlōhē yiśrāᵓēl* (Gen. 33.20), and that this agreed well with the proscription of images which had become a feature of Yahwism during the desert period. Hence behind the account of the putting away of alien gods in Josh. 24, which is there related to the exclusive claims of Yahweh and the adoption of Yahwism by the Israelite tribes, there are traces of the older ritual of the putting away of alien gods in a pre-Yahwistic context at Shechem. The cults of the other *Vätergötter* ('god of Abraham', 'god of Isaac', 'god of Jacob') would coexist with the worship of Yahweh, since they were all cultic expressions of 'Yahweh, God of Israel' – a formula which resulted from the union of Yahweh and 'god of Israel/Jacob' at Shechem. How then did the equation

[1] *op. cit.*, pp. 49-55; see further below, Chapter iv.

of Yahweh with the god of Abraham's clan and the god of Isaac's clan come about? The answer given by Seebass is manifold:

1. The Abraham and Isaac traditions are both attached to Beersheba and cannot be separated out from one another. Further, Isaac along with Ishmael has connexions with Beer Lahai Roi. The Abraham/Isaac traditions thus come from a semi-nomadic setting and belong to the edge of the settled lands of Canaan. The promise which attaches to them is that of descendants (Gen. 12.2; 13.16; 15.5; 16.10; 18.18; 21.13, 18; 26.24). Since the promise of land and only the promise of land is a primary feature of the Israel/Jacob traditions attached to Shechem and Bethel (28.13, 35.12), the two blocks of tradition (Israel/Jacob and Abraham/Isaac) complement each other in respect of promise. Seebass supposes that the Isaac group once worshipped the deity of Beer Lahai Roi in common with the Ishmaelites (21.13, E) and that later the Isaac group moved nearer to the settled land and established itself at Beersheba (cf. 24.62; 25.11b, J).

2. The Abraham/Isaac group had nomadic affinities but were moving nearer to conditions of sedentary life, and the Israel group had finally arrived at Shechem after an experience of the precariousness of nomadic existence (35.2). In terms of an analogous prehistory the two groups were well-fitted to come together and their *Vätergötter* were of the same type.

3. Associated with the Abraham group there was the tradition of a migration into Egypt and this was utilized along with the Abraham/Isaac traditions in general to extend the prehistory of the Israel group. This was done by representing that Abraham and Isaac were grandfather and father respectively of Israel/Jacob, and, in particular, this supplied the Israel/Jacob group with an migration into Egypt which matched the migration of the Moses group into Egypt.

4. The Abraham/Isaac group occupied a territorial area in common with the Moses group and may already have been Yahwists in virtue of their earlier contacts with the Kenites around Beersheba or at Beer Lahai Roi.[1]

XI

I make the following observations on Seebass's treatment of the Jacob traditions:

[1] *op. cit.*, pp. 56-107.

1. It is firmly established that the representation of Jacob as 'father' of the twelve Israelite tribes settled in Canaan does not have biographical significance but is tribal history.[1] This Jacob is not really a father with twelve sons; it is the nationhood of Israel and the community of the tribes which is depicted in the form of family history. This is *prima facie* the reason why Jacob is renamed Israel.

2. It would be possible to argue (as Seebass does) that there is an earlier Israel, a clan leader who settled at Shechem and from whom the figure of the 'father' of the Israelite tribes developed by traditio-historical processes. What evidence of this does Seebass supply? The evidence consists, for the most part, of his interpretation of Gen. 33.20, but this is an unnatural and wrong interpretation. 'ēl 'ᵉlōhē yiśrā'ēl does not point to the association of a *Vatergott* (the god of the clan whose leader is Israel) with the El of Shechem; rather it identifies the El of Shechem with the God of all Israel. The 'Israel' which appears in the expression 'ᵉlōhē yiśrā'ēl is the tribal confederation Israel, not a clan chief called Israel.

3. In considering the issue of the renaming of Jacob as Israel we find that the dubiety whether any evidence of the existence of 'Father Israel' exists damages the credibility of the discussion. The explanation which can be derived from Gen. 32.23 ff. relates to Israel/Jacob who was the 'father' of the twelve tribes and that he was so represented is not in doubt. The explanation of Gen. 35.10 offered by Seebass labours under the disadvantage that it hangs on his dubious explanation of 33.20, and that, even if the existence of 'Father Israel' (a clan leader) is allowed, it still has the appearance of an explanation in which the wish is father to the thought. There is no reason why the renaming in 35.10 should not be explained in the same way as the renaming in 32.23 ff. and 'Israel' understood as a tribal confederacy. Moreover, unless the renaming is related to the enhancement of Jacob's status, it appears to lose its point. If the cult of the god of Israel (a clan leader) at Shechem is a clan cult, and, if the cult of the god of Jacob at Bethel is a clan cult, what incentive is there to legitimate the Bethel cult in terms of the Shechem cult? They both have the same status – they are clan cults established in connexion with the resident El at ancient Canaanite sanctuaries – and neither has any need of legitimation

[1] Cf. above, pp. 11-13.

in terms of the other nor can gain anything from it. Seebass's explanation of the renaming and of the process by which the composite Israel/Jacob originates is a lame one.

4. The assertion in connexion with the renaming discussion that Gen. 35.10 (E) is primary and 32.23 ff. (J) secondary raises important issues of method. The determination of what is primary or secondary in the documentary sources does not necessarily lead directly to historical or traditio-historical conclusions. So far as historical conclusions are concerned Seebass gives no thought to the genre of the patriarchal narratives.[1] He assumes that they are history of a kind and that they give us biographical access to patriarchs who exercised a historical role as clan leaders in Canaan or on the fringes of Canaan. The traditio-historical issue is more subtle and can best be approached by contrasting what Seebass means by 'history of tradition' with what Noth means when he uses the same terminology. We have seen[2] that Noth's history of tradition turns the indications given by the documentary sources upside down (Jacob is the first and Abraham the last). If this is so, documentary criticism does not lead in any simple or direct way to the investigation of the history of the tradition of the patriarchal narratives. Seebass's presuppositions are quite different from this. He supposes that whatever is established as primary in a document by literary-critical analysis is also a primary traditio-historical datum and that whatever is established as secondary by the same method is necessarily of less traditio-historical value. Moreover, by 'traditions' he means 'historically reliable information',[3] so that his history of the tradition of the patriarchal narratives begins with biographical descriptions of the patriarchs themselves.

5. With regard to the *Vätergötter* argument, the conclusions which are reached by Seebass do not follow by cogent p.ocesses of reasoning from the evidence which he assembles. 'God of my father' or 'god of your father' or 'god of his father', whether or not the name of a patriarch is appended, cannot produce a direct reference to the god of the patriarch in question but only to the god of the father of that patriarch. The conclusion which can readily be drawn from this kind of expression is not that *'elōhē 'ābī* or the like was the designation used by worshippers of a clan god and that

---

[1] Cf. above, pp. 2 ff.
[2] Above, pp. 153 ff.
[3] Above, pp. 8 f.

'*ābī* refers to the leader or founder of the clan (i.e., Abraham, Isaac, Jacob, Israel), but that a religious unification which accompanies the genealogical scheme Abraham-Isaac-Jacob is signified. When the patriarchs become three generations of a family, the god of Abraham is also the god of his son and grandson. Hence the contention that *paḥad ʾābīw yiṣḥāq* is more original than *paḥad yiṣḥāq* would seem to be without foundation. A more probable explanation is that the longer designation is secondary and consequent on the genealogical scheme. Seebass therefore has not demonstrated that *paḥad* cannot be the name of the god of Isaac. Again what grounds are there for Seebass's confidence that '*ābīr* (Gen. 49.24) is an attribute of Jacob's god rather than his name? Both explanations are possible, but it is difficult to find decisive reasons for preferring one and excluding the other. As an example of the odd way in which Seebass argues I take his comments on 31.13 on which he remarks:

The god of the Jacob clan is found at the sanctuary of Bethel and the identity of El Bethel with the god of the patriarch is made explicit by 31.5b, 13.[1]

On this the following may be said: (*a*) 'The god of my father' in 31.5b means 'the god of Isaac' or, perhaps, 'the god of Abraham' and does not refer to the god of Jacob's clan. (*b*) In 31.13 there is no mention of a god of Jacob's clan but of a deity who appeared to Jacob at Bethel, and the intention of the verse is to equate this El with Elohim who is an adumbration of Yahweh in the source E. Hence the 'angel of God' says to Jacob, 'I am the God Bethel' or 'I am the God of Bethel'.

6. Seebass's account of the history of the Jacob tradition has credibility only if the existence of a patriarch Israel, who is originally distinct from the patriarch Jacob, is granted. His hypothesis has some points of similarity with an earlier view that the east Jordan Jacob was originally distinct from the west Jordan Jacob, but it has its own special orientation. In effect the Mesopotamian features belong originally to the patriarch Israel and the east Jordan stories to Jacob. The Israel traditions have a span from Mesopotamia to Shechem and the Jacob traditions from east Jordan to Bethel.

7. The same problem of the shadowy patriarch Israel vitiates

---

[1] *op. cit.*, p. 52.

the account of how the Abraham/Isaac traditions are incorporated
into the Israel/Jacob and Moses/Yahweh complexes of tradition.
There is ample evidence of the genealogical scheme Abraham-
Isaac-Jacob, but none of a scheme Abraham-Isaac-Israel. It is this
latter, however, which Seebass postulates and on this hangs the
incorporation of Abraham and Isaac into a composite religious
unity made up of the component parts 'God of Israel' and 'Yahweh,
God of Moses'. There is a lack of evidence to support the conclusion that 'Yahweh, God of Israel' is indicative of the fusion of the
cults of two clan gods, and the relationship of Yahweh to Israel
should rather be elucidated by the assumption that the only Israel
which ever existed was the inter-tribal society bearing that name.
In that case Yahweh and Israel are co-extensive terms. Israel is
the creation of Yahwism (whatever the origins of Yahwism may
be) and Yahwism is operative in the sphere of Israel.

8. I have maintained that if traditions are interpreted as tribal
history, they cannot also be interpreted biographically.[1] If an
individual is the personification of a tribe, he cannot also be an
historical individual. It may be possible for Seebass to rebut the
charge that he is confused with respect to Jacob/Israel, but I do
not see how he can avoid it in relation to Moses. His interpretation
of the figure of Moses is a biographical one, for the most part, and
this cannot be combined with the interpretation of Moses' stay
with the Midianites as tribal history. The latter, according to
Seebass, contains the recollection that the Moses group already
had relations with the Midianites before the exodus from Egypt.[2]
One cannot jump from the understanding of Moses as an historical
individual to the interpretation of him as the personification of a
tribe and then back again to a biographical appraisal.

XII

Kilian[3] indicates his agreement with the methodological views
of Eissfeldt[4] and consequently endeavours to link his traditio-
historical investigations to his source criticism in such a way that
history of tradition is a prolongation of source criticism and can be
expressed in source-critical terms. He traces the processes by

---

[1] Above, p. 177.

[2] H. Seebass, *op. cit.*, p. 84.

[3] R. Kilian, *Die vorpriesterliche Abrahamsüberlieferung literarkritisch und traditionsgeschichtlich untersucht*, Bonner biblische Beiträge, 24 (1966), p. xi.

[4] O. Eissfeldt, *Th.R* 18 (1930), p. 287.

which a *Grundschicht* or *Grundtradition* has grown into the extant text of the Abraham narratives and it is these processes which constitute the history of the tradition. This is an extension of the source-critical method in the sense that instead of being satisfied with a J or an E source (Kilian is not concerned with P in this investigation) he regards the J or E source as the consequence of a growth from a *Grundschicht* or a *Grundtradition*, and the manner of this growth is described and explained. Even if part of the process is said to be pre-literary or oral, the entire development can, nevertheless, be described in source-critical terms, since the *Grundschicht*, as the nucleus of the source J or E, can be expressed as verses or parts of verses of the extant text. If there is an inter-mediate stage between the *Grundschicht* and the source J or E, whether it is described as redaction, expansion or reshaping, whether it is pre-Yahwist (Gen. 13; 16) or pre-Elohist (21.9-21; 22), this too can be expressed in similar source-critical terms.

An important aspect of Kilian's method is the comparison of variants of the same tradition in order to ascertain which is nearest to the *Vorlage*. Although the story about 'the hazarding of the wife' has a pre-Yahwistic *Grundschicht* in Gen. 12 and a pre-Elohist *Grundschicht* in Gen. 20, the form of the narrative in Gen. 26 is the oldest for the following reasons:

1. It has a secular character and it is more probable that a secular tradition would be subsequently theologized than that an original theological tradition would lose its theology.

2. There is a heightening of the danger to which the wife is exposed in chapters 12 and 20 as compared with 26.

3. The transfer of Isaac traditions to Abraham is more probable than the reverse process.

4. The narrower local horizons of chapter 26 (Gerar) is an indi-cation of earliness in terms of saga laws.

5. The directness and simplicity of the narrative in chapter 26, especially the way in which Abimelech finds out the truth about Isaac and Rebecca, as compared with the more artificial devices of 12 and 20, points to the priority of 26.[1]

It will be noted that one of the reasons given (3) is unrelated to a comparison of variants and is a traditio-historical judgement which transgresses the limits of a history of tradition confined to the area between *Grundschicht* and sources.[2] The relationship

---

[1] *op. cit.*, pp. 213 f. [2] See further, below, pp. 182 f.

which Kilian envisages between these variant traditions is one of model and copy. In chapter 20 he finds a *Grundschicht* which is pre-Elohist,[1] just as he finds a pre-Yahwist *Grundschicht* in 12,[2] and he assumes a *Vorlage* which has been developed in different ways and which is best preserved in 26.

Similarly he compares an 'Oath' *Schicht* in 21.22-34 (E, consisting of vv. 22, 23, 24, 27, 31, 33) with its Yahwist counterpart in 26.24-33, and his grounds for allocating priority to 26.24-33 would seem to be traditio-historical (i.e., traditio-historical in a more far-reaching sense than the one with which he operates) rather than literary-critical. He says that these are two variants of one and the same tradition, that there is no relationship of literary dependence, but that rather we have two separate developments of a common tradition. The variants cannot be described simply as earlier and later, since El Olam in 21 is an early feature which has not been preserved in 26.[3] The tradition belongs originally to Isaac and has been secondarily attracted to Abraham. Here again Kilian postulates a *Vorlage* or *Grundtradition* from which the 'Oath' *Schichten* in chapters 26 and 21 are separately developed, and the persistence of the terminology and procedures of source criticism is also illustrated by the conjectural restoration of *Vorlagen* at 19.14aβ, 24-25*[4] and at 18.1b, 3.[5]

A striking feature of Kilian's results is the meagreness of the Abraham traditions which they indicate. Kilian would seem to be in general agreement with Noth[6] that there are hardly any Abraham traditions. The reason for this is that narratives which appear to be about Abraham can be shown in terms of their *Vorlagen* or *Grundschichten* to have nothing to do with Abraham originally and to have been connected secondarily to him by the processes which lie between the *Grundschichten* and the extant text of the Abraham stories. The only exceptions to this are the *Grundschicht* of chapter 15 (vv. 9, 10, 12, 17, 18aba)[7] and the plural *Schicht* of 18.1-8 (vv. 1b*, 2*, 3*, 4, 5, 7, 8).[8] The first contains an ancient promise

---

[1] *op. cit.*, pp. 195-197.
[2] *ibid.*, pp. 10 f.
[3] *ibid.*, pp. 257 f.
[4] *ibid.*, p. 130.
[5] *ibid.*, pp. 148-158.
[6] Above, pp. 132 ff.
[7] *ibid.*, pp. 54-56.
[8] *ibid.*, pp. 148-158.

of land to Abraham, but the place where the promise was made has not been preserved, and the second carries us back to a period when Abraham's clan was settled around Mamre. The *Grundschicht* of chapter 12 is not an original Abraham tradition: Kilian accepts Noth's traditio-historical evaluation, namely that this is a Jacob tradition which has been transferred to Abraham.[1] The sphere of Kilian's detailed investigations lies between a *Grundschicht*, which can be expressed as a nucleus of the extant text, and the extant text itself, or, occasionally between a *Vorlage* (which is assumed and conjecturally restored, but which cannot be expressed as a nucleus of the extant text) and the extant text itself. If in nearly every case the *Vorlage* or *Grundschicht* does not contain an original Abraham tradition, *a fortiori* what develops from the *Grundschicht* does not either, and Kilian's work is principally an explanation of secondary processes by which Abraham was drawn into originally non-Abraham traditions.

Kilian brings to his account of the history of the tradition of the Abraham narratives from *Grundschichten* to the extant text techniques which are not themselves source-critical and it is they which determine largely the shape of his enquiry and the nature of his results. The principle of research into genre (*Gattungsforschung*) which he employs most frequently is the aetiological one and his *Grundschichten* are largely aetiological notices or aetiological stories (chapters 13; 16; 19; 21; 22). The *Grundschicht* of chapter 13 (vv. 2, 5, 7a, 8, 9, 10a, 11a, 14*, 15-17) is an aetiology which explains why Abraham possesses only part of the land, although he had been promised all of it according to the *Grundschicht* of chapter 12 (vv. 1, 4a, 6a, 7, 8) which is the introduction to the aetiology of chapter 13. There is no pre-Abraham or pre-Israelite saga at the foundation of chapter 13. The narrative is not a report of an historical event, but an aetiological solution of a theological problem, namely, a discrepancy between promise and fulfilment. In order to portray the problem in a lively way the narrator made use of the motif of 'strife among shepherds'. Such an aetiology was already redundant by the time that Israel became a state under David. The historical circumstances reflected by the aetiology are those of the period when Israel occupied the hill country west of the Jordan and the Moabites and Ammonites were settled in east Jordan, that is, the period between the settlement and David's

[1] R. Kilian, *op. cit.*, pp. 11, 34.

reign. It was a time when Abraham was attracting to himself sanctuaries which were originally associated with Jacob.[1]

The two Ishmaelite aetiologies contained in the *Grundschicht* of chapter 16 had already grown together in the pre-Israelite period. The first (vv. 11aβb, 12) is a tribal aetiology which explains the name Ishmael and the Ishmaelite style of life. The second (vv. 13, 14a) is a cultic aetiology which explains the existence of the sanctuary and its name. The narrative expansion of these aetiologies (vv. 1b, 2, 4-7a, 11aα, 14b) was not the invention of the Yahwist and was designed to answer a problem which existed before his time. The narrative originated when the Ishmaelite aetiologies were taken up into the Abraham tradition and its form presupposes the prior existence of the aetiologies (e.g., '*ēn mayim*, 'spring of water', in v. 7a assumes *be'ēr* 'well' in v. 14a). The aetiologies are connected with Abraham, because Ishmael had at an earlier stage of the history of the tradition been connected with Isaac. If Isaac and Ishmael are brothers, it is an obvious step to make Abraham the father of Ishmael, and this is facilitated by the circumstance that no father is mentioned in the Ishmaelite aetiology. It was not so easy to incorporate Sarah, since Ishmael already had a mother and narrative skill had to be exercised in order to achieve this. The problem was solved in a masterly way and with great economy (16.1 ff.). The narrator created a story with authentic historical colouring and based on the actual legal practice of the age.[2]

The plural *Schicht* of chapter 19 (vv. 1*, 2 f., 4a*, 5-8, 9abα*, 10 f., 12aα, 12b, 13a, 14aα, 14aβ*, 14b, 15*, 16aαb, 17aα*, 18, 20*, 22b, 23a, 24 f.*, 26, 30-38) is a collection of diverse aetiologies which belonged to the south-eastern fringes of the Dead Sea and explained the barrenness of this region. The story of Lot's wife explains the unusual shape of a particular pillar of rock and the cave story the origins of the inhabitants of the hill country east of the Jordan, and, later, the origins of the Moabites and the Ammonites and their names. The union of the diverse elements took place at a pre-literary stage and neither the once independent aetiologies nor the composite narrative which results from their union has any distinctive Israelite marks; nor is the settlement of Israel in Canaan anywhere presupposed. We are therefore dealing

[1] *op. cit.*, pp. 29-35.
[2] *ibid.*, pp. 84-94.

with a non-Israelite and pre-settlement complex of tradition which
had no original connexion with Abraham, which, in all probability,
originated in east Jordan, but which became known west of the
Jordan and was narrated on both sides of the Dead Sea.[1]

The *Grundschicht* of 21.9-21 (vv. 17*, 18b, 19a, 19b*, 20) corresponds with the Ishmaelite aetiologies in 16.11-14, but the following differences should be noted: (*a*) In chapter 16 the name
Ishmael is explained as the hearing of the mother's complaint, in
21 as the hearing of the cry of the child. (*b*) 16.12 contains a powerful and lively portrayal of Bedouin life, whereas 21.18b is a colourless and general promise, and only in 21.20 can the Bedouin motif
be discerned. (*c*) 16.14a is about a particular well which was hallowed by a theophany, while in 21.19 the particularity of the well
has ceased to be important. What now matters is that God causes
Hagar to *see* a well and to obtain water for her child. (*d*) 16.13 is
about a specific god El Roi, while 21.19 (*'elōhīm*) was perhaps at
the pre-Elohist stage about an unspecified El.

Hence the tradition in chapter 16 is older than that in 21 as is
shown by the following considerations: (*a*) The name Beer Lahai
Roi is known in chapter 16 as a well and an Ishmaelite settlement.
(*b*) The Bedouin character of Ishmael is transmitted in 16.12 as a
divine promise, while in 21.20 it has become part of the narrative.
(*c*) In 16.11 the Ishmaelite aetiology is coupled with the giving of
the name, but in 21.17 ff. the important aetiological moment is
missing. The aetiological concern is thus weakened in chapter 21,
and the aetiology which is originally an explanation of the inauguration of the cult of El Roi at Beer Lahai Roi, is on the way to
becoming a narrative concerning the hearing of the child's cry and
the Bedouin life of Ishmael. The loss of aetiological point had
already occurred at the pre-literary stage and the pre-Elohist narrative expansion and reshaping which connected Ishmael with
Abraham had been consummated in oral tradition. In this narrative
the genealogical link of Ishmael with Abraham and the association
of Hagar with Sarah is simply taken for granted and this indicates
that the narrative of chapter 16 is presupposed, not as a literary
model or *Vorlage*, but in so far as the connexion of Abraham,
Ishmael, Sarah and Hagar had already been established.[2]

The 'Oath' *Schicht* in 21.22-34 (vv. 22, 23, 24, 27, 31, 33) con-

[1] *ibid.*, pp. 132-146.
[2] *ibid.*, pp. 236-249.

tains an aetiology of Beersheba which has been secondarily transferred from Isaac to Abraham[1] and the 'Seven' *Schicht* in the same
passage (vv. 25, 26, 28, 29, 30, 32) is a secondary aetiology for
which there is no *Grundtradition* or *Vorlage* but which has grown
up as a pre-literary narrative out of the name Beersheba. The
Elohist fitted the two narratives together into a composite narrative
working the 'Seven' *Schicht* into the 'Oath' *Schicht*.[2]

The *Grundschicht* of chapter 22 consists of two old traditions, a
pilgrimage aetiology (vv. 3*, 4, 5*, 9*, 14a*, 19aα) and a cult-
foundation aetiology (vv. 5*, 9*, 10b, 11aα*, 12a, 13*), the editing
and expansion of which by the Elohist produced the corpus in
22.1-14a, 19. The pilgrimage tradition concerns a sanctuary which
is approached by a three days' journey in order that prayer may
be offered at it. The cult-foundation tradition deals with the aboli-
tion of human sacrifice through the substitution of a representative
animal. Both traditions belong to the Negeb, but the exact location
of the place to which they were attached was unknown to the
Elohist. It was called '*ēl yir'eh* (*YHWH yir'eh* in 22.14) and a god
of that name was worshipped there by nomads. That such a god
who sees or appears was worshipped in the Negeb is shown by
16.13.[3]

These observations are principally concerned with the history
of the genre and a clear picture of Kilian's understanding of the
Abraham narratives can be gathered from them. Originally non-
Abrahamic aetiological notices are expanded into narratives to
which Abraham is attracted. In connexion with the filling out of
the narrative content the original aetiological point or concern
tends to be weakened or generalized. This loss of aetiological
sharpness can be established by a comparison of variant traditions.
One can also speak in the case of the 'Seven' *Schicht* of 21.22-34
of a secondary aetiology which is aetiological play or invention
rather than an expression of serious aetiological concern (that is,
a display of aetiological virtuosity in exploiting the possibilities of
the name Beersheba).

Kilian tends to explain this narrative expansion functionally
rather than regarding it as free narrative invention,[4] so that it is

---

[1] Above, p. 182.
[2] *op. cit.*, pp. 250-262.
[3] *ibid.*, pp. 263-278.
[4] Above, pp. 183 f., on chapters 13 and 16.

almost a postulate with him that an explanation of expansion or reshaping is only adequate if it can be shown to answer a question or to meet a need of the circle in which the tradition lives and by which it is transmitted. In so far as the narratives have this functional character they have the same kind of indirect historical value which Noth ascribes to them. In other words it is possible to correlate the traditio-historical processes with historical periods and circumstances.

A special type of narrative expansion which does not have an aetiological base is found in the plural *Schicht* of 18.1-8[1] which, according to Kilian, is an 'imitation' of the Sodom narrative in the plural *Schicht*[2] of chapter 19. The close correspondence of 18.1-8 and 19.1-3 can only mean that the original form of 18.1-8 constituted a retelling of the older Sodom-Lot narrative and its transfer to Abraham and his sphere of life. The intention of this transfer was to connect Abraham with the Sodom tradition which was being narrated in Mamre at this period. 18.1-8 cannot therefore be any older than Abraham and is perhaps no older than the period when the Abraham group settled around Mamre.

It should be clear that, according to this treatment, the Abraham traditions are not historiography and that so to evaluate them is a failure to identify the genre. Although Kilian declares his belief in Abraham as an historical individual, his method shows that the apparent historical content consists of narrative expansion of aetiological notices or of originally non-Abraham traditions, and that whatever historical information can be gleaned from these relates to the circumstances mirrored by the traditio-historical processes and does not facilitate the quest after the historical Abraham. An interesting aspect of this is that Kilian attributes to felicitous narrative invention what has elsewhere been regarded as evidence in favour of the historicity of the patriarchal narratives, namely, the authentic second millennium B.C. background which is found in them.[3] Thus of the narrative which connects the Ishmaelite aetiologies with Abraham and Sarah he says that it has authentic historical colouring and reflects the legal practice of the age in which it is set.[4] His view of the narratives as literary creations

[1] Above, pp. 182 f.
[2] Above, p. 184.
[3] Above, pp. 1 ff.
[4] *op. cit.*, p. 91.

rather than historiography is seen in his remark that the flight of Hagar is a narrative device to bring her to Beer Lahai Roi,[1] and in his application of saga laws to the comparison of chapters 12 and 26. The 'hazarding of the wife' tradition in chapter 26 is the older of the two because the area in which the action of the story operates is less extensive in 26 than in 12 (Gerar as opposed to Egypt).[2]

Lot's connexion with Abraham is not an original, historical one, and the Abraham-Lot cycle is entirely the product of traditio-historical processes. 12.4b, 5, which connects Abraham with Lot and both with Harran, is the creation of P. The Abraham-Lot story in chapter 13 is an aetiology and not a report of an historical event,[3] and the association of Abraham with Lot in chapters 18 f. is the consequence of the retelling of the older Sodom-Lot narrative and its transfer to Abraham.[4] Lot is portrayed as a relative of Abraham consequent on the connexion of chapters 12 f. with 18 f. and accompanies him as far as Bethel. In chapter 13* he is still a rich nomad, but in 19* he is a city dweller in Sodom. In the latter chapter he is portrayed in an altogether positive way, whereas in the Israelite tradition of chapter 13* he is accused of greed which is punished with the destruction of Sodom. This is an estimate which is totally foreign to the local saga of chapter 19* before its union with 13*.[5]

In three places Kilian postulates the transfer of original Isaac traditions to Abraham and he arrives at this conclusion by a comparison of the variant traditions. He compares chapter 26 with 12 and 20[6]; 26.24-33 with the 'Oath' *Schicht* in 21.22-34[7]; the *Grund-schicht* in 21.9-21 with 16.11-14.[8] In the case of the first and the third the comparison is orientated towards history of genre and the marriage of methods is not so much a marriage of the source-critical and the traditio-historical as it is a marriage of history of genre and history of tradition. The question should be raised whether in arriving at this type of traditio-historical conclusion (as also is his conclusion that the *Grundschicht* of chapter 12 is an

[1] *ibid.*, p. 92.
[2] Above, p. 181.
[3] Above, pp. 183 f.
[4] Above, p. 187.
[5] *op. cit.*, p. 289.
[6] Above, p. 181.
[7] Above, p. 182.
[8] Above, p. 185.

original Jacob tradition which has been transferred to Abraham[1])
Kilian is not transgressing the limits of his concept of history of
tradition, namely, that it exists in the space between a *Grundschicht*
and the extant sources. When he postulates the transfer of traditions from one patriarch to another he is accepting Noth's concept
of history of tradition which contradicts his view that history of
tradition is a prolongation of source criticism. To some extent
Kilian is saved from this problem by the fact that he is dealing
only with the Abraham traditions, but whenever the secondary
transfer of traditions to Abraham from Isaac or Jacob is contemplated, the implication is that the history of the tradition of the
patriarchal narratives has a character which contradicts the impression conveyed by the extant sources.

XIII

I have already commented on the extent to which Noth's history
of the tradition of the patriarchal narratives is influenced by his
assumption that Shechem was the centre of a twelve-tribe Israelite
amphictyony.[2] The amphictyonic hypothesis also controls his approach to the Abraham traditions: they were not originally located
at Hebron-Mamre and the figure of Abraham only became attached
to that place after it had become the centre of a six-tribe amphictyony. The Lot-Sodom traditions were circulating in the Hebron
area prior to the attraction of Abraham to that place, and so there
is no original connexion between Abraham and that material.[3] The
hypothesis of amphictyony also plays an influential part in Jepsen's
account of the history of the tradition of the patriarchal stories:
there was a six-tribe *ᵃbīr yaᶜᵃqōb* amphictyony of 'sons' of Jacob
and Leah at Shechem and Bethel, a twelve-tribe Yahwistic amphictyony at Bethel, and a six-tribe amphictyony at Hebron-
Mamre.[4]

It is consequently necessary to take some account of recent
criticism of Noth's hypothesis[5] and there are some respects in

---

[1] See above, p. 183.
[2] See above, p. 154.
[3] See above, pp. 139 f.
[4] See above, pp. 163 f.
[5] W. H. Irwin, 'Le Sanctuaire Central Israélite Avant L'Établissement De
La Monarchie', *RB* lxxii (1965), pp. 161-184; G. W. Anderson, 'Israel: Amphictyony: 'Am; Ḳāhāl; 'Ēdāh', *Translating and Understanding the Old Testament*: Essays in Honor of Herbert Gordon May (1970), pp. 135-151; R. de
Vaux, 'La Thèse de "L'Amphictyonie Israélite"', *HTR* lxiv (1971), pp. 415-436.

which this criticism must be regarded as successful. The use of the amphictyonic model from the Graeco-Italian world is not justifiable and consequently most of the features attributed by Noth to a confederation of Israelite tribes under the influence of this model have to be surrendered. The model would seem to have suggested to Noth the central sanctuary, the tribal representatives and the amphictyonic law and of these the only item which I wish to defend is the central sanctuary, although I do it in the full awareness that there is a lack of biblical evidence for such an institution in the period of the Judges. It has further been urged against Noth's use of the amphictyonic model that the number 12 is not one which applies generally to Greek and Italian amphictyonies and that it is adhered to strictly only in the case of the Pylae-Delphic amphictyony (sixth century B.C.).[1] This criticism is sufficient to persuade me that the term amphictyony should be given up, but the hypothesis of a central sanctuary in relation to the Israelite tribes in Canaan seems to me to be more fundamental and not so easily expendable. Noth's critics have urged that a central sanctuary is of the essence of a Graeco-Italian amphictyony and that it was for this reason that Noth was led to postulate a central sanctuary for the Israelite tribes. There are, however, other considerations which still apply in this regard, even when the details of Noth's amphictyonic hypothesis have been surrendered. These were expressed by Noth as follows:

Die religionsgeschichtliche Bedeutung der altisraelitischen Amphiktyonie, so wie wir sie darzustellen versuchten, ist aber noch in einer anderen Richtung zu erkennen. War der Jahwekult anfangs der Bundeskult der israelitischen Stämme, dessen Ort das gemeinsame Amphiktyonenheiligtum mit dem Kultobjekt der heiligen Lade war, so nahm dieses eine Heiligtum von vornherein eine Sonderstellung unter den Heiligtümern des Landes ein, und insofern an den übrigen Heiligtümern die alten lokalen Kulte ungestört weiterleben durften, während der Jahwekult grundsätzlich zunächst seine besondere Rolle als Bundeskult spielte, so war mit ihm zugleich die Tatsache der Einheit seiner Kultstätte aufs engste verbunden. Es handelte sich dabei natürlich zunächst nicht um die Alleinberechtigung des Amphiktyonenheiligtums als Jahwekultstätte, aber es gab faktisch eben nur eine Kultstätte im Lande, an der Jahwe auf alleinige Verehrung prinzipiell Anspruch machen konnte.[2]

Even if the ark cannot be drawn into this argument in the way

---

[1] R. de Vaux, *ibid.*, p. 422.
[2] *Das System*, p. 116.

that Noth supposes (see below), the substance of it is not seriously impaired. Noth's critics are perhaps not sufficiently apprised of the importance of this consideration. In this connexion it should be noted that while there is a broad similarity in the arguments by which they dispose of Noth's detailed hypothesis, there is not the same degree of coherence in the positive alternatives which they offer. If we take their views on the twelve-tribe confederation, we find that it is located in the pre-settlement period by Fohrer[1]: it had significance in connexion with nomadic or semi-nomadic conditions of life and the list was already fossilized at the earliest period of the settlement in Canaan. For Irwin, Gilgal was the first base in Canaan of the Sinai tribes and the twelve-tribe confederation was first achieved at Shechem.[2] Anderson's position is more reserved, but he holds that the incorporation of the tribes into a larger inter-tribal unity rests on the transaction which took place at Sinai and that the twelve-tribe structure certainly antedates the reign of David. He is inclined to believe that what is recorded in Josh. 24 represents a further incorporation of tribes which had not participated in the Sinai events.[3] De Vaux holds that Gilgal was the first sanctuary of the tribes who crossed the Jordan into Canaan and that it was the first station of the ark, but it could not have been a sanctuary of the twelve tribes, since the confederation was not then in existence. Further Shechem was not a sanctuary of the twelve tribes, since they had not yet come together at the time of the events recorded in Josh. 24. The most probable interpretation to be placed on these events is that they represent a pact between the tribes of the north which had not shared the Exodus and Sinai experiences and the Joshua group which offered to them the Yahwistic faith.[4]

On the ark de Vaux observes that there is no specific reference to it in relation to Shechem, and that the notice which associates it with Bethel is suspect (Judg. 20.27 f.).[5] Irwin, however, accepts the Bethel reference – the transfer of the ark to Bethel was occasioned by the threat offered to Gilgal by trans-Jordanian tribes and in view of the presence of the ark the importance which had

[1] G. Fohrer, 'Altes Testament – "Amphiktyonie und Bund" ', *ThLZ* 91 (1966), cols. 801-816, 894-904.
[2] *op. cit.*, p. 183.
[3] *op. cit.*, pp. 141 f., 149 f.
[4] *op. cit.*, pp. 423 f., 427.
[5] *ibid.*, p. 426, G. Fohrer, *op. cit.*, col. 810.

attached to Gilgal and to Shechem (without the ark) was transferred to Bethel.[1] Hence Noth's contention that it was the ark
which constituted the central sanctuary still exercises some influence on Irwin. For Fohrer, on the other hand, the ark does not
enter the history of the Israelite tribes until the period of Shiloh,
when it becomes the symbol of an inter-tribal coalition directed
against the Philistines.[2] If one takes the concept of covenant, one
finds that it is influential in Irwin's account (see below), whereas
for Fohrer the significant theological sense of covenant is said to
arrive only with the Deuteronomists.[3]

Anderson,[4] Irwin[5] and Orlinsky[6] all take the view that the period
of the Judges was a kind of 'dark age' when the tribes lost a
coherence which they had earlier possessed and relapsed into tribalism. With this picture they combine a more idealistic estimate
of the religion of the tribes in this period than Noth had envisaged.
Noth in respect of his history of Yahwism is nearer to Wellhausen
than his critics are. Apart from the existence of a corporate Yahwistic cult with an inter-tribal status, Noth did not see any
possibility of transcending tribal religion in the early period of the
settlement.[7] Orlinsky combines a dark picture of tribal centrifu-
galism with a comfortable doctrine about Israelite religion:

Already in the patriarchal period the Deity was not localized. He accompanied the patriarchal household in its semi-nomadic wanderings, and
made and renewed covenants with them in several different places. In the
period of the Judges the Deity was worshipped in a large number of
places. Shrines were plentifully scattered in virtually every populated site,
and it is likely that but few persons had to cross tribal boundaries to offer
up sacrifice and prayer to God. Amphictyony, a centralized shrine and
cult, is scarcely part of this concept or need.[8]

Irwin supposes that Yahwism was maintained by renewal of
covenant ceremonies at local sanctuaries independently celebrated
by tribes who had no cultic contact with one another. Fohrer's[9]

---

    [1] op. cit., p. 184.   [2] op. cit., cols. 810 f.
    [3] ibid., cols. 897-901.   [4] op. cit., p. 149.
    [5] op. cit., pp. 183 f. Both Irwin and Anderson hold on to a reduced form of
Noth's concept that the ark was the central sanctuary. Wherever it rested, would
be a place of inter-tribal pilgrimage (Irwin) or may have possessed a special
status (Anderson).
    [6] H. M. Orlinsky, 'The Tribal System of Israel and Related Groups in the
Period of the Judges', Studies and Essays in Honor of Abraham A. Neuman
(1962), pp. 375-387.
    [7] See above, p. 190.
    [8] op. cit., p. 386.   [9] op. cit., cols. 814, 901.

view is that Yahwism held its ground in Canaan through the circumstance that a Moses group, which was the bearer of Yahwism, was dispersed throughout the Israelite tribes in Canaan. Anderson may be right in holding that the origins of an inter-tribal structure go back to the Sinai compact, but the complex processes of accommodation to a sedentary culture which required from Yahwism capacities for modification and symbiosis cannot be described only in negative terms of fragmentation and relapse. The contact of Yahwism with Canaanite culture and Canaanite sanctuaries was momentous. Is it enough to say that an inter-tribal Yahwistic cult was lost during this early crucial period of the settlement and that after a long historical interval it re-emerged?[1]

Noth did not suppose that the cults of tribal sanctuaries, some of which were ancient Canaanite sanctuaries, were all Yahwistic. The reform of Josiah, at a much later period, indicates sufficiently how difficult it was to maintain the purity of Yahwism at local sanctuaries. Noth assumed that the processes of settlement brought with them religious confusion and syncretism. What is said in the next chapter about the religion of the patriarchal stories gives some impression of how complicated a matter this can be. Is there not some loss of contact with reality when it is supposed that exclusive Yahwistic cults were a feature of the places where the tribes in separation from each other worshipped throughout Canaan? If the tribalism of the period of the Judges has to be taken seriously, the processes by which tribal religion comes to terms with the sedentary cults of Canaanite sanctuaries and with Yahwism has also to be taken seriously. The view that one can have a plurality of Yahwistic sanctuaries belonging separately to Israelite tribes does not seem to be realistic. Nor is it realistic to suppose that in these circumstances Yahwism could have survived without a public, inter-tribal, cultic institution. The position then is that there is no hard biblical evidence that such a 'central sanctuary' existed, but that, on the other hand, the survival and subsequent history of Yahwism in Canaan still requires the hypothesis of an inter-tribal, Yahwistic cultic institution.

The last observation which I make by way of drawing together the strands of this chapter concerns the two quite different concepts of 'history of tradition' which are discernible in the work re-

---

[1] Cf. A. D. H. Mayes, *Israel in the Period of the Judges*, *SBT*, second series, 29 (1974). Israel as a Yahweh-worshipping group of tribes came into existence

viewed. Noth has an understanding of 'history of tradition' which is irreconcilable with what is intended by Hoftijzer, Kilian and, to some extent, Seebass[1] and Jepsen,[2] when they speak of 'history of tradition'. Noth's concept implies that the manner in which the tradition grows obscures the previous history of its growth, so that the history of the tradition cannot be read off from the end product which is the extant documentary source. This means that one cannot simply inspect the sources and observe an extant stratification which will disclose a record of every stage of the tradition from its earliest beginnings to its fixation in the documentary sources. This, however, is precisely the assumption with which Hoftijzer and Kilian operate and so they postulate a marriage of source criticism and history of tradition which is incompatible with Noth's concept of history of tradition.

This does not mean that Noth's traditio-historical method is entirely independent of source criticism: a definition of the sources is Noth's point of departure, but his method is not a prolongation of source criticism and his results cannot be expressed in source-critical terms, that is, as *Grundschichten* which are nuclei of extant sources. He has a concept of growth of tradition which is organic and which involves transformation and not simply aggregation. This is a view of tradition which has affinities with the expositions of Engnell[3] and Nielsen,[4] and the question has to be asked whether such a view of tradition is compatible with a detailed recovery of the history of the tradition of the kind which Noth undertakes. If every stage of growth involves transformation, it tends to obliterate the earlier stage, and if the logic of this were to be pressed, we should have to conclude that the only one of these successive transformations of which we know anything is the last one – the stage reached at the point of written fixation. So far as I understand Engnell, I take this to be the kind of conclusion which he favours.

---

at Kadesh and the tribes retained their sense of belonging to each other and their common allegiance to Yahweh, although they had no common religious or political structures in Canaan during the period of the Judges.

[1] See above, p. 178.

[2] See above pp, 170 f.

[3] I. Engnell, 'The Traditio-Historical Method in Old Testament Research', *Critical Essays on the Old Testament* (1970), pp. 3-11.

[4] E. Nielsen, *Oral Tradition* (*SBT* No. 11, 1954), pp. 39 ff.

CHAPTER IV

The Religion of the Patriarchs

I

One can see among conservative scholars in the age before Gunkel the thought which is still expressed with many variations to-day that the patriarchs were pioneers of a new religion, who effected a sharp break with preceding religious practice, and who, because of the truth revealed to them, raised religion to a new and even monotheistic level (Oettli, Klostermann, König, Jeremias, Hommel). The assumption that the religion of the patriarchs was nomadic and polydaemonic (Stade, Marti) was contradicted by Franz Delitzsch who maintained that it was an El religion and was monotheistic in tendency. The question whether or not the patriarchs were worshippers of El or of Elim is one around which controversy still rages. The view that the Elim were local Canaanite deities is represented by Baudissin, while the supposition that Yahwism built on a substratum of Canaanite El monotheism and polydaemonic shepherd religion, found in Baentsch, has some similarity with a modern account of the ingredients of Yahwism by Andersen.[1] All in all the seeds of the modern debate on the religion of the patriarchs are already present at this early period.[2]

Gunkel's earlier view had been that El religion was a Canaanite phenomenon and that it was appropriated by Yahwism in connexion with the attachment of that cult to ancient Canaanite sanctuaries which possessed resident El deities. When he resiles from this view,[3] he clearly does so under the influence of Gressmann who had expressly disagreed with Gunkel on this issue.[4] The precise connexion between Gressmann's dissent and Gunkel's change of mind is shown by the circumstance that the pages of Genesis (3) which Gressmann cites are those adduced by Gunkel himself[5] in order to show that there is a divergence between the final opinion which he expresses in the introduction to Genesis (3) and what

---

[1] Below, pp. 215 ff.
[2] For a full account and for bibliographical details see H. Weidmann, op. cit., pp. 11-88.
[3] Genesis (3), p. lx.
[4] 'Sage und Geschichte in den Patriarchenerzählungen', p. 28.
[5] pp. 187, 236, 285.

appears in the body of the commentary.[1] Gunkel therefore ultimately agrees with Gressmann that the patriarchs were worshippers of El and that El religion was not first appropriated by
Yahwism in a Canaanite context. It should be noted, however,
that the account which both give of the history of the genre of the
patriarchal narratives is such that neither can contemplate the
possibility that the patriarchs ever set foot in Canaan or had relations with Canaanite sanctuaries. This is a nice illustration of the
connexion between a determination of the genre of the patriarchal
narratives and an account of the religion of the patriarchs. The
view that El religion is patriarchal will be developed differently by
those who suppose that the patriarchal stories are in some sense
historiography and that the El religion of the patriarchs can be
discussed in a Canaanite context.

Eissfeldt's opinions on the religion of the patriarchs[2] follow from
his conclusions about the historicity of the patriarchal narratives.[3]
Since these narratives give us access to a pre-Israelite period, they
are sources for the religion of the patriarchs, whether interpreted
as tribes or groups, as in the case of Isaac and Jacob, or as historical
individuals, as in the case of Abraham. On the basis of these sources
it can be concluded that the patriarchs participated in the El cult
at various Canaanite sanctuaries. Abraham invoked El Olam at
Beersheba (Gen. 21.33 – YAHWEH is perhaps secondary); Jacob
had relations with the El of Bethel (28.10-22; 31.13); Jacob
fought with an El and called the place Penuel (32.25-33); Jacob
set up an altar at Shechem and called it El Elohe Israel (33.20).
Abraham had a special relationship with the El of Hebron and the
El of Beersheba: El Shaddai (Gen. 17) probably belonged to
Hebron (cf. 18.1) and chapter 15, of which 21.33 is the conclusion,
should be located at Beersheba.[4] El Elyon was the cult established
at Jerusalem[5] and El Shaddai, originally located at Hebron, was,
according to P, the sole El worshipped by the patriarchs and so
had the status of E's Elohim. The equation of Elyon with Shaddai
is post-Davidic. Isaac had especially close connexions with the El
of Beersheba (26.23; 46.1) and with El Roi (24.62), and Jacob with
the El of Bethel, Penuel and Shechem.[6]

[1] Cf. H. Weidmann, *op. cit.*, p. 120, n. 142.

[2] 'Jahwe der Gott der Väter', *KS* iv, pp. 79-91.

[3] Above, pp. 69 ff.   [4] Above, p. 75.   [5] Above, pp. 84 f., 95 f.

[6] 'Jahwes Verhältnis zu 'Eljon und Schaddaj nach Psalm 91', *WO* (1957),
pp. 343-348, *KS* iii (1966), pp. 441-447.

The names *paḥad yiṣḥāq* (31.42, 53) and *'ᵃbīr yaʿᵃqōb* (49.24) are not to be associated with nomadic or semi-nomadic clan cults of which Isaac and Jacob were the founders,[1] but are none other than the Canaanite El whom these patriarchs worshipped: *paḥad yiṣḥāq* is the El worshipped by Isaac at Beersheba and Beer Lahai Roi; *'ᵃbīr yaʿᵃqōb* is the El worshipped by Jacob at Bethel, Shechem and Penuel, and at Beersheba on his way to Egypt (46.1). The patriarchs were El worshippers and the cult of El belongs to Canaan. The pre-Canaanite gods of the patriarchs are not significant as a proto-Yahwism in the way suggested by Alt. The significant religious event was rather the incorporation of El worship and theology into Yahwism and the 'gods of the fathers' *qua* pre-Canaanite clan gods are none other than the idols whom the Israelites were required to put away at Shechem (Josh. 24) or the gods buried by Jacob there prior to his pilgrimage to Bethel to worship El Bethel[2] (35.1 ff.).

The circumstance that L and J, for whom Yahweh is already the God of Abraham, refer to revelations made to Abraham in Canaan not by Yahweh but by an El[3] is to be understood as the shining through of an historical fact which is not entirely compatible with the outline of Israelite religion elsewhere furnished by L and J. The same can be said of the account which these sources give of the relationship between Isaac and Jacob and the Canaanite El (26.24, J; 28.19, J; 32.28-30, L; 33.20, L). In view of the fact that so much is made of the patriarchs not taking Canaanite wives, one might have expected that the origins of their religion would similarly have been represented as non-Canaanite, but, on the contrary, E indicates that the forbears of the patriarchs were idolators (Gen. 31). There is no evidence of any conflict with the Canaanite cult in the patriarchal narratives such as is attested after the settlement. Eissfeldt draws the conclusion that the patriarchs had a positive attitude to the Canaanite El cult and participated in it at the sanctuaries of Bethel, Beersheba, Shechem and Hebron.[4]

Since the patriarchs were El worshippers, it follows that the mention of the 'god of Abraham', 'god of Isaac' and 'god of Jacob' in the patriarchal narratives is a reference to El and not to a pre-

---

[1] Cf. A. Alt, below, pp. 203 ff.

[2] 'Der Gott Bethel', *ARW* 28 (1930), pp. 1-30; *KS* i (1962), pp. 206-233.

[3] The only relevant reference which I can discover is 21.33 (J). Eissfeldt mentions 17.1 (P).

[4] 'Jahwe der Gott der Väter, pp. 83-87.

Canaanite cult of the 'god of the fathers'. The equation of the God of Abraham, Isaac and Jacob with Yahweh may be a post-settlement development associated with the tribal union achieved by the House of Joseph who brought Yahwism to Canaan when they returned from Egypt, but the equation may have been made by Moses himself who is then to be regarded as the creator of Yahwism.[1]

In another article[2] Eissfeldt's enquiry into the religion of the patriarchs is pursued a stage further. '*el 'ᵉlōhē yiśrā'ēl* (Gen. 33.20) is understood as a reference to a clan cult rather than to the experience of an individual and this is in agreement with Eissfeldt's general view that Jacob/Israel is a tribe or group of tribes. What is indicated here is a particular historical circumstance, namely the appropriation of the El cult by the historical entity Jacob/Israel and the erection of an altar at Shechem named '*ēl 'ᵉlōhē yiśrā'ēl* (Eissfeldt assigns 33.18-20 to L as the conclusion of the L narrative in 32.24-33).[3] If in the pre-Mosaic period an El cult was appro-priated by an Israelite tribe or group of tribes, the post-Mosaic confession of allegiance to Yahweh alone reported in Josh. 24 and set at Shechem was possibly and even probably associated with the event narrated in Gen. 33.18-20 which had taken place at Shechem a century or two earlier. The earlier tribal group Israel swore allegiance to El, the later Israel of the twelve tribes swore allegiance to Yahweh, the God who had brought the Israelite tribal group, probably the House of Joseph, from Egypt to central Palestine by way of Kadesh or Sinai and east Jordan. This was the group into which Moses had instilled Yahwism and which brought the cult of Yahweh to Canaan.[4]

The renaming of Jacob as Israel attested by L (32.29) and P (35.10) is closely connected with the adoption of El worship by the Jacob group of tribes. Whatever be the etymology of Israel ('God fights' is probably correct, cf. Gen. 32.29; Hos. 12.4), the renaming has a cultic significance and arises from the desire of the Jacob group of tribes to possess a name of which the name of the God to whom they had pledged themselves was a part. Thus

---

[1] *ibid.*, pp. 89 f.

[2] 'Jakob's Begegnung mit El und Moses Begegnung mit Jahwe', *OLZ* 58 (1963), Sp. 325-331; *KS* iv, pp. 92-98.

[3] In his *Introduction*, p. 194, Eissfeldt assigns only 33.18-19* to L; cf. above, p. 197.

[4] 'Jakob's Begegnung mit El und Moses Begegnung mit Jahwe', pp. 96-98.

Israel is religious terminology, but (contrary to Noth) it does not refer first to a post-settlement amphictyonic entity. Rather it has a historical place, as the sources indicate, in the pre-settlement period when the El cult was adopted at Shechem by the Jacob group of tribes.

On the relation of El and Yahweh Eissfeldt[1] remarks that Canaan was the sphere of El in the first instance and that the supremacy of El was acknowledged by the invading God, Yahweh, who subsequently, however, acquired the rank of king and creator of the world and supplanted El as the highest God. The simple equation of El with Yahweh is found in Josh. 22.22 (*'ēl 'ᵉlōhīm YAHWEH*) where both *'ēl* and *'ᵉlōhīm* are identical with Yahweh; also in Ps. 104, where Yahweh is used throughout except for the one occurrence of El in v. 21. El in the dialogue of the book of Job (3.1-42.5), like Eloah, Elohim and Shaddai, can refer only to Yahweh whose name appears in the narrative outline (1.1-2.13; 42.6-17). In Isa. 40.18, 43.12, 45.22, on the other hand, there is the apologetic intention of representing that Yahweh is El or of claiming the name El for Yahweh. Finally there are a few passages in which El is represented as superior in rank to Yahweh. Of these Isa. 14.13 ('Above the stars of El I shall raise my throne') and Ezek. 28.1 ('I am El, I have a divine seat in the ocean') are outside the pale of Yahwism, but the case is different with Gen. 14.18-24, where Yahweh admittedly does not acknowledge El as his superior, but where, nevertheless, Abraham venerates this El (*'ēl 'ēlyōn*). Abraham, it is true, was not in strict historical terms a Yahwist, but he was regarded by later generations of Israelites as the founder of the faith in the only true God, that is, Yahweh. In Deut. 32.8 f. Yahweh is allotted Israel by El Elyon who is depicted as king of the gods, and the monarchic status of El is also indicated by Ps. 82.2 – Yahweh is in the council of El.[2]

Eissfeldt examines the contention that this sympathetic attitude to El can be explained by the supposition that the worship of El by the patriarchs was pre-Canaanite[3] and that they worshipped El alone. On this assumption the difference between the positive attitude of Yahwism to El worship and the post-settlement hostility to

---

[1] 'El and Yahweh', *JSS* i (1956), pp. 25-37; 'El und Jahwe', *KS* iii, pp 386-397.
[2] *op. cit.*, pp. 26-30.
[3] Above, pp. 195 f.

the cult of Baal, which was indigenous to Canaan, has been explained. Eissfeldt has maintained elsewhere[1] that the patriarchs became El worshippers in Canaan, and he deals here more fully with their relationship to 'god of the fathers' cults. These are to be identified with the 'alien gods' mentioned in Josh. 24.2, 14-15, where it is possible but improbable that the 'gods of the Amorites' include El, and with the gods buried by Jacob at Shechem prior to his pilgrimage to Bethel (Gen. 35.1-7). The nature of these 'alien gods' can be gathered from Gen. 31.53 which refers to the god of Abraham, the god of Nahor and *paḥad yiṣḥāq* ('Fear of Isaac' or 'Kinsman of Isaac'). Eissfeldt accepts that these are Alt's 'gods of the fathers', but does not accept that clan deities described in terms of their relationship to the founders of their cults (i.e., *'ᵃbīr yaʿᵃqōb*, *paḥad yiṣḥāq*) were necessarily the only ones worshipped by the pre-Mosaic Israelites. These gods are, at any rate, quite separate from El who did not acquire significance for the patriarchs until after their entry into Canaan.[2]

If this statement is taken along with the one in 'Jahwe der Gott der Väter', Eissfeldt's position is seen to have changed. In 'El and Yahweh' (1956) he holds that the 'Fear of Isaac' or 'Kinsman of Isaac' is a 'god of the fathers',[3] whereas in 'Jahwe der Gott der Väter' (1963) he holds that *paḥad yiṣḥāq* (31.42, 53) can only refer to the El worshipped by Isaac at Beersheba, and similarly with *'ᵃbīr yaʿᵃqōb*[4] (Gen. 49.24). Even in the earlier article, however, his position over against Alt is sufficiently well established. He says: 'For by this God of Abraham, Isaac and Jacob we are not to understand, as Alt would have it, the father gods of the pre-Mosaic Hebrews merged into *one* figure, but El, who, according to the evidence of Gen. xxi 33, xxvi 23, xxviii 13, xliv 3, revealed himself to all these patriarchs and gave them his promise'.[5] Eissfeldt's final position is that the expressions 'God of Abraham', 'God of Isaac' and 'God of Jacob', when they occur separately, refer to the one God El, that their combination rests on the essential unity of El, that *paḥad yiṣḥāq* and *'ᵃbīr yaʿqōb* refer to the El worshipped by Isaac and Jacob respectively, and that only the 'god of Abraham' and the 'god of Nahor' (31.53) are references to

---

[1] Above, pp. 196 f.
[2] *op. cit.*, pp. 30-32.
[3] Cf. 'El and Yahweh', p. 32, 'gods of the type of the "gods of the fathers" ',
[4] 'Jahwe der Gott der Väter', p. 85.
[5] 'El and Yahweh', pp. 35 f.

'gods of the fathers'. Hence Eissfeldt agrees with Baudissin that El worship belongs to Canaan, but he holds that the reduction of the supreme God El to *ēlim* – local numina – is a mistake. Baudissin has overestimated the importance of the local attachments of El cults and has erected a barrier between the local *numina* and the one God El.

Eissfeldt's conclusion is that the book of Genesis preserves the recollection that the pre-Mosaic Israelites or certain groups of them worshipped the Canaanite God El at several sanctuaries in Canaan. This fits in with the theory that there were successive waves of Israelite immigration into Canaan and that one of the latest of them brought Yahwism with it.[1] The pre-Yahwistic cults established in Canaan included 'god of the fathers' cults, but El worship became authoritative and pushed the other cults into the background. Gen. 33.20 (*'ēl 'ᵉlōhē yiśrā'ēl*) is an indication of this official position of the El cult. In the light of the establishment of Yahwism the El cult was conceived of as an older form of belief which had been raised to a higher level, and the God of Abraham, Isaac and Jacob, who is to be identified with El, was equated with Yahweh.[2]

If, as I have argued,[3] it is impossible to recover a pre-settlement group of Jacob tribes from the book of Genesis, it becomes problematical whether such a history of the religion of the patriarchs as Eissfeldt offers can be reconstructed. If there is no historical access to pre-settlement tribal groups, neither can there be access to the religion of these groups. A description of the religion of Abraham will only carry conviction, if his existence as an historical individual in the second millennium B.C. is presupposed. It is not obvious how Eissfeldt decides which portrayals of patriarchal religion are typical (Jacob, Joseph) and which are sufficiently distinctive to be regarded as the piety of an historical individual (Abraham)[4]. What criteria can be applied which would enable us to distinguish between typical piety and piety which is sufficiently unique to be attributed to an historical individual? The main problem, however, is that of evaluating the sanctuary stories in which the patriarchs feature. Eissfeldt accepts that the El cult

---

[1] Above, pp. 198 f.

[2] 'El and Yahweh', pp. 34-37.

[3] Above, pp. 85 ff.

[4] 'Achronische, Anachronische und Synchronische Elemente in der Genesis', pp. 164 f.

belongs to Canaan and that the patriarchs were not El worshippers prior to their arrival in Canaan.[1] I have already given reasons why Eissfeldt's view that these stories are cultic aetiologies with a superimposition of tribal history should not be accepted.[2] If they do not have this constituent of pre-settlement tribal history, they cannot be used to reconstruct a history of the religion of the patriarchs, whether the patriarchs are tribes or historical individuals. In particular, Eissfeldt's interpretation of *'ēl 'ᵉlōhē yiśrā'ēl* (33.20) must be contested.[3] He has noted that E equates the El of Bethel (or El Bethel) with Elohim who stands for Yahweh in that source in the period before the name of Yahweh has been revealed.[4] Although Eissfeldt allocates 33.20 to L,[5] the same line of interpretation should be followed in that verse. Instead of saying, as Eissfeldt does, that both El and Elohim can be equated with Israel, we should say that El is equated with *'ᵉlōhē yiśrā'ēl* and that the latter is to be equated with the Elohim of E. In that case the verse does not mark the adoption of the name Israel by a pre-Mosaic group of Jacob tribes in order to indicate their allegiance to El, but reflects a post-settlement situation where Israel is the name of the Yahweh-worshipping union of tribes. This suggests that both Jacob and Israel are susceptible of the same cultic solution. What we have to reckon with here is cultic history: a 'god of the fathers' cult, that of *'ᵃbīr ya'ᵃqōb*, has acquired Yahwistic and all-Israelite status and, in these circumstances, the tribes of Israel have become 'sons' of Jacob and Jacob has been equated with Israel.[6]

The patriarchs, according to Eissfeldt, were *gērīm* in the land of Canaan. They were semi-nomads and were 'shadow-possessors' of the land in virtue of the promise of possession which they had received from their God. Eissfeldt describes them as ass nomads,[7] which is not in accord with the indications of the book of Genesis, and is one of the few traces of influence from the side of the archaeological approach to the patriarchal narratives. If the patriarchs were semi-nomadic shepherds and if the El cult was an

---

[1] Above, p. 96.
[2] Above, pp. 85 ff.
[3] Above, pp. 198 f.
[4] 'Der Gott Bethel', p. 209.
[5] Gen. 33.20 is to be allocated to E, according to Gunkel.
[6] Cf. above, pp. 99 f.
[7] Above, p. 82.

aspect of Canaanite culture, it is improbable that semi-nomads would be sufficiently well integrated into that culture to participate in the El cult at ancient Canaanite sanctuaries. Nor does Eissfeldt's view that the patriarchs may have founded El cults at such sanctuaries[1] accord with their cultural status. What is therefore indicated in the notices and stories about the association of the patriarchs with Canaanite sanctuaries is a post-settlement integration of El sanctuaries and, no doubt, as Eissfeldt maintains, El theology into the fabric of Yahwism.

II

Alt is aware that it is a problem to distinguish between what derives from theories held by the authors of the documentary sources and what derives from earlier traditions about a 'god of the fathers' cult,[2] but he maintains that *'elōhē 'abōtēkem* (Ex. 3.13) is not an invention of E[3] and he points to Gen. 31.53 (*'elōhē 'abrāhām wē' lōhē nāḥōr*) and 49.24 (*'abīr ya'aqōb*) as places where the tendency of the sources to unify the references to deities other than Yahweh has been resisted.[4] He recognizes that the genealogical link between the patriarchs is secondary[5] and this implies that wherever 'god of my father' or the like is dependent on the genealogical relationship it must be regarded as secondary. In other words where Isaac refers to the God of his father, Abraham, or Jacob to the god of his father, Isaac, the 'his father' element derives from the genealogical scheme. *'elōhē 'abrāhām, 'elōhē yiṣḥāq* or *paḥad yiṣḥāq* and *'abīr ya'aqōb* are, on the other hand, according to Alt, prior to and independent of the genealogical scheme. They refer originally to clan cults with a common typology of which Abraham, Isaac and Jacob are founders; they are therefore related to persons and not bound to places.[6]

The three patriarchal gods are first united in Ex. 3.15, but the genealogy and the equation with Yahweh is explicit in Gen. 28.13 (*'anī YHWH 'elōhē 'abrāhām 'ābīkā wē'lōhē yiṣḥāq*) and Gen. 32.10 (*'elōhē 'ābī 'abrāhām wē'lōhē 'ābī yiṣḥāq YHWH*).[7] Alt supposes

[1] Above, p. 95.
[2] A. Alt, *op. cit.*, pp. 29, 34.
[3] *ibid.*, pp. 13 f.
[4] *ibid.*, pp. 21, 28.
[5] *ibid.*, p. 27.
[6] *ibid.*, pp. 22 f.
[7] *ibid.*, p. 27.

that *paḥad yiṣḥāq* (Gen. 31.42)[1] and *'aḇīr ya'ᵃqōḇ* (Gen. 49.24; Ps. 132.2, 5; Isa. 49.26; 60.16) are the original designations of the patriarchal deities and that Gen. 15.1 (*'al tīrā' 'aḇrām 'ānōḵī māgēn lāk*) may provide a clue to the original designation of the god of Abraham (Shield of Abraham).[2] He suggests therefore that the expressions *'ᵉlōhē 'aḇrāhām* and *'ᵉlōhē yiṣḥāq* are the result of a secondary unifying tendency (*'ᵉlōhē ya'ᵃqōḇ* is not found in the patriarchal narratives), and he observes that whereas El is used of Canaanite deities Elohim (an appellation for deity in Arabic and Aramaic) has been used for the patriarchal gods. His view is that this is probably not entirely an artificial schematization, to be attributed to a theory of the authors of the documentary sources and similar in tendency to E's use of Elohim, but is rather rooted in earlier tradition and expressive of an awareness of an original difference between the patriarchal cults and the Elim of the Canaanite sanctuaries.[3]

Alt holds that the patriarchs are founders of semi-nomadic clan cults in the period before the Israelite settlement in Canaan and that the descendants of these founders of separate clan cults made their way into Canaan and attached their cults to Canaanite sanctuaries, associating them with the Elim of these sanctuaries in the process. It is difficult to trace the history of these clan cults subsequent to the settlement,[4] but a pre-Yahwistic stage at which the cultic aetiologies of Canaanite sanctuaries were attracted to the patriarchs, who were then described as founders of these El cults, may be postulated. This is described by Alt as a process of legitimation[5] and what is legitimated at this stage would appear to be the process of attaching the 'god of Abraham', 'god of Isaac' and 'god of Jacob' cults to Canaanite sanctuaries and their El cults. To some extent, so Alt argues, the 'god of the fathers' cults maintained their separate existence as can be seen from the passages where references to Canaanite Elim and patriarchal gods lie side by side.[6]

---

[1] Cf. Gen. 31.53, *paḥad 'āḇīw yiṣḥāq*.

[2] *ibid.*, p. 66, n. 179.

[3] *ibid.*, pp. 28-30.

[4] *ibid.*, pp. 50 f.

[5] *ibid.*, p. 9.

[6] The examples given are: *'ᵃnī YHWH 'ᵉlōhē 'aḇrāhām wē'lōhē yiṣḥāq* (Gen. 28.13) and *bēt 'ēl* (28.19) at Bethel; *YHWH 'ēl 'ōlām* (21.33) and *'ᵉlōhē 'āḇīw yiṣḥāq* (46.1) at Beersheba; *ibid.*, pp. 50 f.

At a later stage when Yahwism is imposed on the earlier, still incomplete, amalgam and both 'god of the fathers' cults and the Canaanite Elim are embraced by Yahwism, the cultic aetiologies attached to the patriarchs legitimate the worship of Yahweh at these sanctuaries.[1] In connexion with this thesis of an original difference between Yahwism *qua* national religion and the tribal religion constituted by the coming together of Canaanite El cults and 'god of the fathers' cults, Alt notes that Shiloh, which is attested as a major Yahwistic sanctuary in the later period of the Judges, receives no mention in the patriarchal narratives.[2] On the other hand, Alt attaches significance to the circumstance that the 'god of the fathers' cult in its original conception is related to a group and not to a place, and from this point of view, as also in respect of the element of Promise which it contained, he sees it as an adumbration of the structure of Yahwism.

In some respects Clements' view is near to that of Alt as can be seen in his statement that the terms 'god of Abraham' and 'god of Isaac' were in use among the clans descended from the patriarchs. The ultimate difference in point of view derives from the differing kernels which are postulated for the patriarchal stories: Clements' kernel is historical and Alt's cultic-historical.[3] Clements' conclusions about the historicity of Abraham and the religion of Abraham hinge on his appraisal of the genre of the patriarchal narratives.[4] Like Eissfeldt, Clements supposes that an historical individual, Abraham, can be recovered from the Abraham traditions, and so he too describes the religion of Abraham in religio-historical terms. The primary content of the covenant of Gen. 15 is a divine oath which promises land to Abraham and his descendants (vv. 18-21), while the promise of a great posterity (vv. 4-5) is secondary. This covenant tradition shows that Abraham, who was an eponym and cult founder, led the immigration of Amorite semi-nomads into the region of Hebron where they settled. Here he refounded the ancient cult of Mamre and appropriated, through a divine oath or covenant concluded with the El of that sanctuary, the promise of land to himself and his descendants.[5] If the patriarchal narratives are not historiography or even rudimentary historiography, and if

[1] *ibid.*, p. 60.
[2] *ibid.*, pp. 57 f.
[3] *Abraham and David*, pp. 29, 31 f.
[4] Above, p. 2.
[5] *Abraham and David*, pp. 23 f.

an historical Abraham leading an immigration into the Hebron area in the Amarna Age or just before it[1] is not recoverable from them, the attempt to make such an historical core the starting point of a description of the religion of Abraham is invalid. The distinction between Clements and Alt can be stated quite simply. According to Alt the clans descended from the patriarchs brought into Palestine semi-nomadic cults named after their founders and attached them to Canaanite sanctuaries. According to Clements Abraham's god was the El of Mamre-Hebron, perhaps El Shaddai,[2] and this cult, having been appropriated by Abraham when he settled in the Hebron area in the fourteenth century b.c., was associated with a promise of land. 'God of Abraham' was simply a popular name for this El which was subsequently in use among Abraham's descendants and the same explanation holds for the other so-called 'gods of the fathers'.[3]

Like Alt Rost[4] also begins with the representation of patriarchal religion in the documentary sources and arrives at a view of that religion more or less in accord with Alt's thesis. According to Rost the pre-Mosaic use of Elohim by E is an indication of his view that Yahweh was active in that period, although his name was not known.[5] He notes that E associates the El of Bethel and the El of Shechem with Jacob, and in Gen. 46.1 f., the El of Beersheba with Jacob. J, so Rost holds, transferred the founding of Bethel and Shechem to Abraham in order to connect him with the territory of the northern tribes. This is a source-critical rather than a traditio-historical explanation of the attraction of Jacob traditions to Abraham.[6] Rost observes that the worship of El and of *paḥad yiṣḥāq* existed side by side at Beersheba, and this would seem to imply that Beersheba is originally connected with Isaac and only associated with Jacob subsequent to the establishment of a father-son relationship between Isaac and Jacob. Hence *'ābīw* in *paḥad 'ābīw* (46.2) refers to Isaac.[7]

On Gen. 16.13 Rost remarks that the Hagar-El Roi narrative,

---

[1] 'Abraham', p. 58; *Abraham and David*, p. 45; cf. Gordon, above, p. 5.
[2] *Abraham and David*, p. 33.
[3] 'Abraham', pp. 58 f.
[4] L. Rost, 'Die Gottes Verehrung der Patriarchen im Lichte der Pentateuchquellen', *VTS* iii (1960), pp. 346-359.
[5] *ibid.*, p. 353.
[6] Cf. above, pp. 150 f.
[7] L. Rost, *op. cit.*, pp. 353 f.

in which both the seeing (Roi) and hearing (Ishmael) of God are linked to Hagar, is a cultic aetiology based on the worship of El Roi at Beer Lahai Roi by both Ishmaelites and Hagarites. Gen. 16.13 is an attempt by J to locate the Ishmaelites outside the circle of Yahwistic worshippers – although it was Yahweh who appeared to Hagar she mistook him for El Roi (*wattiqrā' šēm YHWH haddōbēr 'ēlēhā 'ēl ro'ī*). Hence the passage cannot be used to support the view that the patriarchs were worshippers of El.[1] El Olam (21.33) perhaps originates with the union of J and E. I take Rost to mean that El is given the attribute Olam in view of the equation that is made between him and Yahweh (*wayyiqrā' šām bᵉšēm YHWH 'ēl 'ōlām*).[2]

Cross[3] refers to Lewy's[4] contention that 'gods of the fathers' are not nameless gods (*Ilabrat il abim*) and that Shaddai is the name of a patriarchal god who was subsequently combined with El Elyon (cf. Num. 24.16). Cross doubts whether the 'god of the fathers' is nameless, as maintained by Alt, and inclines to the view that clan gods are high gods, or, at least, are related to a high god pantheon and are therefore easily identifiable with the cult of the high god El as practised in Canaanite sanctuaries.[5] He is also disposed to conclude that Olam, Shaddai and Elyon are liturgical names of El, the king of the gods, rather than separate gods. This is similar to Eissfeldt's position.[6] At different sanctuaries the liturgical emphasis falls on different aspects of El: he is the Eternal One (Olam), the Creator (Elyon), the One who dwells in the cosmic mountain (Shaddai). The last named, however, is not localized at any sanctuary.

Cross supposes that '*ēl 'ᵉlōhē yiśrā'ēl* (Gen. xxxiii 20) represents an equation of the Canaanite high god El with a 'god of the fathers', namely, the god of Jacob/Israel[7] and that there is a similar equation in Gen. xlvi 3 (*hā'ēl 'ᵉlōhē 'ābīkā*).*qōneh šāmayim wā'āreṣ*, used of Elyon in Gen. xiv 19, 22, is described as a Canaanite cultic rubric.[8]

[1] *ibid.*, pp. 351 f.
[2] *ibid.*, p. 352.
[3] F. M. Cross, 'Yahweh and the God of the Patriarchs', *HTR* lv (1962), pp. 225-259.
[4] J. Lewy, 'Les textes paléo-assyriens et l'Ancien Testament', *Révue de l'histoire des religions*, 110 (1934), pp. 19-65.
[5] F. M. Cross, *op. cit.*, pp. 228-233.
[6] Above, pp. 196 ff.
[7] Cf. H. Seebass, above, pp. 172 ff.; Eissfeldt, above, pp. 198 f.
[8] F. M. Cross, *ibid.*, pp. 234-244.

On Shaddai Cross is undecided whether it is Canaanite or Amorite in origin and comes to the conclusion that the distinction is not so very significant, since, even if it were Amorite, it would be an attribute of an Amorite high god and could easily be transferred to the Canaanite high god El.[1] Cross explains Shaddai as 'the one of the cosmic mountain' and notes the connexion between El and Baal and Mount Zaphon in the Ugaritic texts.[2] He concludes that Shaddai, whether Canaanite or Amorite in origin, is a cult name of El.[3] Similarly he argues that Yahweh too was originally a cult name of El and speculates that 'ehyeh 'ᵃšer 'ehyeh (Ex. 3.14) has replaced an original *YHWH 'ᵃšer YHWH*. This he relates to a type of formula (*il du olami*, 'El of Eternity') found in fifteenth century B.C. proto-Canaanite inscriptions,[4] and he conjectures that *du yahwī* was originally an epithet of El applied later to Yahweh (*yahwī du yahwī*, 'Yahweh who creates'). Cross observes that *yknnh* is used of El creating or appointing Baal as king[5] and refers to the use of *wayyᵉkōnᵉnekā* in Deut. 32.6 – a verse which speaks of Yahweh as creator. He argues that *du yahwī* is a variant of *du yakāninu* and that *YHWH ṣᵉbā'ōt* is part of a formula '*ēl du yahwī ṣᵉbā'ōt* ('El who creates the hosts of heaven'). Finally Cross, following Eissfeldt,[6] argues that Yahwism adopted a positive attitude to the cult of El, which contrasts with its attitude to Baal, and that, moreover, only such a positive attitude could have achieved the unification of the Palestinian people of patriarchal stock and the other ethnic elements settled in Canaan who participated in the amphictyony.[7]

Cross assumes that it is possible to read the religion of the patriarchs directly from the documentary sources and, consequently, he does not raise the kind of question which is prominent in Alt and Rost. He does not appear to be aware that there is a critical question whether the information which is given by the sources, and of which he makes use, relates to the religion of the patriarchs, or whether it does not rather relate to the religion or theology of

[1] *ibid.*, p. 250.
[2] A. Herdner, *Corpus Des Tablettes En Cunéiformes Alphabétiques Découvertes Á Ras Shamra-Ugarit De 1929 Á 1939* (Mission De Ras Shamra, vol. X, 1, 1963): 4 v 85 (p. 26); 4 v 117 (p. 27); 4 vii 6 (p. 29).
[3] F. M. Cross, *ibid.*, pp. 244-250.
[4] *op. cit.*, pp. 236-239.
[5] A. Herdner, *op. cit.*, 4 iv 48 (p. 26).
[6] Above, pp. 199 ff.
[7] *op. cit.*, pp. 250-259.

the authors of the different documentary sources. This critical obtuseness is illustrated by the following examples:

(a) In Gen. 21.33 *YHWH 'el 'ōlām* tells us nothing about an original relationship of Yahweh to a high God ideology, but only about a doctrine of J that all the deities worshipped by the patriarchs are identifiable with Yahweh.

(b) E also maintains that the patriarchs are worshippers of one God, so that Elohim in E has the same theological function as Yahweh in J. Hence P, who like E maintains that the name Yahweh was first revealed to Moses (Ex. 6.3), equates Shaddai, the God worshipped by the patriarchs according to P, with both Yahweh (Gen. 17.1) and Elohim (Gen. 35.11). *mal'ak hā'ᵉlōhīm* (Gen. 31.11-13, E) identifies himself with *hā'ēl bēt'ēl*.¹ Further in such passages as 33.20 (L, according to Eissfeldt) and 46.3 what is conveyed is not an original affinity between a 'god of the fathers' cult and a high god ideology, but a doctrine of the author of the source, namely, that the patriarchs worshipped only one God. It is arguable that E's intention in 46.3 (*hā'ēl 'ᵉlōhē 'ābīkā*) is simply to say that Isaac worshipped the El of Beersheba. More probably he is saying that the El of Beersheba worshipped by Isaac was none other than Elohim. Hence the verse cannot be used to show that there is an original affinity between the 'god of the fathers' cult and a high god ideology, and so as a source for the religion of the patriarchs. Similarly *'ᵉlōhē yiśrā'ēl* (33.20) is doctrinally equivalent to Elohim and the intention of E is to equate the El of Shechem with this God. Unless one argues like Seebass² that Israel contains a reference to a patriarch Israel who was originally distinct from Jacob, there is no case for concluding that *'ᵉlōhē yiśrā'ēl* refers to a 'god of the fathers' cult. If it were a patriarchal cult the phrase would have to be *'ᵉlōhē ya'ᵃqōb*, for the change of name from Jacob to Israel must be associated with the acquisition of all-Israelite status by the patriarch. *'ᵉlōhē yiśrā'ēl* means 'God of all Israel' and is equal to E's Elohim and J's Yahweh.³

Hence it may be said in general that Cross's phenomenological approach does not clarify the issues. The critical complexities of the sources cannot be coped with in terms of an assumption that

---

¹ 'The god, Bethel', according to the grammar, rather than 'the god of Bethel'; cf. Gen. 35.1; see above, p. 197.

² Above, pp. 172 ff.

³ Contrary to Eissfeldt, above, pp. 198 f.

everything is to be subsumed under a high god ideology, that Yahweh is originally an epithet of El who 'splits off' from the Canaanite high god and ousts him from his place as president of the divine council of the gods.

(c) The equation of El Elyon with Yahweh (Gen. 14.22) can tell us nothing about the religion of Abraham or about the relationship of early Yahwism to the high god of Canaan, because it is a cultic aetiology which post-dates the establishment of the Jerusalem temple. It tells us not about patriarchal religion nor about an original ideological affinity between Yahweh and El, but about the syncretism of Yahwism and Canaanite or Jebusite religion in the cult of the Jerusalem temple. This it legitimates by establishing connexions between Abraham and Melchizedek, the priest of El Elyon.[1]

May,[2] Maag[3] and Andersen[4] are all agreed that 'god of my father' or 'god of thy father' is more primary than 'god of Abraham' or 'god of Isaac' and that Alt is mistaken in his conclusion, based on the latter formula, that the patriarchs were founders of cults. According to May, 'father' in the phrase 'god of my father' has the narrow sense of that word, so that if he finds on the lips of Jacob 'god of my father, the god of Abraham', he concludes that 'god of Abraham' is secondary, because it shows a misunderstanding of the original sense of 'god of my father'. Andersen[5] argues that 'god of my father' or 'god of thy father' has a sense which is independent of and prior to the genealogical scheme Abraham-Isaac-Jacob, and that consequently 'god of my father', as used by Isaac, is not a reference to the god of Abraham, nor 'god of my father', as used by Jacob, a reference to the god of Isaac. Against the view that the unification of kindred patriarchal cults (i.e., the gods of Abraham, Isaac and Jacob) was the cause of the genealogical scheme Abraham-Isaac-Jacob, Andersen argues with May that the concept indicated by 'god of your fathers', which rests on the unification of the patriarchal cults, is the effect of the prior

[1] Above, pp. 95 f.

[2] H. G. May, 'The God Of My Father: A Study of Patriarchal Religion', *JBR* ix (1941), pp. 155-158, 199-200; 'The Patriarchal Idea of God', *JBL* lx (1941), pp. 113-128.

[3] V. Maag, 'Der Hirte Israels: eine Skizze von Wesen und Bedeutung der Väterreligion', *SThU* 28 (1958), pp. 2-28.

[4] K. T. Andersen, 'Der Gott meines Vater', *StTh* xvi (1962), pp. 170-187.

[5] *op. cit.*, pp. 170 ff.

association of the three patriarchs as tribal heroes and then the formalizing of this in genealogical terms. The direction of the argument in relation to the evidence which is adduced is not always clear, and it is impossible on the basis of this evidence to demonstrate that 'god of my father' is always primary and 'god of Abraham' or 'god of Isaac' always secondary. The following review will indicate some of the difficulties and ambiguities:

(*a*) Where the name of a patriarch or the god of a patriarch appears after the formula 'god of my father' or 'god of thy father' or the like, the logic of the conclusion that it has been secondarily appended can be seen:

Gen. 46.1   *lē'lōhē 'ābīw yiṣḥāq*

31.42   *'ᵉlōhē 'ābī 'ᵉlōhē 'abrāhām ūpaḥad yiṣḥāq*

32.10   *'ᵉlōhē 'ābī 'abrāhām wē'lōhē 'ābī yiṣḥāq YHWH*

(*b*) But, unless good reasons can be given to the contrary, the same logic should be applied to cases where 'god of Abraham' or 'god of Isaac' is followed by 'father'. The indication here (if the same logic is applied) is that 'god of Abraham' or 'god of Isaac' is the primary datum and that the reference to 'father' is secondary and consequent on the unification of originally separate if kindred patriarchal cults and the genealogy Abraham-Isaac-Jacob:

Gen. 26.24   *'ᵉlōhē 'abrāhām 'ābīkā*

28.13   *'ᵃnī YHWH 'ᵉlōhē 'abrāhām 'ābīkā wē'lōhē yiṣḥāq*

One is justified in suspecting special pleading on the part of May when he disposes of *'abrāhām* in 28.13 on the ground that 'father' in 'god of thy father' refers always to 'father' in the narrow sense and that Abraham (who is Jacob's grandfather) cannot be original to the verse. In order to accommodate this verse to his thesis he has to postulate an original *'ᵉlōhē 'ābīkā yiṣḥāq*. The further contention that *'ᵉlōhē 'abrāhām 'ābīkā* (28.13) is on the analogy of the late formula *'ᵉlōhē dāwid 'ābīkā* (Isa. 38.5; II Kings 20.5; II Chron. 21.12) does not have great weight. In the case of Gen. 26.24, where no distortion of the sense of 'father' can be alleged, the supposed influence of a late formula is the only reason which May can give for the change of a postulated original *'ᵉlōhē 'ābīkā 'abrāhām* to *'ᵉlōhē 'abrāhām 'ābīkā*.

(*c*) Similar difficulties attend Andersen's arguments[1] as may be seen from a consideration of Gen. 31.42 and 53:

31.42   *'ᵉlōhē 'ābī 'ᵉlōhē 'abrāhām ūpaḥad yiṣḥāq*

[1] *op. cit.*, pp. 174-179.

53    $'^e l\bar{o}h\bar{e}$ $'abr\bar{a}h\bar{a}m$ $w\bar{e}'l\bar{o}h\bar{e}$ $n\bar{a}h\bar{o}r$ . . . $'^e l\bar{o}h\bar{e}$ $'^a b\bar{\imath}hem$
  $wayyi\check{s}\check{s}\bar{a}ba'$ $ya'^a q\bar{o}b$ $b^e pahad$ $'\bar{a}b\bar{\imath}w$ $yi\b{s}h\bar{a}q$

Since $pahad$ $yi\b{s}h\bar{a}q$ occurs in 31.42 there is a *prima facie* case for
regarding it as a primary datum, unless good reasons can be given
to the contrary. Andersen argues that if $pahad$ $yi\b{s}h\bar{a}q$ had been
original in 31.42, the phrase in 31.53b would have been $pahad$
$yi\b{s}haq$ $'\bar{a}b\bar{\imath}w$ and he appeals to $'^e l\bar{o}h\bar{e}$ $'abr\bar{a}h\bar{a}m$ $'\bar{a}b\bar{\imath}k\bar{a}$ (28.13). But
in so doing he contradicts May (and himself in so far as he appears
to agree with May), for May has maintained that the original of
the phrase in 26.24 is $'^e l\bar{o}h\bar{e}$ $'\bar{a}b\bar{\imath}k\bar{a}$ $'abr\bar{a}h\bar{a}m$. Andersen says that
Alt has to explain how $'\bar{a}b\bar{\imath}w$ interposed itself in 31.53b ($pahad$
$'\bar{a}b\bar{\imath}w$ $yi\b{s}h\bar{a}q$), but he has the more formidable task of explaining
how $pahad$ $yi\b{s}h\bar{a}q$ arose. He has to postulate the following development:

  $pahad$ $'\bar{a}b\bar{\imath}w$ > $pahad$ $'\bar{a}b\bar{\imath}w$ $yi\b{s}h\bar{a}q$ > $pahad$ $yi\b{s}h\bar{a}q$

Andersen holds that 31.53a ('god of Abraham and god of Nahor')
is late and should be regarded as an expansion of vv. 51-52 – the
gods of the two parties to the treaty take over the witnessing function of the cairn (vv. 51-52). When 31.52a was formulated, Isaac
was not yet the father of Jacob and so the original of v. 53b is
$wayyi\check{s}\check{s}\bar{a}ba'$ $ya'^a q\bar{o}b$ $b^e pahad$ $'\bar{a}b\bar{\imath}w$.

The traditio-historical judgement that Jacob was connected with
Abraham before he was connected with Isaac is applied to the
interpretation of $'^e l\bar{o}h\bar{e}$ $yi\b{s}h\bar{a}q$ in 28.13. Since Abraham and Jacob
are linked before Isaac and Jacob are linked, $w\bar{e}'l\bar{o}h\bar{e}$ $yi\b{s}h\bar{a}q$ (which
apparently supports Alt) is to be regarded as a secondary addition
to the verse. Even if Andersen's view of the history of the tradition were correct in this respect (he supposes that the Abraham tradition is linked to the Jacob tradition for the first time in 31.53a), it
would not invalidate Alt's view that $pahad$ $yi\b{s}h\bar{a}q$ is an indication
that Isaac was the founder of a patriarchal cult. An interpretation
of 31.53 which followed Alt would assume the prior existence of
the Abraham-Isaac-Jacob genealogy and the unification of the
patriarchal cults, in which case $'^e l\bar{o}h\bar{e}$ $'abr\bar{a}h\bar{a}m$ is to be identified
with $pahad$ $yi\b{s}h\bar{a}q$. Such a unification and identification of the
patriarchal cults with Yahweh is given in 28.13 and 32.10. With
regard to $'^a b\bar{\imath}r$ $ya'^a q\bar{o}b$ Andersen[1] agrees with Eissfeldt[2] that this is
a reference to El and not to a patriarchal cult. Hence no 'god of

[1] *op. cit.*, p. 179.
[2] Above, pp. 200 f.

Jacob' is attested except in the late formula 'God of Abraham, God of Isaac, God of Jacob'.

Maag[1] argues that 'Israel' is a patriarch distinct from Jacob and he relies principally on Gen. 33.20 (*'ēl 'ᵉlōhē yiśrā'ēl*) and also on references to a patriarchal god which he finds in Gen. 49.24, 48.15 and Ps. 80.2 ('Shepherd of Israel'). In 49.24 Maag deletes *'eben* and observes that *rō'ēh yiśrā'ēl* is then parallel to *'ᵃbīr ya'ᵃqōb*. 'Shepherd of Israel' is another patriarchal cult called after its founder. In Gen. 48.15 Jacob refers to *hā'ᵉlōhīm hārō'eh 'ōtī* and in Ps. 80.2 there is a mention of *rō'ēh yiśrā'ēl*. Israel was a patriarch along with Abraham, Isaac and Jacob and only with the establishment of a central sanctuary at Shechem did Israel acquire a national status. Andersen[2] is sympathetic towards Maag's thesis and thinks it probable that a tradition about a patriarch Israel once existed and was suppressed by the Jacob traditions, but he is aware of the difficulties which are involved in making out such a case. Maag's supposition[3] that the Jabbok tradition belongs originally to Israel and only secondarily to Jacob is speculative (Israel originally fought with a river demon and the identification of this demon with Yahweh is later interpretation). It is more probable that the name Israel in this passage (Gen. 32.23-33) has an original connexion with the national status which had been acquired by Jacob. The only direct piece of evidence which Maag has is Gen. 33.20 and Andersen is aware that this has a highly contentious character. Thus Andersen recognizes that *'ēl 'ᵉlōhē yiśrā'ēl* is not necessarily a reference to a patriarchal cult and he notes the other possibility that it may be associated with a pre-settlement El amphictyony.[4] But since the reference is attached to Shechem, *'ᵉlōhē yiśrā'ēl* should probably be equated with Yahweh and what is then indicated is a fusion of El religion and Yahwism in a post-settlement, amphictyonic context.[5]

In his article 'The Patriarchal Idea of God' May[6] holds that the Elim of the patriarchal narratives are not local deities, but are manifestations of a high god El or of gods in El's pantheon.[7] The cult of the god Bethel[8] may have been founded by Jacob and the

---

[1] *op. cit.*, pp. 8 f.; cf. Seebass, above, pp. 172 ff.
[2] *op. cit.*, pp. 180 ff.
[3] *op. cit.*, pp. 79 ff.   [4] This is Eissfeldt's view, above, pp. 198 f.
[5] Above, pp. 202 f.   [6] *op. cit.*, pp. 119 f.
[7] Agreeing with Eissfeldt, above, pp. 196 ff., especially p. 201; also Cross, above, p. 207.   [8] Above, p. 197.

place where it was established named after the deity.[1] Shaddai is a general title of El which is not connected with any place and El Shaddai is equated with El Elyon in Num. 24.16.[2] El Shaddai is El *qua* head of the pantheon and this explains why P represents that Yahweh appeared to the patriarchs as El Shaddai (Ex. 6.3). May uses the same passages as Haran[3] (Num. 1.5, 12; 2.12; 7.30, 35; 10.18) to show that the title Shaddai is pre-Mosaic. In these passages the names of fathers and sons, who are said to have been contemporary with Moses, are given and the name *šᵉdēʾūr* contains Shaddai as a theophoric element.[4] Shaddai, according to May, is related to Akkadian *šadū* 'mountain' and is to be interpreted in the light of such cultic and mythological phenomena as the *ziggurat*, Zaphon, the mountain of El and Baal, and Sinai or Horeb, the mountain of Yahweh. The later identification of Yahweh and Shaddai is the more easily explicable in view of the mountain associations of both.[5]

Hyatt[6] accepts Alt's theory about patriarchal religion as 'basically correct' and advances an hypothesis that Yahwism originated as a 'god of the fathers' cult. He supposes that *ʾᵉlōhē ʾābī* (Ex. 15.2), which appears in the context of the Song of the Sea, is probably a genuine reminiscence going back to the Mosaic age[7] and that the aetiology of Eliezer in Ex. 18.4 (*kī ʾᵉlōhē ʾābī bᵉʿezrī*) suggests that the original form of the name may have been *ʾēl ʾābī ʿezer*. He concludes that the name contained the formula 'god of my father' which is an allusion to the 'god of thy father' in the context of Moses' experience at the burning bush (Ex. 3.6).[8] Thus the singular *ʾābīkā* is to be retained in Ex. 3.6[9] and what is indicated by these references to 'god of my father' and 'god of thy father' is that Yahweh was the patron deity of one of Moses' ancestors. His mother (*yōkebed*, Ex. 6.20; Num. 26.59) apparently has a theophoric name with a shortened form of YHWH. The expansion of *ʾᵉlōhē ʾābīkā* in Ex. 3.6 (*ʾᵉlōhē ʾabrāhām ʾᵉlōhē yiṣḥāq wᵉʾlōhē*

[1] H. G. May, *op. cit.*, p. 126.
[2] Cf. Cross, above, p. 207.
[3] Below, p. 218.
[4] H. G. May, *op. cit.*, pp. 121 f.
[5] *ibid.*, pp. 122 f.; cf. Cross, above, p. 208.
[6] J. P. Hyatt, 'Yahweh as "the God of my Father"', *VT* v (1955), pp. 130-136.
[7] *ibid.*, p. 134.
[8] *ibid.*, p. 135.
[9] *ibid.*, p. 133.

ya'ᵃqōb) is the result of later theological reflection when Yahweh became amalgamated with the patriarchal deities after the Hebrews entered Canaan.

Hyatt conjectures that Moses' family had come to Egypt from Midianite territory and that this explains why he sought asylum in Midian. Moreover, his sharp reaction to the brutal treatment meted out to the Israelites in Egypt is to be explained by the circumstance that he and his family had not been long there and were not reconciled to the conditions of life. Hence the Kenite hypothesis is true in that the part of the Hebrew community to which Moses belonged had Midianite connexions, and that Moses' knowledge of Yahweh was derived from this ancestral source, but it is wrong in supposing that the knowledge was mediated to him by his father-in-law, Jethro. In the encounter at the burning bush Yahweh, 'the god of his father', was revealed to him with great power, and so he did not summon the Hebrews in Egypt to the worship of an entirely new deity.[1]

Another account of the origins of Yahwism in relation to patriarchal religion is given by Andersen. He disagrees with Eissfeldt's[2] view that the gods who are to be destroyed (Gen. 35.1-4; Josh. 24) are to be identified with the patriarchal gods, and he maintains that the cult encountered by Yahwism when it entered Canaan was constituted by a fusion of El and the patriarchal gods. The patriarchal cults lived on at the local sanctuaries and only the cult of the amphictyonic sanctuary was Yahwistic. It was only after a long interval that the cult of Yahweh penetrated the local sanctuaries and then the patriarchal gods were identified with him. Andersen assumes the correctness of Noth's view[3] that the Exodus and Sinai traditions were originally unrelated, and so he argues that if Yahweh comes from Sinai, he does not come from Egypt. Yahweh belongs originally to the Sinai traditions and has been inserted secondarily into the patriarchal and Exodus traditions. Who then was the original God of the Moses tradition?[4]

Andersen holds that the equation of *'ᵉlōhē 'ābīkā* (Ex. 3.6) with Yahweh (May and Hyatt) is erroneous and that YHWH in Gen. 32.10 is an addition to the text which misinterprets 'god of my

---

[1] *op. cit.*, pp. 135 f.
[2] Above, p. 200.
[3] M. Noth, *Überlieferungsgeschichte des Pentateuch*, pp. 48 ff.
[4] K. T. Andersen, *op. cit.*, pp. 181-184.

father'. This argument is based on the supposed primacy of 'god of thy father' over against 'god of your fathers' (Ex. 3.13, 15, 16). If this is not accepted, it is arguable that the God who reveals himself to Moses in 3.6 is none other than the one who declares himself to be Yahweh in 3.16. Andersen conjectures that there was a tradition according to which it was not Yahweh but a patriarchal god (*'elōhē 'ābīkā*) who called Moses to his work of liberation.[1]

Andersen rejects Hyatt's account of Ex. 18.4,[2] but in the aetiology of Eliezer (*kī 'elōhē 'ābī b'ezrī*) he finds an equation between El and 'god of my father' and he holds that this identification is also given in Gen. 31.13 and 46.3. He explains the aetiology of Eliezer as a confession made by the people of Israel (an El amphictyony),[3] or, at first, by a smaller group, in the pre-Yahwistic period in order to give thanks for their emancipation from Egypt. This confession has been utilized to explain the name Eliezer, but that this was not its original function is shown by the words 'and saved me from Pharaoh's sword'. The confession is older than the context of Ex. 18.1-12 which is Yahwistic and *nṣl* in vv. 8, 9, 10 refers back to the *nṣl* of the confession. Hence not only Yahweh but Moses also is secondary in relation to the Exodus tradition. Thus Andersen agrees with Noth[4] that Moses cannot be regarded as the leader of the Israelites in Egypt or as the one who led them to freedom through the desert, and against Hyatt he argues that the patriarchal god who is associated with the Exodus is not Yahweh. The assumption that Yahweh first acquired the characteristics of the patriarchal gods in Canaan is simpler, for the equation of Yahweh with 'god of my father' in an Egyptian setting is not an adequate explanation of the thundering God of Sinai (i.e., on the premise that Yahweh cannot be both God of the Exodus and God of Sinai). It was in a Canaanite context that Yahweh was adopted by those whose cult was a fusion of the patriarchal gods and El and so became for the first time the God of the Exodus.[5]

Andersen's treatment of Gen. 31.13 (cf. 31.5) and 46.3 requires special comment. According to Eissfeldt[6] Gen. 31.2, 4-18aα are to be allocated to E (cf. Elohim, vv. 7. 9, 16; *mal'ak hā 'elōhīm*, v. 11). What is therefore indicated by 31.13 (cf. 31.5) is not simply that 'god of my father' is to be equated with the El of Bethel or with

---

[1] *ibid.*, p. 185.
[2] Above, p. 214.
[3] Above, pp. 197 f.
[4] M. Noth, *op. cit.*, p. 190.
[5] K. T. Andersen, *op. cit.*, pp. 185-187.
[6] O. Eissfeldt, *Introduction*, p. 201.

El Bethel, but that both are to be equated with Elohim. Since E uses Elohim where J would use Yahweh, it is arguable that the genealogy Isaac-Jacob and the unification of the patriarchal cults in terms of Elohim is involved in 'god of my father' (31.5). Similarly 46.3 is E and Elohim identifies himself as *hā'ēl 'ᵉlōhē 'ābīkā*. Since *hā'ēl* is the El of Beersheba, the genealogy Isaac-Jacob is presupposed. An important aspect of these equations is the circumstance that E does not use the name Yahweh when he is portraying pre-Mosaic situations. In view of this they do not necessarily give us access to the kind of pre-Yahwistic situation which Andersen is postulating, namely, a syncretism resulting from the fusion of the El cult and the patriarchal gods prior to the advent of Yahwism. Nor does Ex. 18.4 necessarily stem from a period when Yahweh had not yet become the God of those who had equated their patriarchal gods with El.[1]

III

According to Haran[2] the patriarchs do not participate in the El cult at ancient Canaanite sanctuaries and do not set foot in Canaanite towns. Rather they are themselves the founders of sanctuaries on the edges of Canaanite towns.[3] Abraham founds a tree sanctuary and invokes El Olam near (*bᵉ*) Beersheba (Gen. 21.33). Jacob acquires a piece of land facing the town of Shechem (*'et pᵉnē hā'īr*), builds an altar and invokes *'ēl 'ᵉlōhē yiśrā'ēl* (33.18-20). Jacob consecrates as an altar the stone on which his head had rested when he had his dream and received the promise of Canaan for his descendants, and founds the cult of the god Bethel (Gen. 28.11-22). The site may also have been a tree sanctuary (35.8), although in this case it is not stated that Jacob planted the oak which is said to have been renamed 'oak of weeping' to mark the burial of Deborah, Rebecca's nurse, there.

Haran finds significance in the circumstance that Baal worship is not mentioned in connexion with the patriarchs and becomes an issue only after the settlement of the Israelites in Canaan, and also in the presence of theophoric names with an El component among the pre-Mosaic Hebrew tribes. Among these he reckons Israel and he suggests that Jacob, Joseph and perhaps Isaac are

[1] Cf. M. Haran, below, p. 218.
[2] M. Haran, 'The Religion of the Patriarchs', *ASTI* iv (1965), pp. 30-46.
[3] Cf. Eissfeldt, above, pp. 95, 203.

abbreviated theophoric names of the same type as Ishmael. He also holds that onomastic combinations with Shaddai appear at about the same period (Num. 1.5, 6, 12).[1] Such points of contact as there are between patriarchal and Canaanite religion are explicable on the ground that El is a general Semitic term for deity and do not preclude the possibility that the Elim whose cults were established by the patriarchs at different places in Canaan were brought by them into that country. In this connexion Haran notes that El Shaddai (the El worshipped by the Patriarchs according to P) is not attached to any place in Canaan, and the only El whom he regards as Canaanite is El Elyon.[2]

Pre-Mosaic 'Hebrew' religion also included the worship of Yahweh and the cult of a household god ('god of my father', 'god of thy father', 'god of his father'). Haran questions the value of speculation about the origins of the god Yahweh, including the Kenite hypothesis, and he confines himself to the statement that Yahweh was one deity among others worshipped by the pre-Mosaic 'Hebrews', and that only as a consequence of the contribution of Moses did Yahwism achieve its commanding position as the religion of later Israel. On the other issue he argues that 'god of my father' and the like has a quite distinct religious significance from 'God of your fathers' or 'God of Abraham, God of Isaac and God of Jacob'. He notes passages where the plural 'fathers' might be expected but where the singular 'father' is found (Gen. 31.53; Ex. 15.2; 18.4), and he interprets this as evidence of the tenacity of an old formula which is indicative of a particular religious phenomenon. He observes that in the extant documentary sources 'god of thy father' is equated with El Shaddai (Gen. 49.25) and with El (Gen. 46.3). The equation with El Shaddai indicates that 'god of thy father' is taken as a reference to Yahweh and the same is shown by the combination of 'god of thy father' with 'God of Abraham, God of Isaac and God of Jacob' in Ex. 3.6, since the latter formula can be equated with P's El Shaddai and E's Elohim and so ultimately with Yahweh.

Haran supposes that 'god of thy father' and the like originally referred to a household cult which was a feature of patriarchal religion and in separating the formula from 'the God of your fathers' and 'God of Abraham, God of Isaac and God of Jacob'

---

[1] Above, p. 214.
[2] M. Haran, *op. cit.*, pp. 32-35.

he rejects Alt's hypothesis. Neither 'the God of your fathers' nor 'God of Abraham, God of Isaac and God of Jacob' relate to pre-Yahwistic clan cults as Alt supposes. 'God of Abraham, God of Isaac and God of Jacob' is not the result of a fusion of independent cults and their equation with Yahwism. Rather these expressions were used by Moses when he was commending Yahwism to the Hebrew tribes in order to establish a link with their past, and from the book of Exodus onwards the two formulae are equivalences of Yahweh. E's account, however, as Haran observes, implies that they existed before the disclosure of the name Yahweh to Moses, and E's point is rather that the God hitherto known by these names is none other than Yahweh (Ex. 3.6, 13, 16). It is not therefore clear that Ex. 3 supports Haran's statement that these formulae served from the first 'as mere characterizations of Yahweh himself'. Haran describes *paḥad yiṣḥāq* (Gen. 31.42, 53) and *'ᵃbīr ya'ᵃqōb* (49.24) as doubtful traits. About the first he says no more than that it may reflect a concept peculiar to the patriarchal period. On *'ᵃbīr ya'ᵃqōb* he says that it is difficult to decide whether it is a survival from pre-Mosaic times or whether it was retrojected from a later period (it appears as 'poetic diction' in Isa. 49.26; 60.16; Ps. 132.2, 5). Haran's general conclusion is that the religion of the patriarchal period probably embraced El Shaddai, associated with other Elim, and a household cult. It can also be assumed that Yahwism in its primary pre-Mosaic form was present.[1]

In speaking about pre-Mosaic 'Hebrew' tribes and 'Hebrew' religion Haran is assuming that the patriarchs and the patriarchal narratives can be set in an 'ethnic-national' framework. This ethnic frame of reference lies outside Canaan among the Hebrew-Aramaean tribes of the upper Euphrates area, that is, Paddan-Aram (Gen. 25.20; 28.2, 5, 7). This ethnic group consists of all the 'sons of Eber', the eponymous forefather of the Hebrews (Gen. 10.21) and comprehends the people of Joktan (10.26-30), Nahor (22.20-24) and Lot (i.e., Moab and Ammon before their settlement in their respective countries). Also included are peoples later considered to be descendants of Abraham prior to their ultimate separation from one another – the tribes of Ishmael (25.13-16), Keturah's sons (25.1-4) and the tribes of Esau. Consistent with this ethnic frame of reference outside Canaan is the circumstance that the patriarchs marry Mesopotamian wives (Gen. 24; 28.1-5) or,

[1] *op. cit.*, pp. 35-39.

at least, non-Canaanite wives (26.34 f.; 28.8 f.) and as evidence of 'common religious possession' the following details are adduced:

(*a*) Theophoric names with an El element are found among all the 'sons of Eber'.

(*b*) El Shaddai, in particular, is allied to a Hebraic, non-Israelite, background. The name is used by Balaam (Num. 24.4, 16) and occurs frequently in the book of Job.

(*c*) The practice of circumcision separated the Hebrew tribes from their environment and emphasized their distinctiveness over against the lands where they sojourned.[1]

Haran views the patriarchs as individuals of extraordinary spiritual stature who gave a decisive impetus to earlier Hebrew religion. At the same time he maintains that Jacob was the founder of a tribe. He is undecided whether the Elim are first revealed to the patriarchs or whether the patriarchal contribution is rather the attaching of them to holy places.[2] His observation that El worship is not necessarily set in an urban Canaanite context would seem to be correct. Beersheba, he remarks, was no more than an encampment in the 'patriarchal age' and Beer Lahai Roi was on the edge of the desert. Yet both places were El sanctuaries. El is a general Semitic appellation for deity and cannot be assigned a specific Canaanite reference. It should not therefore be assumed that the ideology of the Canaanite high god El is everywhere presupposed in references to El worship in the patriarchal narratives.[3] This line of argument is reinforced by onomastic considerations – the name Ishmael is that of a desert tribe which is associated with Beer Lahai Roi and Jacob and Isaac are abbreviations of types of names found outside Canaan in the second millennium B.C. and especially at Mari and in the Execration Texts.

It is not clear, however, that Haran draws the right conclusions from this set of observations. He tends to say that the patriarchs brought these Elim with them to Canaan,[4] although he stops short of categorical assertion. For example, 'Thus the names of the Elim became revealed only to the patriarchs or are attached by them to holy places for the first time'.[5] This would appear to leave the

---

[1] *op. cit.*, pp. 40-43.

[2] *ibid.*, pp. 43-45.

[3] Cf. J. Bright, *A History of Israel* (2), pp. 95-102.

[4] Cf. G. E. Wright, *Biblical Archaeology*, p. 52. Wright holds that El was both an Amorite and Canaanite deity.

[5] *op. cit.*, p. 44.

alternatives open: either the Elim revealed themselves for the first time to the patriarchs in Canaan or this was a type of religion which the patriarchs brought with them to Canaan. On the other hand, the argument on the basis of Jacob-El and Isaac-El indicates that the origins of the worship of El to which the patriarchs were attached lies outside Canaan (the only Canaanite, urban El acknowledged by Haran is El Elyon).

Another possible interpretation of the facts assembled by Haran is that the Elim are local *numina* in which case the older view (Baudissin) would be vindicated over against the one which now tends to prevail (Eissfeldt, Cross), namely, that these Elim are, more or less, manifestations of the Canaanite high god El and can all be subsumed under his rich theology. Consistent with the view that the Elim are local *numina* are the vestiges of lower levels of religion which are preserved in the references to stones and trees which are divinized.[1] Thus the fact that sanctuaries are outside Canaanite towns does not prove that they are not ancient Canaanite sanctuaries, although it may indicate that their origins are pre-urban. Even if the patriarchs are represented as founders of these cults, the evaluation of this depends on the kind of judgement which has been made about the historicity of the patriarchal narratives. If one is bound to Haran's view that these narratives are essentially historical and inform us directly about the 'patriarchal age' and the religion of the patriarchs, the circumstance that the places where the patriarchs founded El sanctuaries lie outside Canaanite towns will be seen as agreeable to the semi-nomadic mode of life and status (*gērīm*) which are attributed to them in Canaan. If one is not bound to this judgement about historicity, other possibilities open up. We can say that the representation that the patriarchs are semi-nomads who wander about Canaan is an indispensable part of the literary scaffolding of the stories and has to be maintained. This does not preclude the possibility that these accounts of the connexions of the patriarchs with sacred trees and stones in the vicinity of Canaanite towns both preserves vestiges of lower levels of Canaanite religion and at the same time reflects a post-settlement process involving the integration of Yahwism with El cults at ancient Canaanite sanctuaries.

If the patriarchs brought these Elim into Canaan, it is difficult

[1] W. R. Smith, *The Religion of the Semites* (*3*) (1927), pp. 185-212 (Shechem, Bethel, Mamre).

to explain their motivation for localizing such cults at different places in Canaan. In what respect can this be regarded (as Haran maintains) as a refining of earlier Hebrew religion? The localizing of earlier Hebrew religion at places in Canaan might rather lead to the fragmentation of the unity of the postulated pre-Canaanite El worship of the Hebrews. Haran attributes to the patriarchs a religion which is so discrete and pluralistic that it is hard to see what right it has to be regarded as a preparation for Mosaic Yahwism. The spiritual stature which he accords to the patriarchs is not borne out by the new departure in religion which he attributes to them. It may be that the reason why P unified pre-Mosaic religion in terms of El Shaddai was that El Shaddai had no local Canaanite attachment, but this unification, on Haran's own hypothesis, whether by means of E's Elohim or P's El Shaddai, was not a patriarchal achievement. In what respects does the attaching of the worship of El to Canaanite localities or the possession of a 'god of my father' household cult constitute a refining of earlier Hebrew religion? The link between the attaching of the patriarchs' God to Canaanite localities and post-settlement Yahwism is only achieved by Haran in so far as this attachment is a symbolic realization of the Promise that Canaan will be possessed. Only, however, in the Bethel narrative (Gen. 28) is a direct connexion established between the founding of a sanctuary and the Promise of Canaan. Since Haran has differentiated 'god of my father' and the like from 'the God of your fathers' and 'God of Abraham, God of Isaac and God of Jacob', he cannot bring this 'god of my father' cult into any significant relationship with post-settlement Yahwism. Alt's and Noth's 'god of the fathers' cult is, on the other hand, connected with post-settlement Yahwism and integrated into it in so far as the promise of the earlier clan cult is taken up into Yahwism and reinterpreted as the realized promise of the land of Canaan.

I sum up this chapter by reiterating that accounts of patriarchal religion are conditioned by views which are held concerning the genre of the patriarchal narratives. Gressmann and Gunkel suppose that the semi-nomads on the fringes of Canaan from whom these stories issued were worshippers of El, but because they define the stories as *Märchen*, they postulate a double remove from historical patriarchs on the soil of Canaan. A double remove, because, in the first place, the stories belong to a semi-nomadic, cultural context outside Canaan and because, in the second place, the characters of *Märchen* are literary creations and not historical persons. Cross and Haran, on the other hand, who are also inclined to the view that the El or Elim worshipped by the patriarchs are pre-Canaanite or Amorite, hold that the patriarchal narratives are essentially historiographical and that, on this basis, the religion of the historical patriarchs in a Canaanite context can be described. Eissfeldt has a similar view of the genre, but he maintains that El worship is a Canaanite phenomenon and that the patriarchs make their first contact with this cult of the Canaanite high god subsequent to their entry into his territorial and cultural sphere. Then there are those who, more or less, follow Alt (Andersen, May, Hyatt) and set out from the premise that the patriarchal narratives are not history but cultic history. Their concern is not with the historical patriarchs or with their religion, but with the patriarchal cults and the processes by which they were integrated with the El cults at Canaanite sanctuaries and with Yahwism.

What I am exploring in the final chapter is the extent to which the theology of the patriarchal narratives is bound up with their historicity or with our capacity to speak directly, on the basis of the available sources, about the religion of the patriarchs. One of the reasons why the issue of historicity has been taken so seriously by modern scholars is their conviction that a theology of the patriarchal stories can only be built if there is a foundation of historicity. Thus, for example, Wright who says:

Yet to this writer any Biblical interpreter who loves theology but not in equal measure 'the flesh and bones of history' is certain to fail in his interpretative effort. Various modern forms of gnosticism or docetism can indeed hide behind the revival of Biblical theology.[1]

Similarly de Vaux:

The problem is not only urgent for the historian. It matters also very much for the historian of religions and for the theologian, for the faith of Israel is founded on acts of God.[2]

Bright's[3] disquiet with Noth's handling of the patriarchal narratives is associated with his persuasion that fundamental theological

---

[1] 'Modern Issues in Biblical Studies: History and the Patriarchs', *ET* lxxi (1959/60), p. 293.
[2] R. de Vaux, 'Method in the Study of Early Hebrew History', p. 17.
[3] *Early Israel*, pp. 55, 92.

issues are at stake in connexion with the degree of historicity which is attached to the patriarchal narratives.

I accept that these are substantial considerations and that a danger of docetic trends in biblical interpretation has always to be taken with the utmost seriousness. It is a matter of no small importance in the field of biblical theology that there should be some kind of historical infra-structure on which kerygmatic traditions rest, and that these should be seen to have an anchorage in the historical existence of men and women who had ultimate concerns not essentially different from our own. The relationship between history and theology in the biblical field is, however, a complex one, and the task of extracting a theology from the patriarchal narratives has to be stretched beyond questions about the degree of historicity which attaches to them. If it were concluded that the narratives give us direct access to the religion of the historical patriarchs, that Abraham, Isaac and Jacob were proto-Yahwists or even monotheists, practising a religion which has meaning for us and demands our respect, this would not of itself assure the narratives a present theological significance. Even if we were to envisage that all historical questions could be finally settled and that the conclusions reached were emphatically positive, this would achieve no more than a secure infra-structure on which the theological edifice could rest. The next chapter represents an attempt to uncover and discuss these deeper theological issues.

CHAPTER V
Some Theological Considerations

Gunkel's first major work published in 1895[1] is fructified by insights which he shared with the Göttingen school of *Religionsgeschichte*. The point has been made that *Religionsgeschichte* does not indicate, in the first place, a comparative study of religion and that what is intended is rather a new historical orientation of the study of biblical religion.[2] There can be no doubt, however, that the methods employed by Gunkel in *Schöpfung und Chaos* attach a new importance to a Babylonian religious and mythological hinterland for the study of the primaeval history in Genesis 1-11.

The response of Wellhausen to what amounted to a new dimension of exegesis was, on the one hand, to admit that the new connexions which Gunkel had traced were real, and, on the other hand, to assert that the only important and significant exegetical level was that on which he had hitherto focused attention and that Gunkel's extension of the exegetical task would uncover no more than relics or fossilized remains.[3] Wellhausen's conviction was that Gunkel's exegetical antiquarianism would not yield any important results. What was significant exegetically lay on the surface of the documents: the only thing that mattered was to discover the meaning which was conveyed by those who were responsible for the documentary sources of the Pentateuch. Hence it was right that exegesis should, in this sense, be superficial, that it should operate on one level only and that the exegete should not be distracted by the antiquarian remains which might be discoverable below the surface of the documents. The only question which had to be answered was this: What meaning did the authors of the documentary sources intend to convey?

For Gunkel the deepening of the exegetical task had much more significance than Wellhausen would allow and there can be little doubt that his concept of 'tradition' in this exegetical setting brought a great enrichment to the understanding of the first eleven chapters of Genesis.[4] Thus he observes:

[1] H. Gunkel, *Schöpfung und Chaos* (1895).
[2] H. Weidmann, *op. cit.*, pp. 95 ff.; W. Klatt, *op. cit.*, pp. 54 ff.
[3] J. Wellhausen, *Skizzen und Vorarbeiten*, vi (1899), p. 233.
[4] *Genesis* (1) appeared in 1901.

Therefore I have not been content to maintain the Babylonian origin of biblical material, but have discussed in detail in what distinctive way the appropriated material was taken up and transformed in Israel.[1]

Again:

> The reason why Babylonian influence on Israel so enchanted me is that it is more than a curiosity, more than antiquarian notices.[2]

These stories had been transmitted; they had distant origins and they had a long history behind them in the course of which they had travelled through the world of the ancient Near East. Not only the stories but the concepts and the vocabulary in them could only be fully elucidated if the richness of their tradition were discovered and understood. In reply to Wellhausen's criticism Gunkel says:

> We know very well the emphasis of an older school which, in the last analysis, will enquire only into the religion of the people of Israel, and which maintains that to deal with Israel's contacts with peoples of higher culture has no theological interest but perhaps an antiquarian interest; who recognize in general that Israel was influenced by foreign cultures, but who do not apply this recognition to the particulars of exegesis . . . because they have no eye for the impressive structure of the history of peoples and religions which stand behind such connexions; who, indeed, also occasionally speak about tradition, but who, when they speak about exegesis, nearly always have only the author in mind.[3]

The primaeval history was a particularly promising area for the inauguration of a new exegetical method, for these stories had an international character and they had been mediated to Israel through Canaanite culture. Here was a case for enquiring into the nature and degree of Israel's participation in the culture of the ancient Near East. Gunkel intended to demonstrate by his method that there was, on the one hand, a hinterland of mythology and international culture without a full awareness of which the interpretation of these stories would be impoverished and incomplete, and, on the other, to show that such an indebtedness to international culture and involvement with mythology was compatible with the distinctiveness of Old Testament religion.

If one considers more carefully the theological objectives of

---

[1] *Schöpfung und Chaos*, p. vi.

[2] *Deutsche Literaturzeitung* (1904), 1109 f. (W. Klatt, *op. cit.*, p. 75, n. 3).

[3] *Zeitschrift für wissenschaftliche Theologie*, vii (1899), pp. 610 ff. (W. Klatt, *op. cit.*, p. 72, n. 10).

Religionsgeschichte it becomes evident that it was the intention of the Göttingen school to make the supernatural redundant in theological discussion and to account for the distinctiveness of biblical religion without postulating a dichotomy of natural and supernatural.[1] They were persuaded that this dichotomy must disappear and that 'revelation' could not survive as the theological category which it had been in the pre-critical era of biblical scholarship. Gunkel was not altogether prepared to dispense with revelation but neither was he anxious to flaunt it or to produce it as a solution for otherwise insoluble difficulties or as a device for patching threadbare arguments. Revelation was no longer to be thought of as the descent of timeless truths from heaven, but as a special aspect of the historical process. Religion, including biblical religion, was part of a great web of causal relationships, and so biblical religion emerged as an integral part of the total historical process. In this sense there is an emphatic rejection of the supernatural. The distinctiveness of biblical religion is preserved by saying that in its case the historical conditioning is of such a kind that the product is special and superior and that, to this extent, we may still speak of revealed religion. What Gunkel intends here is certainly nothing akin to a *Heilsgeschichte*, but he is invoking something like a Providence which so orders this part of the general historical process that a religion having a claim to truth superior to that of all other religions emerges. Klatt notices that there is a certain unevenness in Gunkel's approach and that, despite the theoretical foundations which he lays, there is an apologetic anxiety which he is not able to remove and which gives rise to special pleading. It also appears to be true that Gunkel became more and more exercised to refute the charge that he had reduced all religions to the same level and to justify the evangelical usefulness of his method by insisting that he had not compromised the distinctiveness of biblical religion.[2]

It is his awareness of the historical interrelatedness of religions which brings Gunkel into conflict with Wellhausen's account of the origins of Israelite religion.[3] Wellhausen had offered what was very largely a self-contained account and Gunkel rejected the pre-

---

[1] W. Klatt, *op. cit.*, pp. 74-77.

[2] W. Klatt, *ibid.*, pp. 76 f., 148.

[3] J. Wellhausen, *Reste arabischen Heidentums: Skizzen und Vorarbeiten*, iii (1887); cf. W. R. Smith, *The Religion of the Semites (3)* (1927).

mise that the development of Israelite religion was entirely from within itself. He remarks:

> In reality in the earliest period in which we encounter it, it already has a history and is a product of that history. It has taken up decisive motifs from the religion of Canaan. It is therefore at the period reflected by our sources a complicated phenomenon.[1]

Wellhausen had assumed that the religion of Israel had originated and developed in a setting which was itself innocent of culture and which was cut off from outside cultural influences. If there were any parallels which would enhance the understanding of the earlier levels of its development, these were discoverable in pre-Islamic religion or in the religious practices of modern Bedouin. It was, one might say, almost a perfect experimental situation for the study of the evolution of a religion, and all the forces and influences which prompted it were exercised from within. It was a small world and one free from complexity in which, according to Wellhausen, Israel's religion developed along special lines. In this insulated historical context the understanding of Israelite religion would not be helped by a consideration of the larger historical and cultural setting in which the little community lived and had its being. Israel's world became bigger, more realistic and more complicated as a consequence of Gunkel's new departure.

There are reasons why the working out of the new approach of *Religionsgeschichte* is ultimately less impressive in relation to the patriarchal narratives than it is in *Schöpfung und Chaos*. In *Genesis (I)*, in association with the theory that the patriarchal stories are an international genre and may have their origin in myth, one can see the same possibilities of a deep exegesis as existed in the case of the primaeval history. The stories are a Canaanized expression of a widely disseminated art form and there seems no limit to the extensions of the area of study which are desiderated in order to place the stories in their total cultural setting. Once again, as in *Schöpfung und Chaos*, a vast new hinterland of investigation full of possibilities is opened up to the interpreter. At this point in the development of Gunkel's thought about the patriarchal narratives the whole world of the ancient Near East and other cultures besides are brought to bear on the discovery and definition of the themes which are the scaffolding of these narratives and on the characters,

---

[1] *Schöpfung und Chaos*, p. 157; cf. W. Klatt, *op. cit.*, pp. 58 f.

in different guises but essentially the same, by whom they are peopled.

The impression which is gained from *Genesis* (*1*) is that the study of the patriarchal stories is an ample task which carries the investigator far beyond the geographical and cultural limits of early Israel. For the stories are not Israelite and they do not reflect the cultural attainments or the corporate consciousness of the early Israelite community. Rather they were picked up by Israel in Canaan and they had arrived there because there was an international commerce in such stories. But the deepening of the exegetical task which can be contemplated in connexion with the tradition of these stories turns out not to be very significant in relation to *Religionsgeschichte*, for, according to Gunkel, their interest and merit does not lie in their religious content. It is more difficult here than in Gunkel's study of the creation myths to combine the widening and deepening of the area of study with a final illumining of the nature of the distinctiveness of Israel's religion, where the breadth of the base of the investigation served to enhance the final pinnacle of attainment of a religion whose 'revealed' character could be demonstrated not by disengaging it from history and culture but by exhibiting its right to a place of pre-eminence in the widest possible historical setting.

The patriarchal narratives are much less promising material for an impressive illustration of the thesis of *Religionsgeschichte*. They afford Gunkel great opportunities but these are along the line of literary and aesthetic appraisal: it is the story as a literary genre and the patriarchal stories as classic examples of their kind to which he devotes his criticism. It is not accidental that he examines the structure of the stories with minute care, that he takes the narrative machinery to pieces and describes each piece in great detail; that he puts the machinery together again and tells us how it works. Into this task goes his highly developed aesthetic sensitivity, his sympathy with creative literary achievement and his joyful submission to the sovereignty of imagination and 'poetry'.

The change of ground in *Genesis* (*3*) results in a narrowing of the horizons of the patriarchal narratives. The settled conclusion that they take their origin in *Märchen* disengages them, to a large degree, from the international cultural context in which Gunkel had set them in *Genesis* (*1*). They now tend to be traced to the semi-nomadic culture of the ancestors of the Israelites who owned flocks and herds and lived on the southern and eastern edges of the arable land of Canaan. So described the stories have lost the cosmopolitan glamour which was attributed to them in *Genesis* (*1*); they are no longer products of a widely disseminated culture; they are no longer forms of art with a claim to universality. Instead they are to be seen as reflecting the culturally impoverished conditions of life among clans which do not yet enjoy the benefits of possession of arable land or the order of a settled existence. It is a narrow existence, touched by constant economic insecurity and necessarily destitute of impressive manifestations of material culture. The narratives reflect the urgent preoccupation of these semi-nomads with certain basic needs on which their survival hinges. There are the relationships with their settled neighbours which are not always frictionless; there is disagreement about wells which supply the indispensable commodity of water. But it is only incidentally that the narratives are sources for a history of culture and the point which Gunkel made in *Genesis* (*1*) can be made no less resoundingly in *Genesis* (*3*): the patriarchal stories are not historiography; they are *Märchen* – tales told to entertain and to give pleasure which are peopled by creatures of the imagination, by products of literary invention. For as long as the patriarchs are depicted as living out their lives outside the boundaries of the arable land of Canaan, we may suppose that they reflect the nomadic or semi-nomadic, pre-sedentary and pre-Canaanite stage of Israelite life. When the stories move into Canaan proper, we are to understand that this is a secondary sphere subsequent to the settlement of Israel in Canaan. The attachment of the patriarchs to the ancient pre-Israelite sanctuaries of Canaan is the stage of the Canaanization of the patriarchal narratives.

Whether we take the view of *Genesis* (*1*) that the patriarchal narratives originate in myths or that of *Genesis* (*3*) that they originate in *Märchen*, the striking thing about Gunkel's account from the point of view of *Religionsgeschichte* is that the literary history and the religious history of the stories fall apart: the literary merit of the narratives and their dramatic power are entirely severed from their religious content.[1] The only trace of an exception to this that can be found in Gunkel is his tendency to agree with Gressmann that the patriarchs in their semi-nomadic condition were worshippers of El and that this was a superior religion to the worship of Baal

[1] Above, pp. 26 f.

of which there is no mention in the patriarchal narratives. Apart from this the stories in the form on which Gunkel lavishes his careful and discerning aesthetic analysis are, according to Gunkel himself, destitute of religious worth. Their value as absorbing stories, as imaginative products, as fragrant poetry, bears no relationship to their religious value. This is a great loss. If religious worth were to be attributed to the stories, one would hope that the religion would be integrated with their total aesthetic impact – that the imaginative forms themselves would be bearers of religious insights. Instead Gunkel's view is that the religious content of the narratives originates in separation from the processes of creative literary composition – it is an accretion of piety, a veneer of edification. It is the collectors of the stories not their creators who confer on them the level of religious refinement of which Gunkel approves. The religious content which they now possess has been given to them by J and E who are not individuals but schools of collectors, so that we have to envisage a cumulative process by which written collections of traditions are aggregated and the final result is J and E.[1] The morality[2] and religious concepts in the extant narratives tell us about the character of Israelite religion in the period between 900 and 750 B.C.[3] The unifying theological framework of Promise and Election belongs to this period as does the praise of the faith of Abraham. Secular motifs are suppressed and piety predominates in such late pieces as the account of Abraham's migration (Gen. 12), Jacob's prayer in which the crafty shepherd takes on the traits of a saint (32.10-13), the account of the concluding of the covenant in chapter 15 and the story of the sacrifice of Isaac in chapter 22.[4] Abraham's conversation with God concerning Sodom may betray prophetic influence (Gen. 19).[5] One aspect of this reorganization of the patriarchal narratives is that they are unified in terms of 'Israel' and become a common body of national stories. In Gunkel's view this presupposes the advances towards a more articulate nationhood which took place under the first kings and, in particular, the sense of national self-identity which was created by the achievements of the Davidic era.[6]

---

[1] *Legends*, pp. 130-133; *Genesis* (*3*), lxxxv f.
[2] Cf. *Genesis* (*3*), pp. lxxii-lxxiv, where the moral refinement of the stories is associated with the processes of oral tradition.
[3] *Legends*, pp. 137-142; *Genesis* (*3*), pp. lxxxix-xci; cf. W. Klatt, *op. cit.*, p. 153.
[4] *Legends*, pp. 108 f., 114, 117; *Genesis* (*3*), pp. lxx f; lxxiii f., lxxv.
[5] *Legends*, p. 142; *Genesis* (*3*), p. xci. [6] *Legends*, pp. 137 f.; *Genesis* (*3*), pp. lxxxix f.

Comparable views on the derivation of the religious content of the patriarchal narratives are found in Jepsen and Kilian. According to Jepsen[1] we can speak of a single author of the patriarchal narratives (J) who worked in the reign of Hezekiah and to whom the shaping (*Gestaltung*) of the narratives is to be attributed. That Jepsen can describe the contribution of J as *Gestaltung* is an indication that he is a historian of tradition of a different stamp from Noth. If the *Gestaltung* is the work of J, then the tradition itself does not have a *Gestalt* in Noth's sense. Noth's view is that the shape and structure of the tradition are seminally determined, and he leaves no room for the major contribution by an author J which is posited by Jepsen. The tradition grows from a 'seed' or 'kernel' and its final shape is the organic outcome of possibilities which were already contained in the 'seed'. Hence the structure of the patriarchal narratives which is now given to us in the extant text is the culmination of the history of the tradition and is not the creation of an author. There are two aspects to this fundamental divergence of opinion as between Jepsen and Noth:

(*a*) The extant organization of the patriarchal narratives is viewed by Jepsen as the consequence of a work of editorial compounding by J. The order in which the narratives appear is a consequence of his decisions and he has throughout smoothed the transition from one set of traditions to another and thereby created a new and complex unity.

(*b*) In addition J has made substantial contributions to the extant content of the patriarchal narratives, so that 'tradition' for Jepsen, in relation to these narratives, can mean a residual or fragmentary deposit which has been reshaped or expanded by J. Thus the following passages, according to Jepsen, have been composed or formulated (it is difficult to ascertain what precisely is intended by 'formulated') or reshaped or expanded by J: Gen. 12.1-3, which sets out the universal implications of Abraham's call, is J's contribution; 12.4-8 may have some basis in tradition but it has been formulated by J; 12.9 and 13.1-4 are supplied by J as a framework for the story of Abraham in Egypt. 13.5-13 has been shaped by J with a view to preparing the way for chapter 19. 13.14-18 has been formulated by J. In chapter 15, which is based on the tradition of a revelation given to the founder of the Abraham cult, vv. 13-16 were inserted by J. In chapter 16 a variant version

---

[1] A. Jepsen, *op. cit.*, pp. 278-281.

of the Hagar story (vv. 8-9) has been inserted by J. J is responsible
for 18.16-33 and 19.27-28, while chapters 20-22 consist of north
Israelite material incorporated in the patriarchal narratives by J
in the time of Hezekiah. 22.15-18 is complementary to 12.1-3 and
by means of it J gives expression to the idea that the blessing of
12.1-3 is confirmed as a consequence of Abraham's obedience.
Chapter 24 may be based on old tradition, but its structure is
entirely attributable to J and expresses his belief in divine guidance.
25.21-34 was given by tradition but was shaped by J; 26.1, 2-5,
12-18, 23-25 was inserted by J in order to fill out the context and
chapter 27 was possibly formulated by J. 28.10 is a connecting
piece formulated by J; 28.11-22 has been expanded by J through
the inclusion of the promise of blessing (vv. 13aβ-14, 15b). 29.1-3
is to be attributed to J and is the same family history as in chapter
24. All that was given by the tradition was that Jacob had married
two sisters, Leah and Rachel. Similarly in 29.31-30.24 only the
names of Jacob's children and the order of their births were given
in the tradition. 30.25-43, which had links with an old tradition,
probably owes its formulation to J. In chapter 31 J has connected
a Gilead-Mizpah tradition with a family history of Jacob which
he himself shaped. Elements of tradition are contained in 32.2b-3,
25-33 and in 33.17, 18-20, but the remainder of these chapters is
the work of J. In chapter 34 a tribal tradition or a tradition concerning local history has been transformed by J into a family
history. Chapter 35 is the work of J: he collected certain local and
tribal traditions (vv. 8, 16-20, 21-22a) and contributed the conclusion of the Bethel narrative (vv. 7, 14, 15), and as a preparation
for this, vv. 1-5. The Joseph narrative was already a complete
entity when it was taken over by J, but he inserted chapter 38 and
reshaped chapters 45.25-46.5. He probably contributed 46.1-4 and
perhaps also 48.15-16, 49 and 50.22-26.

Jepsen's conclusion is that the main parts of the patriarchal history is the work of J[1] and that the theology of history to which they
give expression is attributable to him.[2] With regard to the bearing
of all this on the theology of the patriarchal narratives the following
observations may be made:

1. Some of the theological material in the patriarchal narratives
is not saga material and cannot be regarded as belonging to the

[1] A. Jepsen, op. cit., p. 281.
[2] ibid., p 278.

history of the tradition of these narratives. This is clearly the case with 15.13-16 with its reference to bondage in Egypt and the possession by Israel of the Promised Land. Abraham is represented as having had the shape of the distant future disclosed to him. Similarly 18.16-23 has the appearance of a piece which has been constructed to give deliberate expression to a theological doctrine. The matter is different with chapter 20, where we have to reckon with a reshaping of saga material under the influence of piety and theology (the comparison of chapters 26 and 20 makes this point clearly). As for chapter 24, this is one place where Jepsen's theological appraisal of the patriarchal stories makes common cause with von Rad,[1] for both see in it a special concept of Guidance which is attributable to J. There is, however, an important distinction to be drawn here. This concept of Guidance, according to Jepsen, is ultimately traceable to the cult of *paḥad yiṣḥāq*, whereas von Rad sees it rather as a new and more secular concept of Guidance to be correlated with the 'hiddenness' of Yahweh. Hence Jepsen's statement that J contributes theophanies to the patriarchal narratives[2] is entirely at variance with von Rad's understanding of J's theology.

2. Unlike Noth[3] Jepsen does not adopt Alt's typology of the 'god of the fathers' cult and, as a consequence, the unifying theme of Promise is not viewed by him as given by the tradition itself but as contributed by an author (J), and this is a similar position to that of Gunkel. The theology of history which Jepsen attributes to J is expressed in terms of Promise, Blessing and Guidance.[4] Since Promise only attaches originally to the cult of the 'god of Abraham', it follows that where this is carried over to Isaac (26.2-5, 23-25) and Jacob (28.11-22) the extension is attributable to J. But even in relation to Abraham the deliberate, thematic formulation of Promise is to be attributed to J (12.5-8; 13.14-18; 21.1, 2a, 6, 7b; 22.15-18). Moreover, Promise in all these cases is coupled with Blessing and since Blessing, according to Jepsen, derives from the cult of *'abīr ya'aqōb*, this amounts to a theological enrichment effected by J. Guidance, as expounded in chapter 24, represents, according to Jepsen, a theological expression of J's own

---

[1] Below, pp. 241 ff.
[2] *op. cit.*, p. 278.
[3] Below, pp. 239 ff.
[4] *op. cit.*, p. 278.

belief. Hence J has compounded the separate theological contribution of the three 'god of the fathers' cults, each of which, according to Jepsen, has a different theme. J is said to have done his work in the reign of Hezekiah, but it is not evident that the period in which he works puts its stamp on his theology, nor does a clear impression of the distinctiveness of J's theology emerge from Jepsen's treatment. In von Rad, on the other hand, it is highly significant that J's theology is interpreted in the context of the reign of Solomon, since it is accorded a distinctiveness which matches the intellectual and cultural climate in which J is supposed to have worked. Jepsen says that chapters 20-22 were incorporated by J from a northern Israelite source in the reign of Hezekiah, and so we may suppose that J identified himself with the piety of these chapters. To some extent Jepsen's position is that J's theological position is discernible in those passages characterized by refinements of piety or didactic, theological formulations (15.13-16; 18.16-33; 20), and in so far as this is so, his understanding of the theology of the patriarchal narratives has some resemblance to that of Gunkel.

Kilian's[1] concept of a development from *Grundschichten* to pre-Yahwist or pre-Elohist narratives, whether pre-literary or literary, and then to the sources J and E has important implications for our understanding of these sources. J and E are not merely collectors of traditions, and the scope of the 'traditions' is not more than the extent of the *Grundschichten*. The rest is secondary expansion, reshaping, and reorientation. J and E play a significant part in this process as authors and make an important material contribution to the content of the extant Abraham narratives. For example, the singular *Schicht*[2] of chapter 18 is attributed to J who has introduced the reference to the tent (v. 1) in order to create the nomadic setting preparatory to the introduction of the etymological aetiology of Isaac (vv. 9b-15), and who has replaced a more general promise of son and posterity. Sarah has also been introduced by J and the effect of his contributions is to heighten the miraculous element. Abraham is shown in vv. 17 f. as the man who trusts in Yahweh and this feature emerges strongly in vv. 22 ff. Above all J's theological intention appears in the way that he handles the three men, who are explained by him as Yahweh and his two

[1] Above, pp. 180 ff.
[2] vv. 1b, 2*, 3b*, 6*, 9aβb, 10-15, 17, 18, 20 f., 22b, 23-33; *op. cit.*, pp. 96 ff.

messengers. J thus incorporates chapter 18 into the faith of Israel. If the plural *Schicht* of chapter 18 was the taking up of a foreign element into an Israelite context, the J edition was its 'nationalization' with all the attendant consequences.[1]

According to Kilian the most important thread running through the J narrative is that of Promise and it is in terms of this that J's work achieves compactness and consistency. The result of Kilian's analysis indicates that only in chapter 15 do we have an original Abraham tradition containing a promise of land, and that the promise which appears in chapter 12 belongs to a Jacob tradition which has been transferred to Abraham. In chapter 18 promise cannot be original if the plural *Schicht* is an imitation of a Sodom-Lot tradition,[2] but it has, according to Kilian, been appropriated from a genuine Abraham tradition. If these are the facts, it is not clear that Kilian is entitled to say that the promise of posterity is characteristically associated with Abraham.[3] At any rate, Kilian holds that it is J who has made Promise the *leitmotiv* of the Abraham narratives: in the ordering and succession of promises not only an inner principle or structure is revealed but also an outer one, namely the journey of Abraham from north to south and his settling in Mamre which J regards as final.[4]

Similarly the Elohist is also represented as having made important material contributions to the Abraham narratives. In chapter 20 he supplies vv. 3a, 4a, 6*, 7*, 8*, 10, 12, 13?, 16, 17a. It is E who endeavours to free Abraham from the reproach of having told a lie (v. 12) and who exculpates him from all blame (vv. 12 f.). Also he is concerned with the integrity of Sarah (vv. 4a, 6aβb) and for this reason God appears to Abimelech (v. 3a) immediately after she is brought into his *harim* (v. 2). Hence E omits a notice about an illness among the people of Abimelech which is to be postulated between v. 2 and v. 3. Revelation in the night by means of dreams is an Elohist trait (vv. 3a, 6aa*, 8aa*) as is the intercessory activity of Abraham (vv. 7a*, 17a). The E narrative is the final stage of a process of oral expansion and reshaping and the hazarding of the wife in the E source follows immediately on the Elohist introduction to the Abraham narratives in chapter 15. Hence E like J

---

[1] *ibid.*, pp. 158-160.
[2] Above, pp. 182 f., 187 f.
[3] *op. cit.*, p. 153.
[4] *op. cit.*, pp. 301-305.

represents that the hazarding of Sarah took place when she was a young woman.[1] In 21.9-21 the Elohist[2] is concerned to portray Abraham as a good man (v. 11) who is obedient to God (vv. 12 f.) and who cannot be faulted for the expulsion of Hagar and Ishmael. The appearance of the angel or messenger of God in v. 17 is a theological trait of E. Abraham is localized at Beersheba and the introduction of a human warmth into the story (vv. 11-13) absent from chapter 16 is made easy for E by the foundation which has been laid in the pre-Elohist narrative[3] which has changed the Ishmael tradition into a Hagar tradition in which Hagar wails for her child.[4]

E like J imposes an artistic and conceptual unity on the Abraham narratives. The connectedness of chapters 20, 21 and 22 is indicated by the circumstance that they set Abraham in the south where Isaac belongs and by their common possession of the distinctive features of E, including linguistic features. The E *Schicht*[5] of chapter 15 originally constituted the introduction to chapters 20-22 and was displaced from its original position and connected with the J *Schicht* of chapter 15 when J was combined with E. The expulsion of Hagar and Ishmael is particularly oriented towards the birth of Isaac by whom Abraham's line is to be continued (21.12). In chapters 20-22 Abraham always appears along with Isaac and in connexion with originally Isaac traditions – there are no Isaac traditions in E in which Abraham does not feature.

While the crisis over posterity in J is concerned with the deferred fulfilment of the Promise, that is, the absence of a child for Abraham and Sarah, the crisis in E arises in connexion with the offering of Isaac. Hence in E the promise of descendants is not put in question because no son is born; it becomes problematic after the child is born. Although there is no explicit promise of land in E, this does not indicate that E's attitude to the Promised Land was different from that of J. In the E narratives Abraham is at home in Beersheba and only in Gerar is he a stranger (20.1b). There is no reason to suppose that the Abraham narratives in E were of greater scope than those which have been preserved. Only the promise of

---

[1] *ibid.*, p. 200.

[2] The contribution of E is vv. 9, 11, 12, 13, 14*, 16*, 17*; *op. cit.*, pp. 236-248.

[3] This consists of vv. 10, 14*, 15, 16*, 18a, 19b2*, 21, together with the *Grundschicht* (vv. 17*, 18b, 19a, 19b*, 20).

[4] *op. cit.*, p. 246.

[5] This consists of vv. 4aα*, 5, 6, 13*, 14*, 16; *op. cit.*, p. 68.

the birth of Isaac, the giving of a name to the child and a notice about the birth of Ishmael are to be postulated. These will have been left out when J was combined with E. The Abraham of E does not have the northern connexions of J's Abraham (Gen. 12). Since he belongs to the south, Ishmael and Hagar are around him, but not Lot, neither as the son of Haran nor as the eponym of the Moabites and the Ammonites nor as the one who accompanies Abraham.[1]

The fundamental weakness of *Religionsgeschichte* as a theological method is connected with the dichotomy of *Literaturgeschichte* and *Religionsgeschichte*. *Religionsgeschichte* is incapable of overcoming the barrier to Old Testament theology which is created by its own critical method. Gunkel's description of the way in which the patriarchal narratives acquire their religious content (and the accounts of Jepsen and Kilian are the same in principle) is such that they are doomed to theological obsolescence. If Old Testament theology is concerned with a progression or flow of religious ideas, an ascent from lower to higher, then everything has been swallowed up by the intervening centuries. Religious ideas which were superior in the age of the collectors of the patriarchal narratives have become inferior with the passage of time. One may wish to posit certain historical points of high attainment, to say that these were peaks of religious and moral insight and to prize these ideas as normative for ever. But this escape route is not really open. If what constitutes the theology of the patriarchal narratives is a superimposition of superior religious ideas, these are part of a historical flow from which they cannot be abstracted. By saying that higher religious ideas are superadded to the patriarchal narratives by collectors or by the authors of the documentary sources one is already indicating the transience of these ideas and condemning them to obsolescence. This, however, is not a difficulty which besets only the method of *Religionsgeschichte*. Any critical approach to the Old Testament has the greatest difficulty in bridging the gulf between historical particularity and temporal imprisonment, and the sphere of universal validity to which theology, including Old Testament theology, claims to belong. It would be fair to say that the problems created for Old Testament theology by the advent of the critical era of scholarship have not yet been solved. The old pre-critical theology is dead and buried,

[1] *op. cit.*, pp. 311-313.

but it has not been completely replaced by a new kind of theology resting on sound critical foundations. *Religionsgeschichte* is a valid critical activity and its results may be more or less accurate, but Gunkel is mistaken in supposing that this way of describing the religious content of the patriarchal narratives can confer on them abiding theological significance. Moreover, Gunkel's method is exposed to the real danger of confusing theology with a mere style of piety or with a theoretical concept of spirituality.

It is out of considerations such as these that Tradition has become an important concern of Old Testament theology. We have to enquire how the patriarchal narratives were able to retain their theological seriousness over a span of time and in changing historical circumstances, and this may be regarded as one of the issues with which the traditio-historical approach tries to grapple. One virtue of the approach, as it is exemplified by Noth, is that *Literaturgeschichte* and *Theologie* do not fall apart as in Gunkel. The most significant adjustment that is made is the shift of emphasis from religious ideas to a credal theme, but this does not signify the reinstatement of a pre-critical dogmatic Old Testament theology. What Klatt[1] has to say about von Rad's use of the 'Little Creed'[2] may not be entirely beside the point, but his suggestion that a Barthian dogmatic may be determining the shape of Old Testament theology will not stand up to close scrutiny. It is one thing to express critical disagreement with the hypothesis of the 'Little Creed'; it is quite another to cast doubts on the genuineness of von Rad's enterprise as an essay in criticism and to ascribe it to crypto-dogmatic motives. The most important cleavage of opinion between Gunkel and Noth – also, as we shall see, between von Rad and Noth – derives from their different attitudes to the element of Promise in the patriarchal narratives. According to Noth, this credal theme is the kernel of the patriarchal narratives; according to Gunkel, it is a theological scaffolding supplied by the collectors. Gunkel's view is that the theme of Promise and Fulfilment is superimposed and is a device employed in the interests of a secondary theological unification. As such it is an aspect of a process of *Vergeistlichung*. Noth's view is that Promise is the most important characteristic of the seed from which the patriarchal stories grow and the one which above all else controls and determines the nature of their growth. Promise is seminal and organic

---

[1] W. Klatt, *op. cit.*, p. 160.   [2] Above, p. 153.

in relation to the patriarchal narratives and this implies that their literary history and theology are inseparable. The history of the tradition of the patriarchal narratives is unitary without any falling apart of literary and theological components.

It is true that, according to Noth, there is a slackening of the connexion of the patriarchal stories with their original credal centre, but his account of the history of their tradition remains, nevertheless, a single one. The west Jordan Jacob traditions give expression to the claims of the Israelite tribes to possess the Promised Land of Canaan: the promise made to the cult founder Jacob by his god had been fulfilled for the Israelite tribes by Yahweh. In this way the stories have been integrated with another article of the 'Little Creed' and the assertion that Yahweh bestowed Canaan on Israel is seen as the fulfilment of the promise contained in the patriarchal traditions. These west Jordan, Jacob traditions are then about credal claims to the possession of Canaan and they represent that the patriarchs had contacts with sanctuaries which subsequently became centres of Yahweh worship and places of assembly for Israelite tribes. The east Jordan, Jacob stories, on the other hand, are no longer dominated by these credal claims and ancient Canaanite sanctuaries do not feature in them. They are more mundane and they reflect more general concerns of co-existence between Ephraimite colonists in east Jordan and their Aramaean neighbours. The title to the land of Canaan is no longer an issue in these narratives, but the frictions which arise within a community as a consequence of processes of cultural change are reflected in the story of Jacob and Esau.

The change in the character of the east Jordan, Jacob tradition over against its west Jordan counterpart should not be interpreted as a total loss of theological content. Sanctuaries and theophanies recede into the background and pressing, everyday concerns prevail. The men who appear in these stories have received a new access of liberty; they are free to make mistakes, to be overcome by evil, and a new psychological area of investigation is opened up. The mystery of our humanity deepens and in its labyrinthine recesses we discover complex motivation and residual darkness and chaos. The more profoundly human the stories become, the greater is their theological potential. It is along these lines that von Rad has made his distinctive contribution to the theology of the patriarchal narratives.

It should be noted, however, that von Rad is not a historian of tradition in the same sense or of equal profundity to Noth, and that, in the creative contribution which he ascribes to J, there is a suggestion of the same kind of falling apart of *Literaturgeschichte* and *Theologie* as has been observed in Gunkel. According to von Rad[1] J has used as the scaffolding of his narrative the themes of the 'Little Creed' and has thereby created out of the discrete and heterogeneous material which he had at his disposal a coherent theological structure which did not previously exist. J's creativity, however, for the most part, is not concerned with the super-imposition of a superior religious content. Rather than interfering internally with the traditions out of which he shapes his new theo-logical structure, he supplies significant linking passages here and there, although there are narratives such as the wooing of Rebecca (Gen. 24) and the complex Joseph story[2] which are better regarded as reflecting directly the intellectual and theological climate of J's time than as units of tradition which he took over and incorporated in his master plan. There is a dichotomy of literature and theology in von Rad in so far as the patriarchal narratives acquire their theological importance only as a consequence of the place which is accorded to them in J's comprehensive theology of the Hexateuch. Gunkel argues that the important religious content is given to the patriarchal narratives for the first time at the stage of collecting, while von Rad argues that they assume theological significance as a consequence of J's creative work. Noth's position, on the other hand, is quite different. Promise is a theme which is seminal in relation to the patriarchal narratives themselves. According to Gunkel Promise is a theological framework supplied by the col-lectors (by the authors in the case of Jepsen and Kilian), and according to von Rad it is a theme which has no connexion with the patriarchal narratives until they are related to it by J in terms of the first article of the 'Little Creed' within the context of his comprehensive theology of the Hexateuch.

J's theological enrichment of the patriarchal narratives as con-

---

[1] G. von Rad, 'The Form-Critical Problem of the Hexateuch' (see above, p. 112); *Das erste Buch Mose: Genesis* (Das Alte Testament Deutsch, herausge-geben von W. Herntrich und A. Weiser), 1956; translated by J. H. Marks, *Genesis* (Old Testament Library), 1961.

[2] 'Josephgeschichte und ältere Chokma', *VTS* i (1953), pp. 120-127; trans-lated by E. W. T. Dicken, *The Problem of the Hexateuch and Other Essays*, pp. 292-300.

ceived by von Rad has not much to do with a superimposition of superior religious ideas and this is a decisive distinction between him and Gunkel. Whatever one may suppose to be intended by von Rad's designation of his Old Testament theology as a theology of traditions, he has stated unambiguously that religious ideas do not constitute the content of his theology.[1] To a large extent, so von Rad maintains, the deepening of the theological significance of the patriarchal narratives achieved by J is brought about without any material alteration in the narratives themselves. This transformation has therefore little to do with the superimposition of more refined religious ideas. It is a matter of widening the relationships of the narratives, that is, of locating them within an Hexateuchal structure in such a way that the meaning of the parts is inseparable from the meaning of the whole. Hence the question of context is brought to bear on the exegetical task in a new way and it becomes evident that the interpretation of the stories is affected by where one draws the boundary in respect of total context. It is also clear that 'context' is intended to cover not only the extent of the material assembled for consideration, but also the point in time at which the hermeneutical task is performed. The passage of time is therefore taken into account and the fact that there is a continual temporal flow is a variable which affects the meaning of the material under consideration. It is this particular hermeneutical basis of von Rad's theology which offends Eichrodt[2] and the nature of his arguments against it show that his own theology of the Old Testament is still essentially based on the presuppositions of *Religionsgeschichte*. He will not have what he calls 'existential exegesis'[3] and instead clings to a static exegesis and to a corresponding normative body of religious ideas. In the last analysis these constitute the content of his theology.[4]

The validity of this insight of von Rad is not necessarily impaired if one dissents from some of the critical decisions which are associated with it. If one were to follow Noth rather than von

---

[1] G. von Rad, *Theologie des Alten Testaments*, Band I: *Die Theologie der geschichtlichen Überlieferungen Israels* (1957); translated by D. M. G. Stalker, *Old Testament Theology*, vol. i (1962), pp. 105 ff.

[2] W. Eichrodt, *Theology of the Old Testament*, vol. i, translated by J. A. Baker (Old Testament Library), 1961, pp. 512-520 (see below, n. 4).

[3] *ibid.*, p. 515.

[4] W. Eichrodt, *Theologie des Alten Testaments*, Teil I, 6th ed. (1959); Teil 2/3, 5th ed. (1964); translated by J. A. Baker, *Theology of the Old Testament*, vol. i (1961), ii/iii (1967).

Rad and hold that the structure of the Pentateuch is the consequence of a growth from the seminal theme of Promise and not a novel creation of J, the point about context which von Rad is making would still be worthy of consideration. According to von Rad the patriarchal narratives, in so far as they were attached to localities and sanctuaries and derived their point from these local attachments, had become irrelevant and ineffective in the period when J gave a new structure to the complex of traditions with which he worked. In so far as the stories were merely locally bound tales about sanctuaries which had acquired holiness and terror as a consequence of appearances of Yahweh to the patriarchs at them, they had no longer a high theological seriousness in the time of J.[1] This author, according to von Rad, was at work in the reign of Solomon and in addressing his theology to the climate of that age he aimed at relating the patriarchal narratives to the whole of his theology of the Hexateuch in such a way as to release them from the divinized world to which they originally belonged and to give them a new level of theological significance.[2]

In the context of a theology which is marked by its fitness for the 'humanism' of the Solomonic enlightenment Yahweh is no longer the God of the theophany whose effective working is to be correlated with his appearances at special times and places, and yet Yahweh has fulfilled his Promise to Israel gloriously, almost, it might seem, doing his work by stealth, remaining hidden and yet making Israel into an empire with a place in the world, with its tenure of Canaan uncontested and its foot on the neck of surrounding kingdoms. There is a secularity about this fulfilment. It can be accounted for in terms of David's military skill and political acumen; it seems only too worldly – the product of human cleverness and ambition. Moreover, the style of life which it has ushered in is a confident humanism. Its cultural products are historiography which stems from a sense of national pride and achievement and a composition like the Joseph story which reveals an openness to the themes of international wisdom literature.

The Joseph story and the Rebecca story are, according to von Rad, particularly revealing examples of the civilization and theo-

---

[1] The loosing of the patriarchal narratives from their original local and aetiological moorings, the dissociation of the deity from sanctuaries and the 'hiddenness' of God in the Rebecca and Joseph stories are noted by Gunkel (*Legends*, pp. 104-106; *Genesis* (*3*), pp. lxviii-lxx).

[2] G. von Rad, *Genesis*, pp. 27 ff.

logical temper of J's age. It is a time which makes room for the full expression of human capacities and activities, in which men have come of age and act decisively and effectively in order to shape their world. No longer do they await or expect the decisive intervention of God at every critical juncture. They have freedom and power and there is a vast new area of human interest accessible to literature. Even theology need no longer be monopolized by God and yet this does not represent the demise of theology, for the fulfilment which has been experienced can be related to the Promise which was heard in the Patriarchal narratives. The Settlement tradition – the final, resounding article of the creed – had begun to sound hollow in the face of the difficulties of Israel's early days in Canaan: disorganization, disunity and weakness in the face of danger did not correspond with the affirmation that Yahweh had given Israel the land of Canaan. The old creed which no longer had its secure cultic anchorage or the social and theological climate which had supported its life seemed no more than a matter of antiquarian interest, but then it was brought to life and restored to vigour in the new context of the Davidic fulfilment.

A change of context can bring about a change of theological significance. This insight has repercussions for Old Testament theology beyond the limits of the Hexateuch as is evident from von Rad's treatment of the theme of Promise. The possibilities of Promise can be stretched out beyond the Davidic fulfilment and may embrace a larger context, even one inclusive of the New Testament, without exhausting the Promise which is contained in the patriarchal narratives. The stretching out of the Promise is to be correlated with a material and temporal extension of the context. Yet the Old Testament is an end in itself and belongs to Israel. We ought not to assert that the Old Testament is Christian scriptures or that the Old Testament is fulfilled in the New Testament. What we may say instead is that the meaning of the Old Testament depends on the total context within which that meaning is sought. If this context includes the New Testament, Old Testament theology is oriented towards Christianity; if it includes rather the Talmud, the Old Testament is oriented towards Judaism.

List of Works Cited

ALBRIGHT W. F. 'Abraham the Hebrew', *BASOR* 163 (1961), pp. 36-54.

ALT A. 'Der Gott der Väter', *BWANT* III, 12 (1929); translated by R. A. Wilson, 'The God of the Fathers', *Essays on Old Testament History and Religion* (1966), pp. 1-77.

'Die Wallfahrt von Sichem nach Bethel', in piam memoriam Alexander von Bulmerincq, *Abhandlungen der Herder-Gesellschaft und des Herder-Instituts zu Riga*, vi 3 (1938), pp. 218-230; *KS* i (1962), pp. 79-88.

ANDERSEN K. T. 'Der Gott meines Vater', *StTh* xvi (1962), pp. 170-187.

ANDERSON G. W. 'Israel: Amphictyony; 'Am; Ḳāhāl; 'Ēdâh' ,*Translating and Understanding the Old Testament*; Essays in Honor of Herbert Gordon May (1970), pp. 135-151.

BAENTSCH B. *Altorientalischer und Israelitischer Monotheismus* (1906).

BREKELMANS C. H. W. 'Het "historische Credo" van Israël', *Tydschrift voor Theologie* iii (1963), pp. 1-11.

BRIGHT J. *A History of Israel* (1959); 2nd ed., 1972.

CLEMENTS R. E. *Abraham and David: Genesis xv and its Meaning for Israelite Tradition* (*SBT* 2nd series, no. 5, 1967).

'Abraham', *Theologisches Wörterbuch zum alten Testament*, Lieferung I (1970), Sp. 53-62.

CROSS F. M. 'Yahweh and the God of the Patriarchs', *HTR* iv (1962), pp. 225-259.

EICHRODT W. *Theologie des Alten Testaments*, Teil I, 6th ed. (1959); Teil 2/3, 5th ed. (1964); translated by J. A. Baker, *Theology of the Old Testament*, i (1961), ii/iii (1967).

EISSFELDT O. 'Die Bedeutung der Märchenforschung für die Religionswissenschaft, besonders für die Wissenschaft vom alten Testament',) *Zeitschrift für Missionskunde und Religionswissenschaft*, 33 (1918), pp. 65-71, 81-85; *KS* i (1962), pp. 23-32.

'Die Schichten des Hexateuch als vornehmste Quelle für den Aufriss einer israelitisch-jüdischen Kulturgeschichte', *PrM* 23 (1919), pp. 173-185; *KS* i, pp. 33-43.

'Die kleinste literarische Einheit in den Erzählungsbüchern des alten Testaments', *Theologische Blätter*, 6 (1927), pp. 333-337; *KS* i, pp. 143-149.

'Der Gott Bethel', *ARW* 28 (1930), pp. 1-30; *KS* i, pp. 206-233.

'Gabelhürden im Ostjordanland', *Forschungen und Fortschritte*, 25 (1949), pp. 9-11; 28 (1954), pp. 54-56; *KS* iii (1966), pp. 61-66, 67-70.

'Israel und seine Geschichte', *ThLZ* 76 (1951), Sp. 335-340; *KS* iii, pp. 159-167.

'El and Yahweh', *JSS* i (1956), pp. 25-37; 'El und Jahwe', *KS* iii, pp. 386-397.

'Jahwes Verhältnis zu 'Eljon und Schaddaj nach Psalm 91', *WO* (1957), pp. 343-348; *KS* iii, pp. 441-447.

EISSFELDT O.   'Genesis', *The Interpreters' Dictionary of the Bible*, ii (1962), pp. 366-380.
'Jahwe, der Gott der Väter', *ThLZ* 88 (1963), Sp. 481-490; *KS* iv (1968), 79-91.
'Jakobs Begegnung mit El und Moses Begegnung mit Jahwe', *OLZ* 58 (1963), Sp. 325-331; *KS* iv, pp. 92-98.
'Achronische, anachronische und synchronische Elemente in der Genesis', *Jaarbericht van het Vooraziatischegypitsch Genootschap*; *Ex Oriente Lux* 17 (1963), pp. 148-164; *KS* iv, pp. 153-169.
Einleitung in das alte Testament, 3rd ed. (1964); translated by P. R. Ackroyd, *The Old Testament; an Introduction* (1965).
'Stammessage und Menschheitserzählung in der Genesis', *Sitzungsberichte der sächsischen Akademie der Wissenschaften zu Leipzig*, Phil.-Hist. Klasse 110, 4 (1965), pp. 5-26.
'Jakob-Lea und Jakob-Rahel', *Festschrift für Hans Wilhelm Hertzberg zum 70 Geburtstag am 16 Januar*, 1965; *KS* iv, pp. 170-175.

EMERTON J. A.   'The Riddle of Genesis xiv', *VT* xxi (1971), pp. 403-439.

ENGNELL, I.   'Traditionshistorisk metod', *Svenskt Bibliskt Uppslagsverk*, ii, 2nd ed. (1962), 1254-1261; translated by J. T. Willis, 'The Traditio-Historical Method in Old Testament Research', *Critical Essays on the Old Testament* (1970), pp. 3-11.

FOHRER G.   'Altes Testament – "Amphiktyonie und Bund" ', *ThLz* 91 (1966), Sp. 801-816, 894-904.

GLUECK, N.   'The Sixth Season of Archaeological Exploration in the Negeb', *BSAOR* 149 (1958), pp. 8-17.
'The Seventh Season of Archaeological Exploration in the Negeb', *BASOR* 152 (1958), pp. 18-38.

GORDON C. H.   'Abraham and the Merchants of Ura', *JNES* xvii (1958), pp. 28-31.
'Hebrew Origins in the Light of Recent Discovery', *Biblical and Other Studies*, edited by A. Altmann (1963), pp. 3-14.
'Abraham and Ur', *Hebrew and Semitic Studies presented to G. R. Driver* (1963), pp. 77-84.

GRESSMANN H.   'Sage und Geschichte in den Patriarchenerzählungen', *ZAW* 30 (1910), pp. 1-34.
'Ursprung und Entwicklung der Joseph Sage', EUCHARISTERION. *Studien zur Religion und Literatur des Alten und Neuen Testaments. Hermann Gunkel zum 60 Geburtstage* (*FRLANT* 19, I, 1923), pp. 1-55.

GUNKEL H.   *Schöpfung und Chaos in Urzeit und Endzeit. Eine religionsgeschichtliche Untersuchung über Gen. 1 und Ap. Joh. 12* (1895).
Genesis, *HKAT*, 1st ed. 1901; 2nd ed. 1902; 3rd ed. 1910.

The Legends of Genesis (1901); translated by W. H. Carruth.

'Ziele und Methoden der Erklärung des alten Testamentes', *Zeitschrift für praktische Theologie* xxvi (1904), pp. 521-540; *Reden und Aufsätze* (1913).

A review of Max Reischle, *Theologie und Religionsgeschichte* (1904), in *DLZ* 25 (1904). Sp. 1100-1110.

Die israelitische Literatur, Kultur der Gegenwart, I, 7, 1st ed. (1906), pp. 51-102; 2nd ed. (1925), pp. 53-112.

Das Märchen im Alten Testament (1917).

'Jakob', *Preuss. Jahrbuch* 176, 3 (1919), pp. 339-362.

'Die Komposition der Joseph-Geschichten', *ZDMG* lxxvi (1922), pp. 55-71.

GUTHE H.   *Geschichte des Volkes Israel*, 3rd ed. (1914).

HARAN M.   'The Religion of the Patriarchs', *ASTI* iv (1965), pp. 30-46.

HERDNER A.   Corpus Des Tablettes En Cunéiformes Alphabétiques Découvertes À Ras Shamra-Ugarit De 1929 À 1939 (Mission De Ras Shamra, vol. x, i, 1963).

HOFTIJZER J.   *Die Verheissungen an die drei Erzväter* (1956).

HUFFMANN H. B.   Amorite Personal Names in the Mari Texts: A Structural and Lexical Study (1965).

HYATT J. P.   'Yahweh as the "God of My Father" ', *VT* v (1955), pp. 130-136.

'Were there an ancient historical Credo in Israel and an independent Sinai Tradition?', *Translating and Understanding the Old Testament*, Essays in Honor of Herbert Gordon May (1970), pp. 152-170.

IRWIN W. H.   'Le Sanctuaire Central Israélite Avant L'Établissment De La Monarchie', *RB* lxxii (1965), pp. 161-184.

JEPSEN A.   'Zur Überlieferungsgeschichte der Vätergestalten', *Wissenschaftliche Zeitschrift für der Karl Marx Universität Leipzig*, Gesellschafts- und Sprachwissenschaftliche Reihe, 2/3 (1953/54), pp. 265-281.

KILIAN R.   *Die vorpriesterlichen Abrahamsüberlieferung, literarkritisch und traditionsgeschichtlich untersucht* (Bonner Biblische Beiträge, 24, 1966).

KLATT W.   *Hermann Gunkel: zu seiner Theologie der Religionsgeschichte und zur Entstehung der formgeschichtlichen Methode* (*FRLANT* 100, 1969).

LEWY J.   'Les textes paléo-assyriens et l'Ancien Testament', *Revue de l'histoire des religions*, 110 (1934), pp. 19-65.

LUTHER B.   'Die israelitischen Stämme', *ZAW* 21 (1901), pp. 1-76.

'Die Persönlichkeit des Jahwisten', in E. Meyer, *Die Israeliten und ihre Nachbarstämme* (1906), pp. 105-173.

MAAG V.   'Der Hirte Israel: eine Skizze von Wesen und Bedeutung der Väterreligion', *SThU* 28 (1958), pp. 2-28.

MAY H. G.   'The Patriarchal Idea of God', *JBL* lx (1941), pp. 113-128.

'The God of my Father': a study of Patriarchal Religion', *JBR* xi (1941), pp. 155-158, 199-200.

MAYES A. D. H.   *Israel in the Period of the Judges* (*SBT* 2nd series, 29, 1974).

248   STUDIES IN THE PATRIARCHAL NARRATIVES

MAZAR B.   'The Historical Background of the Book of Genesis'
JNES xxviii (1969), pp. 73-83.

MEYER E.   *Die Israeliten und ihre Nachbarstämme* (1906).

MOWINCKEL S.   'Rahelstämme und Leastämme', *Von Ugarit nach
Qumran BZAW* 77 (1958), pp. 129-150.
*Tetrateuch-Pentateuch-Hexateuch: die Berichte über die
Landnahme in den drei altisraelitischen Geschichtswerken
(BZAW* 90, 1964).

NIELSEN E.   *Oral Tradition: a Modern Problem in Old Testament
Introduction (SBT* 11, 1954).
Shechem: A traditio-historical Investigation (1959).

NOTH M.   *Das System der zwölf Stämme Israels, BWANT* 4, 1
(1930).
Überlieferungsgeschichte des Pentateuch (1948); trans-
lated by B. W. Anderson, *A History of Patriarchal
Traditions* (1972).
'Mari und Israel: eine Personnennamen Studie',
Beiträge zur historischen Theologie (Albrecht Alt Fest-
schrift), 16 (1953), pp. 127-152.
Geschichte Israels, 2nd ed. (1954); translated by S.
Godman, *The History of Israel* (1958); revised by
P. R. Ackroyd (1965).
'Der Beitrag der Archäologie zur Geschichte Israels',
VTS vii (1959), pp. 262-282.
'Thebes', *Archaeology and Old Testament Study*, edited
by D. Winton Thomas (1967), pp. 21-35.

ORLINSKY H. M.   'The Tribal System of Israel and Related Groups in
the period of the Judges', *Studies and Essays in Honor
of Abraham A. Neuman* (1962), pp. 375-387.

VON RAD G.   *Das formgeschichtliche Problem des Hexateuchs,
BWANT* 4, 26 (1938); translated by E. W. T. Dicken,
'The Form-critical Problem of the Hexateuch', *The
Problem of the Hexateuch and other Essays* (1966), pp.
1-78.
'Josephgeschichte und ältere Chokma', *VTS* i (1955),
pp. 120-127; translated by E. W. T. Dicken, *The
Problem of the Hexateuch and other Essays* pp. 292-300.
*Das erste Buch Mose; Genesis (Das alte Testament
Deutsch*, 1956); translated by J. H. Marks, *Genesis* (Old
Testament Library), 1961.
Theologie des alten Testaments, i: *die Theologie der
geschichtlichen Überlieferungen Israels* (1957); trans-
lated by D. M. G. Stalker, *Old Testament Theology*, i:
The Theology of Israel's Historical Traditions (1962).

REDFORD D. B.   *A Study of the Biblical Story of Joseph, VTS* xx (1970).

RICHTER W.   'Beobachtungen zur theologischen Systembildung in
der alttestamentlichen Literatur anhand des "kleinen
geschichtlichen Credo" ', *Wahrheit und Verkündigung*
(1967), pp. 175-212.

ROST L.   'Das kleine geschichtliche Credo', *Das kleine Credo
und andere Studien zum alten Testament* (1965), pp.
11-25.

'Die Gottes Verehrung der Patriarchen im Lichte der Pentateuchquellen', *VTS* iii (1960), pp. 346-359.

ROWLEY H. H. 'Recent Discovery and the Patriarchal Age', *BJRL* 32 (1949/50), pp. 44-79.

From Joseph to Joshua: Biblical Traditions in the Light of Archaeology (1950). The Schweich Lectures of the British Academy for 1948.

SAGGS H. W. F. 'Ur of the Chaldees', *Iraq* xxii (1960), pp. 200-209.

SCHÖKEL L. A. *La Palabra Inspirada* (1966); translated by F. Martin, *The Inspired Word* (1967).

SEEBASS H. *Der Erzvater Israel* (*BZAW* 98, 1966).

VAN SETERS J. 'The Terms "Amorite" and "Hittite" in the Old Testament', *VT* xxii (1972), pp. 64-81.

Abraham in History and Tradition (1927).

SMITH W. R. *The Religion of the Semites*, 3rd ed. (1975).

SOGGIN J. 'Ancient Biblical Tradition and Modern Archaeological Discoveries', *BA* xxiii (1960), pp. 95-100.

SPEISER E. A. 'The Biblical Idea of History in the Common Near Eastern Setting', *IEJ* 7 (1957), pp. 201-216.

'The Wife-Sister Motif in the Patriarchal Narratives', *Biblical and Other Studies*, edited by A. Altmann (1963), pp. 15-28.

STEUERNAGEL C. *Die Einwanderung der israelitischen Stämme in Kanaan* (1901).

THOMPSON T. L. *The Historicity of the Patriarchal Narratives* (*BZAW* 133, 1974).

DE VAUX R. 'Les Patriarches Hébreux Et Les Découvertes Modernes', *RB* liii (1946), pp. 321-348.

'Les Patriarches Hébreux Et L'Histoire', *RB* lxxii (1965), pp. 5-28.

'Method in the Study of Early Hebrew History', *The Bible in Modern Scholarship*, edited by J. P. Hyatt (1965), pp. 15-29.

'La Thèse de "L'Amphictyonie Israelite"', *HTR* lxiv (1971), pp. 415-436.

Histoire Ancienne D'Israël: Des Origines Á L'Installation En Canaan (1971).

Histoire Ancienne D'Israël: La Période Des Juges (1973).

VRIEZEN TH. C. 'The Credo in the Old Testament'. Volume of the Sixth Annual Congress of the Society for Old Testament Study in South Africa (1962), pp. 5-17.

WEIDMANN H. *Die Patriarchen und ihre Religion im Lichte der Forschung seit Julius Wellhausen* (*FRLANT* 94, 1968).

WEIPPERT M. *Die Landnahme der israelitischen Stämme in der neueren wissenschaftlichen Diskussion* (*FRLANT* 92, 1967); translated by J. D. Martin, *The Settlement of the Israelite Tribes in Palestine* (*SBT* 2nd series, 21, 1971).

WEISER A. *Einleitung in das alte Testament*, 4th ed. (1957); translated by D. M. Barton, *Introduction to the Old Testament* (1961).

WELLHAUSEN J. *Skizzen und Vorarbeiten: Reste arabischen Heidentums* iii (1887); vi (1899).

WESTERMANN C.   *Arten der Erzählung in der Genesis: Forschung am alten Testament: Gesammelte Studien* (1964), pp. 9-91.

WHYBRAY R. N.   'The Joseph Story and Pentateuchal Criticism', *VT* xviii (1968), pp. 522-528.

WINCKLER H.   *Die babylonische Geisteskultur in ihrer Beziehungen zur Kulturentwicklung der Menschheit: Wissenschaft und Bildung* 15 (1907).

VAN DER WOUDE A.   *Uittocht en Sinai* (1960).

WRIGHT G. E.   'Archaeology and Old Testament Studies', *JBL* lxxvii (1958), pp. 39-51.

'Modern Issues in Biblical Studies: History and the Patriarchs', *ET* lxxi (1959/60), pp. 292-296.

Biblical Archaeology, 2nd ed. (1962).

Shechem: The Biography of a Biblical City (1965).

WUNDT W.   *Völkerpsychologie*, 2, III; *Mythus und Religion* (1909).

YEIVIN S.   'The Age of the Patriarchs', *Rivista degli Studi Orientali*, xxxviii (1963), pp. 276-302.

Index of Authors

Index of Old Testament Passages

Subject Index